Chronicum Holocenum

Chronicum Holocenum

Holocene Current Events for Primates

Truth and the Greatest Stories Ever Told by Primates
Religion and other Plagiarized Gobbledygook

RAYMOND ROBERT MARTIN

ISBN: 0997865903
ISBN 13: 9780997865905
Library of Congress Control Number: 2016912412
BenedictMartin, Tarpon Springs, FL

For Molly Clare, and Julie, Lower Brule Sioux; Brian, Freda and Allan, Raymond and Mary, Patricia and Ken, and Everyone of you who likes Freedom

Preface

This book is kind of self-explanatory. I wrote down some events that happened since the ice melted after the last ice age, up until my present time. I am not a writer, I spent 20 years working as a commercial aircraft mechanic, followed by 20 years working as a Medical Technologist in various places in the United States, mostly on a graveyard shift. I wrote this just to provide myself and you the reader with events that may or may not be of interest to you, but it helped me to understand what is going on today in the world. Feel free to insert your own ethnic timeline as you see fit.

650,000,000 BC   The entire planet Earth is a giant white frozen "snowball"

As Time Goes By

You must remember this,
a kiss is just a kiss,
a sigh is just a sigh,
the fundamental things apply,
As time goes by.

And when two lovers woo,
they still say I love you,
on that you can rely,
no matter what the future brings,
As time goes by.

Moonlight and love songs never out of date,
hearts full of passion, jealousy and hate,
woman needs man and man must have his mate,
that no one can deny

It's still the same old story,
a fight for love and glory,
a case of do, or die
the world will always welcome lovers
as time goes by.

As far as I can tell and the only thing I am reasonably sure of is I am alive and I am here. I exist inside a living body. I breathe air into my chest through my nose; there is a heart that pumps inside my chest. I am held to the ground somehow. As I exist in here, thoughts come into my mind, move through my head then disappear. I am able to see out through my eyes, to the outside world around me. I can touch and feel things around me, I can smell, I can taste, I can hear and I can make sounds with my mouth. I can put thoughts together into speech, to communicate with other things that are also here, and especially with my cat. I don't think she knows what I am saying to her, but sometimes I'm not so sure, she talks back and I can differentiate some of her different meows. I have two legs with two feet, two arms with two hands that have fingers and thumb. I can grasp things, and I can move around on the ground by walking on my legs, and I can swing on a branch on a tree. I eat things when I have hunger, sometimes more than I should.

I look up into daytime sky and see the bright yellow sun above me in a blue colored sky, and often at night when the heavens are bright, with the light from the glittering stars, have I stood here amazed, and asked as I gazed if their glory exceeds that of ours. It is beautiful, what is going on here, how did I get here, where am I from, where was I before I was here, and where do I go when I die and am no longer here? One day leads to another. Did someone or something make all of his and me up, or is it all in my head? I don't know. Only time will tell.

I am a primate, descended from a long line of evolutionary enhanced primates. I did not make or create myself. I was born to two parents, a female and a male, Faye and Ray, each of whom were also born through two parents back into time past. A few years ago I began to take an interest in my families' ancestry. My parents were "only" children, and my father only knew little of his father. His father came back from WW I and had married my grandmother, then he was gone leaving my grandmother to raise my father. I think it was just a "grudge fuck", because he was Irish and had just fought the Germans in WWI. My paternal grandmother was part Austro-Hungarian. My paternal grandmother's ancestry was a mixture of maternal Irish and her paternal line was from somewhere in the Austro-Hungarian Empire. They arrived in Jersey City, New Jersey after the U.S. Civil war and after the Prussians defeated Austria around 1870. Her father, aunt and uncle were named Franz, and Joseph and Theresa, which were names of some of Austria's royalty. Their last name was Benedict, which was the name of the Austrian General who lost to the Prussians. I like to think they skipped town due to that relationship, but it was more likely that they left because the Austrian Empire abolished serfdom a few years before. The US was the New World, the land of opportunity, and milk and honey. Her father, a conductor on "Jersey Transit" died of pneumonia when she young so she remarried another Irishman, who went back to Ireland around 1916 and stayed until the early 1920's. On the maternal side, my mother's father had immigrated to America from Scotland to make his living as a football player. He went on to coach the US Soccer team in the First World Cup in South America. He was good as a left forward player, but when I knew him as a kid I watched him slowly deteriorate with Parkinson's' disease into his senior years. Whenever I saw Cassius Clay, Mohammad Ali, the boxer, on TV, I think of my grandfather, both suffered the debilitation of Parkinson's after sporting careers. Another DNA mutation that needs to be fixed and understood. My grandfather, the footballer, had many older brothers and a younger sister in Scotland. One brother immigrated to Brooklyn and worked as a machinist at the Brooklyn Navy yard during World War II, working on the USS Missouri battleship. Back in time, some of that side of the family built ships on the Clyde, fought in the Royal Artillery of the British Army against the French Emperor Napoleon; one fought in the British Army against Boers in South Africa so that the House of Hesse could secure diamonds for the bankers in London, and yet another fought in the Dardanelles against the Ottoman Empire in World War I, but mostly they were dyers and machinists in the textile mills around Paisley and Glasgow. They were Scots. The football player married my maternal grandmother whose parents were from the same town as his in Scotland. Her parents had emigrated to Massachusetts in the 1870's, maternal great-grandfather worked as a machinist in the textile mills in Massachusetts and then they all eventually moved to Brooklyn, NY. A lot of the textile mills at that time were built in the area around Newark, N.J. Needless to say, I am from a small family with little extended family around, but with a traceable ancestral past. I began to wonder who these people were and where they came from, what they did. I used ancestry online and obtained records from Scotland's People websites, then put together a pretty clear lineage back a couple hundred years, for one side of my family. The paper records become less exacting the further back in time one goes, and sometimes civil war and fire destroy archives. Through genetic testing at Oxford University, I learned that my father's paternal (Y) DNA lineage is haplotype R1b.

Genetic testing tests certain areas on the genes of an individual then compares the same area to other people in the data base. National Geographic has a world-wide data base. These genes are on the X and Y sex chromosomes of primates, a male inherits an XY sex chromosome and a female inherits an XX chromosome. These chromosomes mutate slightly over the ages, which allows genetic experts to differentiate the results into different groups. We, as humans, all had a common ancestor back in time who lived in Africa, this could be considered the trunk of the tree, then we all branched off as time evolved.

The R1b Y lineage is sometimes called Oisin, pronounced O'Sheen, or it is sometimes called Ruslan, or just R1b. This Y DNA marks my ancestral line as being one of the inhabitants of Western Europe or the area around the Black Sea. Erin, and Albu, is where they came from. The paper trail of birth, death and marriage certificates allows for the paper trail, along with the census. Thank God and Western European government for the paper trail.

This R1b haplotype of Y DNA is also the same as those responsible for the early cave paintings in Europe, the Neolithic Aurignacion Culture of Cro-Magnon man. The cave paintings are of animals in that era. One example is the "Yellow Horse" painting. During the ice age, this haplotype resided in the Basque region of Spain, around the Pyrennes' mountain range and in southern France. The R1b hunter-gatherers migrated eastwards and westwards across Western Eurasia south of the Ice sheets following the big game animal migrations. My mother's maternal X mitochondrial DNA is mtDNA J. This female haplotype J is sometimes called Jasmine after the Persian flower. This Jasmine, mtDNA J, originated in the headwaters of the Tigris and Euphrates Rivers in what was known as Mesopotamia around 9000 B.C., near the ancient city of Byblos in the area that is now known as Turkey and Syria. My mother's ancestors were from the Strathclyde region of what is now Renfrewshire, Scotland; near the Clyde River and Glasgow. The journey from Mesopotamia to Scotland occurred with the spread of farming thousands of years ago. I continued researching history and archeology books in my spare time still wondering where and when they came from. I had to start looking at tribal, ethnic movements in the past to continue backwards. Primarily I focused on the history that pertained to my family search, so I did not focus on the Yanomamo Indians of the rain forest, or the Zulu tribe of south Africa. Anyone could use the DNA testing to find where the roots of their tree were. As I did this, I pulled together historical events, along the way.

I, as everyone else does, also wonder about the sky and God. My parents sent me to a Catholic parochial school run by the Sisters of Divine Charity where they beat the God of Abraham into my brain until I was a young teenager, then I went to Public High School in NYC and Senior-etta Rosenbaum taught me Spanish.

My father drank a lot of alcohol when he was not running his gin mill or teaching people how to fly airplanes. He was a flight instructor during WW II, in the US Army Air Corps in Waco, Texas. In 1943 he was going on to fly "The Hump" over the Himalayas to bring supplies to the Chinese fighting the Japs, but he hurt his arm and had a partial paralysis preventing him from using the yoke in the heavier transport planes, so he mustered out. Most of the men he taught to fly had just graduated from West Point, they received their training and went into the bombers over Europe, he said most never came back from their missions. His grandmother remarried so he had some half cousins, one of them flew with "The Flying Tigers" in China against the Empire of the Sun. I spent my off time when I was not slaving for him or doing homework, impaling horseshoe crabs on driftwood spears along the beach or hunting water rats in an old ammunition barge that was beached across the street from the gin mill. Sometimes his students would crack up the airplanes and the planes would have to be reskinned with fabric and coated with dope. I would hang out at the hangar at his airport and get high from the dope being used to recover the fabric of the wings and fuselage, and act as a gopher. Sometimes he would take me flying and we would fly past the Statue of Liberty and look up at her face as we headed up the Hudson River. We circled the Empire State building and would then fly through the Narrows, and east out over the North Atlantic Ocean skirting the scud coming in off the sea. I guess I am lucky we didn't have to ditch in the Atlantic, and get attacked by a Great White. One time his friend went Tuna fishing and came back with a 30-foot shark instead of a Tuna. They had to use a large boat lift to get it on to shore, where they lift out the large pleasure boats at the end of the season. He pulled out all the teeth and made keychains for everyone. Childhood was a trip, I learned how to read and write thanks to my parents and the brutality of the Roman Catholic church, and I also learned that if you repress and ignore your being, your own truth, you can become mentally and emotionally disturbed, but you can cope with this and cover it up with sex, drugs and alcohol, and of course rock and roll, for a while, that is. Then you have to get your head out of your ass or die. I married a Native American woman, a Sioux, who was born in South Dakota, but given up for adoption to a Jewish family. She passed away a few years ago from the same plague as the Irish have experienced. I used to ask her if her relatives really did massacre the 7th Cavalry, and she would stare at my long hair. She still was resentful of the white man in her country. We raised an American daughter.

Life, a duality, both divergent and convergent to be used, good and bad. I sometimes think about God, and I don't know why. Perhaps it's the deep down belief that I am alone in this universe, but surrounded by other primates and lifeforms at the same time, but I just don't know. Looking at history, it seems the idea of God has accompanied primates in their tribes and ethnic affiliations in all of recorded history. The concept of God waxes and wanes, ebbs and flows like a tide about humans. Religion appears to be a "spell" cast by something that completely adsorbs the mentality of higher primates. This little story chronicles some of the history of both religion and organizations and European and Middle-Eastern events over time that I encountered in my ancestry search.

Time goes by and so must be divided into some sort of grouping, in order to make sense of when things were or when things are. By using a number-line we can make something or some event zero, and count back or forward from that zero point in time as a reference. The zero point used here is the birth of a Jewish child, Jesus Christ. He is quite significant because it is said he was the only person to have ever been killed and then after three days he physically rose from the dead, spoke to people, and then ascended into the sky to join his father. B.C. means before Christ; A.D. is Latin for Anno Domini, meaning after Christ. As such, the recorded time scale for most Holocene current events are greatly influenced by the Middle East where Jesus was born. Most of these Holocene events that I cover here occurred between earth longitude -19 degrees East and +79 degrees East longitude, with some further west and some further east towards the rising sun.

HOLOCENE

In our current Holocene period and before 9000 B.C., there were no animals and no people living in Scotland, England, Wales and Ireland. Scotland was populated between 9000 B.C. and 1000 A.D. The last ice age was called the Weichsel Ice Age. It was divided into three stages. The Weichsel Early Glacial was from 115,000 B.C. until 60,000 B.C., and the Weichsel High Glacial was from 58,000 B.C. until 15,000 B.C. The Weichsel Glacial Maximum was around 20,000 B.C.; the Weichsel Late Glacial Ice Age was from 12,500 B.C. until 10,000 B.C. After 10,000 BC, the earth entered the period known as the Holocene period. The earth has been mostly cool and dry for its entire existence. The Weichsel Ice Age lasted about 100,000 years. We have not had ice for about 12,000 years. During the ice ages, water is contained frozen in the ice, so that the sea levels of the world's oceans were lower than they are at present in the early 21st century, about 340-450 feet lower. The continents would have ended further out to sea than they do now in places. There was an additional lost island off the Northwest Coast of Ireland and inlets and bays would not have existed. Ireland and the British Isles were all connected to each other and to the mainland of Europe.

Before 85,000 B.C., all the humans, Homo sapiens, lived on the continent we know as Africa. Around this time some started to migrate out of the Rift Valley, Africa, heading east. During the Weichsel Early Glacial Ice Age, at around 70,000 BC, a super volcano named Toba exploded near Sumatra in the Western Pacific and left a 70 mile by 20-mile crater behind. The ash thrown into the sky blackened the atmosphere and a ten-year volcanic winter followed depressing the cold global temperatures even further. This volcanic winter killed off most vegetation and mammals, even as far south as Africa was. The Homo's who were not Homo sapiens closer to Toba became extinct. The aftermath of this explosion left only about 5,000 to 10,000 Homo sapiens alive with maybe 2,000 of child bearing age. There were many diverse African male and female DNA haplotypes amongst these 10,000 people. After 70,000 B.C., a small group of a few hundreds of these Homo sapiens left the Rift Valley in search of greener pastures. They left the Rift Valley and headed northeast to the horn of Africa where Ethiopia is today. Here they crossed the straights to Yemen below the Red Sea, then over to the Persian Gulf Marsh, then up to Mesopotamia, the area between the Tigris and Euphrates River. Many of their ancestors continued east towards the Himalaya Mountains, some went North but mostly they continued walking east along the coast line of the Indian Ocean, to finally reach Asia, the Malay peninsula, and Australia.

Neanderthals existed around continents from around 450,000 B.C. until around 40,000 B.C. The Homo sapiens would have overlapped and encountered Neanderthals for tens of thousands of years.

The female mtDNA haplotype L3 was the female haplotype lineage to leave Africa. M an N were her daughters. Only two female mtDNA lines, M an N left the Rift Valley and Africa behind. The male lineage Y haplotype that left Africa was CT. CT-168 or M-168 is the genetic marker for all non-African males. Sub-Saharan African males are all Y haplotype A and or B, they are not CT-168. All the other Y haplotypes in the world today are derived from CT-168, they are C, D, E, F, G, H, I, J, K, L, M, N, P, Q, R, S, and T.

Haplotype CT had descendants' C and F, each with mutation P-143. Male haplotype F had the defining mutation F M-89. This clan of male haplotype F was called the "Seth" clan. The sons of Seth were GHIJK. The haplotype K, KM-9 arose about 50,000 years ago. The haplotype K2, KM-526 arose about 43,000 B.C. Haplotype R, R-M207 arose about 30,000 B.C. in Central Asia. Haplotype R1, R-M173 arose about 25,000 years ago in Central Asia. Haplotype R1b, R-M343 arose in Western Asia about 18,000 B.C. R1b1a2, R-M269 is the R1b clan that covers most of Western Europe with frequencies of 85-95 % in Scotland, Ireland, and Wales. Migrations occurred east to west and west to east south of the ice wall as these hunter-gatherers followed the migrations of the herds of large animals. These people lived in caves, under animal skins, or under the stars.

Seth clan is a super clan found over a wide range of Europe and Asia. Seth lived in the Middle east about 50,000 years ago. Seth lived in the Upper Paleolithic or Old Stone Age. It is just an arbitrary name given to him. He hunted big game as a hunter-gatherer. The name Seth is named after the Egyptian God of the desert. In hieroglyphics, he appears as an animal with the body of a greyhound, a forked tail and square topped ears. Haplotype K broke off from the Seth clan and evolved to K2, then K2b, then P and finally R, R1a and my own R1b. R1a and R1b are associated with Scythians, and Cimmerians. The R1b tribes were primarily spread throughout Western Europe, with R1b also inhabiting the lands north and south of the Black Sea, east of the Sea of Azov, and continuing east to the western and northern shores of the Caspian Sea. R1a was spread to the north of the R1b, west to present day Poland and the eastern regions of Germany, then out east across Russian steppes to Siberia. Haplotype I and N settled in the far northern reaches of Europe, in Scandinavia. Male haplotype J1 and J2 is associated with Semite tribes, along with the haplotype G and E in the Levant, Anatolia areas.

Female mtDNA M and N left Africa. Female mtDNA N eventually mutated and some became mtDNA R, then mutated into female mtDNA J around 9,000 BC in the headwaters of the Tigris and Euphrates Rivers in Mesopotamia, and eastern Anatolia. Jasmine haplotype J is associated with the invention of farming as they both arose at the same time and place. Growing food was self -learned around 9,000 B.C.

Homo sapiens encountered groups of Neanderthals in their hunter-gatherer migrations. The Neanderthals had been around for a very long time compared to human primates. The Homo sapien primates mated with the Neanderthals sometimes producing off spring. 1-4% of all non-African Homo sapiens DNA is inherited from Neanderthals. African DNA does not contain Neanderthal DNA.

The ice would eventually melt and some would drain into Mesopotamia creating the Fertile crescent. The Garden of Eden. It must have had abundant wildlife and enough to supply all needs for the hunter-gatherers if they continually moved. The fertile crescent was thought to cover a wide expanse from what is now Egypt to the Persian Gulf and Anatolian Mountains in Turkey. The area was not desert as much of it is today. Saudi Arabia was desert then as it is now, but the Persian Gulf was freshwater and marsh like, extending up to the foothills of Anatolia. Today the depth of the Persian Gulf or Arabian Gulf is 295 feet at the deepest point with a drop off into the Indian Ocean south of the Strait of Hormuz. In the past with the water tied up in the glaciations, the Persian Gulf would not have been flooded by the Indian Ocean, but would have been above Sea Level, the ground watered by the Tigris and Euphrates Rivers, then a waterfall into the Indian Ocean. The same was true for the Red Sea, which is only 450 feet deep today.

In 58,000 B.C., men and women walked into Britain, maybe 20 or 30 families across the dryland called Doggerland. There were no Neanderthals found in Britain after 58,000 BC. These families fled south again as it was still getting colder until the glacial maximum was reached in 20,000 B.C. The area was not occupied again until around 9,000 B.C.

In 40,000 B.C., the majority of the group that had left the Rift Valley was still living in the Levant and Mesopotamian Fertile Crescent. They had been there for 20,000 years, moving east but not North or North east or Northwest. They had spread east along the coast of the Indian Ocean. In 40,000 B.C. the Neanderthals were dying off or turning into the Abominable Snowman, or Bigfoot or Sasquatch and were not seen much anymore. Nessie was still trapped under the ice in Scotland. At that time, the ice age glaciers were still covering most of the Northern hemisphere. North of the Mediterranean Sea it was cold and there is tundra south of the face of the ice walls. In 33,000 B.C. more of haplotype R1b clan moved into Western Europe from the east. The Neanderthals had died off leaving the area uninhabited.

In 30,000 B.C., the ice wall had been there for almost 100,000 years. The temperature on top of the ice wall was -60 C. There is always high pressure air overhead, cloudless blue skies and hurricane like winds and gales blowing over the slick ice. The ice sheet is 5,280 feet thick (tall) in places. It is a mile high at the face of it. At the southern edge of the ice sheets, at the mile-high faces, the atmospheric pressure was low, there was stormy weather, sleet, hail, snow, rain, cold, clouds, and wind gusts, but it was slightly warmer than on top of the ice sheet. South of the wall was arctic tundra, then steppes, then grassland with large animals like the wooly mammoth, auroch, wisent, saber-toothed tiger, reindeer, stag horn deer, and horses. Primates were living in caves, hunting these animals for food, and they drew pictures of the animals on the walls of the caves. Both the Chauvet cave paintings, near Chauvet, France, and the Lascaux cave paintings were painted 27,000 years ago and 15,000 years ago by the Aurignacion stone age culture. Hunters followed these herds back and forth in the grassland south of the ice walls. The ice extended as far south as the Loire Valley along the Loire River in France. Otzi, the ice man who thawed out a few years ago died in 33,000 B.C. It is believed he was from the Middle-east and he stole some of the cave paintings and was tracked down by a group of French police high in the Alps.

The cave men were artistic hunter-gatherers who could control fire and make weapons from wood and flintstones. After 24,000 B.C., the cave men retreated farther south again as they were coming up on the peak period of the last ice age, the LGM, last Glacial maximum. In 20,000 B.C. the ice age peaked and there were really fantastic colors, snow in the summer time, and the unicorn was born. It was the loveliest of all animals and remains today as the national animal of Scotland. After 20,000 B.C., until 12,500 B.C. the glaciers melted and slowly retreated north. As the ice receded after 20,000 B.C., plants grew, animals followed, then men followed animals back north to Ireland and Scotland. In 10,000 B.C., it started to get warmer, glaciers continued to recede until 9,400 B.C. In 9,400 B.C. the cold melted water covering Canada was slowly draining into the Mississippi River, blocked by ice dams further north. The dams couldn't hold the pressure, they broke and the entire area of cold water in northern Canada drained into the Arctic Ocean over a period of 36 hours. This massive amount of clean cold water raised the sea levels 9 feet. There must have been world-wide enormous death and destruction, well maybe not destruction, because this was the Stone Age and everything was made out of stone, like in the Flintstones. The Mediterranean coast line must have been devastated. The Persian Gulf marshland must have seen tsunamis. This could have been the inspiration of the Bible Story of Noah and his ark. This fresh water from the thawed ice diluted out the salinity of the oceans and the Atlantic conveyor currents stopped, meaning the Gulf Stream stopped flowing, plunging the earth back into ice again for 1000 years. This period was called "The Younger Dryas" or the Loch Lomond Stadial. The system balanced out again in 8400 B.C., the Gulf Stream restarted, and global warming has continued to this day in the 21st century with some up and down variations.

The time period from 9600 B.C. to 8800 B.C. was a cold dry period. It was a pre-boreal period existing of grasslands and scrubs, willow, aspen, alder, hazel, juniper and pine trees. The prime game for hunting was reindeer. The wooly mammoth and the saber tooth tiger were becoming extinct. When birch trees began to spread it drove the reindeer further north to the colder areas. The Younger Dryas caused drought in the Levant and the Fertile Crescent, this prompted the primates to learn how to grow and domesticate plant life, which helped in domesticating animal life. In 9000 B.C. farming was self-learned by the inhabitants of Upper Mesopotamia. The mtDNA haplotype credited with this discovery is Jasmine, haplotype J. During this cold, dry period they started growing wheat, barley, rice, corn, flax, peas, lentils, and chickpeas by careful observation of what grew best. Flax was used for oil and fabric. In hunter-gatherer societies, children were not weaned until they were 4 years old, so women only had kids every four years. Women lived to their mid-twenties. With the domestication of animals that yielded milk and crops, children were weaned earlier and the growth of populations took off correspondingly. With enough meat and farm products, the Fertile Crescent must have been like the Garden of Eden, but when the talking reptilian snake got involved, the garden of Eden must have turned into a living hell, and God kicked them out of paradise or enslaved them within. Abrahamic creation stories were made about how Adam and Eve were kicked out of paradise over the forbidden fruit, the apple of their eye.

From 8800 B.C. to 5800 BC the climate was warm and dry. It was a 3000 year, Boreal period. Old growth forests increased in size and density as the ice wall melted. Deciduous trees abounded bringing forth new animals to hunt in the forest, red deer, roe deer, elk, wild boar, brown bear, wolf, badger, auroch, horse, wild cat, lynx, beaver, otter and hare. The forests became an extensively diverse mosaic of an environment north of the Med. There was a wider selection to hunt when compared to the reindeer herds, but the reindeer provided more meat per kill. These Mesolithic Stone Age hunters used micro-lithe tools including stone axes and scrapers to take the animals apart. In 8000 BC, the last wooly mammoth and saber tooth tiger died off and became extinct. Farming slowly spread north and east. The cat was domesticated in 7500 BC, the horse in 4000 BC or earlier. Utilizing the horse allowed for a wider range to hunt and travel, and enhanced killing. As the vast woodlands north of Mesopotamia and the Mediterranean Sea were pretty much empty and the Fertile crescent began to feel population pressure, people began to be attracted to the suburbs. Primates move and there was movement into Anatolia, across the Bosporus, and up between the Caspian Sea and Black Sea to the open spaces there. Massive tribes formed on the steppes called the Cimmerians, and the Scythians utilizing the horse for movement.

Albu, the Island off the Coast of Western Europe

In 8000 BC, near Edinburgh, Scotland there was and is a cave called Crammond Cave; it was first occupied at this time by Homo sapiens. Erin (Ireland) was by then an island, separated by a slowly widening sea from Albu. Albu was still attached to the western European continent by an area known as Doggerland. Erin was not yet occupied with humans. Beginning in 7000 BC, Erin slowly began to be populated. R. Martin, an R1b, flies his yellow J-3 Piper Cub from the Pyrennes Mountains of Espana and looks for a suitable green field to land on in the Emerald Isle, he meets Erinn, then others follow over the next 1000 years and the first colonization of Ireland begins. The date, of about 6,000 BC, coincides with the date for the beginning of the world which appears in "The Annals of Ulster", written started in 431 AD. Albu means white in the proto Indo-European language, the islands were called white, or Albu, because of the chalk, white cliffs of Dover, which are visible from France across the English Channel.

In 6500 BC, Doggerland began to disappear beneath the waves of the North Sea. Doggerland was the land bridge connecting Europe to Albu. Doggerland disappeared due to an earthquake that occurred further north off the coast of Norway. This earthquake at the bottom of the Storegga trench in the North Sea caused an area the size of present day Scotland to break off and slide to the deeper part of the Sea. Albu became isolated from Europe, and over the next 1000 years the Doggerland islands completely fell under the rising sea. Doggerland was an inhabited hilly area full of trees and lakes and small rivers. Holland still builds dykes to protect its coast from the encroaching North Sea. After 6000 BC the sea levels' rise decelerated because of the lack of melting ice. By 5500 BC Doggerland was completely gone. The English Channel was fully open between 5800 BC and 5400 BC. Between 5500 BC and 2500 BC the ocean's sea levels rose 21 feet. Between the year 2500 BC and the present, 2016, the sea levels rose 5 feet. Farming reached the Hungarian plane at the same time Doggerland disappeared in 5500 BC.

During this Mesolithic period (10,000 BC to 4200 BC), 3,000 to 10,000 people, at most, occupied all of Scotland, Wales, Ireland, and England. After 4,200 BC, there were about 100,000 people there. Migrants crossing the English Channel brought farming and domestic cattle technology along with accompanying belief systems between 4,200 BC and 3,800 BC, explaining the population growth over this 400-year period. This is the period when my maternal haplotype mtDNA J arrived in the islands with the farming. Haplotype J1b1 is particular to the Scots. 3% of Scots have mtDNA J as their maternal lineage. The period from 3800 BC until 2500 BC, saw the development of the indigenous population intensify. There was great population homogeneity between all the areas of the islands. This is the period when the great monuments were built. Land was beginning to be cleared, and farming established. Gobekli Tepe, some sort of religious, cultural artifact in upper Mesopotamia, Turkey was built from 10,000 BC until 8,000 BC, this is also associated with the rise of farming. The Newgrange burial vault, in Ireland was built around 3,200 BC. Stonehenge in south western England was started about 3,100 BC and continually upgraded until 2,000 BC. The population of Britain and Ireland in 2000 BC was thought to be 300,000 people, with 250,000 in Britain and 50,000 in Ireland. These stone buildings all correspond with the arrival of farming, Stonehenge was used to keep track of the time, through alignment of the stones with the sun's rays on a particular day each year. For comparison, the Great Pyramid of Giza was built around 2,580 BC until 2,560 BC.

2500 BC marked the end of the Neolithic age and the beginning of the metallurgy era. In 2500 BC, the copper age began. The Bronze Age (2100 BC -to- 600 BC), arrived about 400 years later, in 2100 BC. Britain had large mineral deposits of tin, necessary to make Bronze. After 2500 BC, the large old growth forests were still slowly being cut and burned back with the new metal tools, agriculture continued to take root. Maritime beaker pottery culture was introduced in three phases between 2500 BC and 1600 BC. Burials were made in beakers and they were used as storage, etc. This was the first pottery used after the Stone Age ended. Barrows were created. Tools and weapons and jewelry were starting to be crafted. Boats also were beginning to be built with planks around 1600 BC, by inventing and utilizing the metal tools necessary for carpentry. Cornwall and Devon had the mines containing casserite (tin ore), and became heavily defended. This mineral was rare and without it there would not have been a Bronze Age. Cornwall, and the Cassiterrite Islands off its coast became an important maritime export center for tin to the Mediterranean civilizations.

Around the year 1600 BC, agriculture and farming the land intensified even more, not only did metallurgy continue to grow but management of the farmland became more defining with large manmade boundaries, irrigation ditches, draining ditches and hill forts coming into existence. The manpower required for this was obtained through coercive means by a rising warrior aristocracy within tribes. The life of this nonproductive aristocracy centered on the feast and combat. Leaders arose who could enhance this lifestyle. There was now an elite class that controlled the bulk of the population, enabled in this by the continued surplus food supplies. Trade across the channel and the North Sea also intensified, and it became a center of civilization on both sides. There was a continuous flow of goods between the continent and the islands. Wooden boats made of wooden planks and cut wood were improved over the previous 400 years. Trade with the Mediterranean developed, exporting tin in exchange for other goods. The climate was warm and dry before 1250 BC. In 1177 BC, a group of unknown peoples attacked the Eastern Mediterranean coastline civilizations and these Eastern Med civilizations collapsed. This group of peoples were known as "The Sea Peoples" and may have included the sea faring peoples of Britain and Gaul and the Iberian Peninsula, the Cimmerians from the Bible. Temperatures were again plummeting and this may have put pressure on the hordes of Sea Peoples to take to the sea for survival. By 1100 BC, the Atlantic Seaways were being fully appreciated and trade from western Spain, southern and western Gaul, Albu and Erin was increased. Climate was good up until around the years 1250 BC to 1100 BC. It was warm and dry before this time. After this time the climate deteriorated. It became colder, wetter, and stormy. This drop in average temperature by about 4 degrees Fahrenheit drove farming lower to only lowland areas and the drop in temperature created blanket bogs and moors in areas. The Icelandic volcano Hekla erupted around 1159 BC- 1141 BC. This contributed to the decline in temperatures. People turned more towards animal husbandry during these cold times. Small stone walls, and reaves enclosed farmland. Defensive earthwork rings were constructed and surrounded the settlements. The concept of private ownership began in this period of time around 1000 BC. Different social hierarchies developed. Although burial of the dead remained, excarnation became the norm around 600 BC. Bronze weapons were deposited in rivers and still water around 800 BC for some reason.

In 800 BC, the Iron Age began in Albu and Erin. The very early Iron Age (800 BC-600 BC), was still a period of cold, wet weather. There was continued intensified agriculture and the sea trade continued as previously. In the period known as the Early Iron Age (600 BC-400 BC), the climate started to improve again it became warm and dry again. The sea trade networks appear to have disintegrated, except for ports on either side of the channel. Deciduous forests began to reclaim the landscape, suggesting there had been a decline in the population previously. Iron swords dominated, and regionalism crystallized. There were three distinct regional zones; the Eastern Zone stretching from the Firth of Forth down to the Thames, with open villages and enclosed homesteads. The largest iron ore mines existed on the southeast coast south of the Thames River, in an area known as the Weald. The Western Zone stretched from the Hebrides, the Highlands, down the western coast of Scotland, down through England to Wales and Cornwall. The Western Zone had strongly defended homesteads, with enclosed earthworks. Cornwall and Devon had the mines containing cassiteride (tin ore) and southern Wales had iron ore mines both were heavily defended in this Western zone. The third Central Zone lay in between the two east and west zones and were dominated by hill forts with scattered settlements around them.

Around this same time, in Iron Age Europe, the Hallstat culture with its chiefdoms developed, and Celtiberian civilization became established. Many Celtic tribes of the Hallstat culture migrated to the islands, and became dominating. Trading was along the rivers in western Gaul to the Mediterranean in Massila (Marseilles), and from central Iberia to the coasts. Tribes moved into the area of Belgium and north to southern Jutland. Trading continued with Britain but not as much as earlier, for some reason.

Tin was still one of the most valuable commodities, along with silver and gold. Tin was used to make Bronze. There were the mines in Cornwall, Britain and there were mines for tin in Iran. The Greek Herodotus learned of the "islands of the Cassiterides" when trading in the Greek port of Massila. The Greeks were interested in the mines in Britain. La Tene art was developed by the Hallstat culture and these valuable art pieces traded all over Europe. The LaTene culture made fast chariots made of Bronze that elite warriors used and were buried with. Craft skills developed and spread throughout Western Europe. At the end of the fifth century, (401 BC), and into the fourth century, (390 BC), the Celtic social system that had maintained the warrior elite broke down into a melee of folk-wanderings to the west, south and southeast. Hordes of Celts moved out of native territory to set up new homes in distant lands, many moved to Erin and Alba. Most of La Tene migrations only went as far west as Alba and not into Ireland. Also many tribes moved along the Danube River to the Carpathian basin. The Celtic British King Brennius led an army of Celts to Rome and sacked the city in 390 BC. There were Celtic invasions of Greece (279 BC), Anatolia (280 BC), and down the boot of Italy. The groups that attacked Greece were driven out and most settled in Anatolia. They became known as the Galatians and are recorded in the New Testament of the Hebrew Bible.

In the second century, (199 BC), Belgic Gaul, (Belgium) began to mint gold coins that have been found in areas of southern Britain. There were Celtic military alliances between Britain and Belgic Gaullist tribes. Trade had increased again across the channel, and Britain was starting to receive French wine and Roman luxuries. In Ireland, there was not as much trade with continental Europe but there was a development of "Royal sites", like Tara in County Meath, Navan in County Armagh, Rathcrghan in County Roscommon, and Knockaulin in County Kildare. These sites were the residences of kings, and elite Celts.

The first century (100 – 1 BC), saw the demise of Celtic civilization in Gaul, and a brief invasion of Britain by Rome. Roman civilization was approaching epic proportions, after expanding into Greece, Anatolia, Iberia, and North Africa. Rome now turned its attention northward to the area west of the Rhine River and East to the Atlantic Ocean, the area known as Gaul, named after its Gaelic Celtic inhabitants. Iberia was first invaded by the Latin Romans in 218 BC during the second Punic War. They fought the Celts, the Carthaginians and the Greeks that were living there. This Roman invasion lasted 200 years, and culminated at the same time Gaul was defeated. Under Emperor Augustus, Iberia became the Roman province of Hispania. In 58 BC, Roman armies invaded Gaul under the command of Julius Caesar. Caesar was an epileptic and he wrote a book about his conquests in Gaul under the title, "The Gallic Wars" Gaul was conquered in 50 BC, and was essentially under the complete control of Rome by 27 BC. In 12 BC, Rome had its first census within Gaulish territory. This year also saw the dedication of an altar to Rome and Augustus at Lugdunum (Lyon). Sixty Celtic tribes from Gaul attended. Gaul was transformed into a Roman province, roads were constructed, aqueducts built and the written history of the area of Gaul began.

The trade between Britain and Gaul was envied by Julius Caesar, and he landed in both the years 55 BC and 54 BC. He conquered a few tribes and some others swore allegiance to Rome, then he left. For the next 97 years, Britain remained free of Roman interference. Trade continued across the channel, and people came and went. Rome controlled trade on the east side of the channel. Britain had a great quantity of mineral wealth within its land and Rome needed these riches to further its ambitions. In 43 AD, Britain was again invaded in force by Rome, conquered, and occupied until 410 AD.

In 43 AD, there were approximately 2-4 Million people living in Britain, divided into many different Britannic and Celtic tribes. A person's identity would have been in relation to his or her lineage and tribe.

The Roman Legions landed at Dover, Kent County in 43 AD. The white cliffs of Dover can be seen from Gaul on a clear day. There were 40,000 Roman men in four legions who landed, plus auxiliaries from around the Empire. They took the leading city of the area Colchester, and quickly established a core area under Roman military control in south east Britain. The tribes in the periphery to this core zone were brought to heel, and a Roman military road was built through their territory, called the Fosse Way. The Fosse Way ran southwest to northeast, from around Exeter, on the Devon coast to the Humber at Lincoln, in the northeast. By 51 AD, parts of Wales were under Roman control. The Romans attacked the Welsh island of Anglesey which was a Druid stronghold, containing sacred groves just prior to Celtic Queen Boudicca's revolt, in 60 AD. In 60-61 AD, a revolt against Roman rule was led by the Celtic Queen Boudicca of the Iceni tribe, who lived around Norfolk, on the east coast. She and her followers slaughtered the retired pensioners of the legions, and fought and defeated the legions. She burnt the port of Londinium, Camulodunum, and the town of Verulamium. She brutally killed Romans, while impaling prisoners. This may have been due to the slaughter of the Druids in their Anglesey sanctuary or in retribution for the treatment of her daughters by the Romans. The Romans eventually put down the revolts, then took devastating reprisals on the native Celtic population. Possibly 80,000 Britons died in this revolt. Roman expansion stopped for the next ten years in the province of Britain but resumed again in the 70's AD.

In the 70's AD, Wales, and the north of Britain were conquered, and in 84 AD Roman armies had penetrated to the north of Pictland. The last major battle of resistance was at Mons Graupius near Inverness, Scotland. Romans sailed to Orkney and around the top of Pictland then down the west coast. They never invaded Hibernia. A few years after this, Pictland was abandoned by the Romans, and the Romans withdrew to the Tyne-Solway line. This is where the legions built Hadrian's wall, across Britain from west to east, coast to coast. The Romans ventured further north in 139 AD, and built the Antonine Wall from the Clyde River to the Firth of Forth, but abandoned it 20 years later in 159 AD. By 160 AD, Hadrian's Wall was the northern limit of the empire, and part of the Limes system that bounded their empire. There was continuous fighting between the Romans and the tribes to the north of the Wall until the Romans left. By the mid second century there were still four legions plus auxiliaries trying to maintain control of the island, primarily in the north and in Wales. In 208 AD, Emperor Severus, a north African Berber, led incursions into Caledonian Pictland, far into the Highlands with 40,000 legionnaires but eventually withdrew back to Hadrian's Wall, unable to counter the guerilla tactics of the Caledonians. He died at York in 211 AD. He killed every man, woman and child he could, including pregnant female Caledonians. Some of the cavalry used in the north were Sarmatia's, there were Thracians, Syrian archers on the wall, Roman Latin infantry, German auxiliary infantry conscripts and some units from Roman North Africa.

Celts were head hunters. They cut off the heads of their enemies and placed them in a cedar oil jars where they would display them to strangers, they also hung the heads around the necks of their horses like a necklace. By possessing the head of a deceased enemy represented to them that they had power over the deceased. Many Roman heads were taken and displayed during the Roman occupation of Celtic lands.

In the second century, the south of Britannia was pacified and it became a non-military civilian zone. Many new people entered Britain and it became cosmopolitan. Slaves were used for construction and farming. Baths and shrines were built by imported masons, and there was an influx of skilled professionals. Greek slaves were imported because they were literate and educated. Entrepreneurs migrated there from Gaul and the Rhineland. Londinium was built where the Thames River was narrow enough to have a bridge built across it and still experience the tidal changes from the Thames estuary. This became the city of London. Atlantic maritime coastal trade continued and increased exponentially, trade was carried by ship primarily from the mouth of the Rhine River to the Thames estuary and from Dover (Dubris) to Boulogne (Gesoriacum), Gaul across the Strait of Dover. This area was patrolled by the marines of the classis Britannica (British Roman Fleet). Trade with Hibernia resumed in the second century. The main port of trade in Hibernia was Drumamagh, east of the royal center of Tara. In the second and third century AD, those people under Roman control would have more ways to express their identity than lineage and tribal associations. For instance, they could now identify as being a slave of Rome, a craftsman of Rome, a scribe of Rome, a merchant of Rome, in addition to being a tribal member, if any of their tribe was left, but not a citizen of Rome.

The third century in the Roman Empire was a time of turmoil. There were exponential population increases in Germanic tribes outside the Roman limes, exerting pressure to get into Roman territory. In the early third century, there were manpower shortages, due to the Antonine plague followed by the Plague of Cyprian, so Roman citizenship was extended to the provinces enabling provincials to join the Roman army; Franks, and other German tribesmen were beginning to be let in to be settled inside Gaul. In 260 AD, Frankish and Alemanii tribe hordes completely overran Gaul and Hispania. Saxon and Frankish raiders took to the North Sea. In 260 AD, the "Gallic Empire" came into being during the years of the Imperial crisis in Rome; it lasted until Rome again took control in 274 AD. This folk-wandering process continued for the next 150 years until eventually the Western Roman Empire collapsed.

The classis Britannica disappeared in the late third century. In 285 AD, Rome hired a man named Carausius to rid the English Channel sea lanes of pirates, which he did, but then he made himself Emperor of Britain and parts of Gaul. He enlisted Franks and Germanic tribesmen as mercenary soldiers, Gaulish sailors for his Navy and he kept Rome out for 7 years, until he was killed by one of his officers, Allectus, who then took on his role. Rome sent Constantius I (250-306 AD) to retake Britain in the year 296 AD. Constantius I was the father of Constantine the Great who was also known as Saint Constantine. In the north, in the highlands of Caledonia, the tribes that had coalesced into the one tribe called the Picts were Celts but they were Celtic tribes that were indigenous, arriving well before the more recent Scots and Briton Celtic tribes. The Picts had arrived around 3000 BC. The dialect of Gaelic they spoke was similar to the Britons and Scots but interpreters were needed for communication. The Romans called them Picts because they wore a lot of blue tattoos on their arms and legs. They were the Picti, "the people who draw pictures on themselves". The Picts built the most excellent wooden ships that permitted them to trade with Denmark and the Continent. The Pict economy was based on using these ships for trade, cattle, and agriculture; they lived in 28 small kingdoms, which were part of eight provincial Pict kingdoms. The 8 provincial kingdoms were grouped into three nations with a high king for each. Craig Phadrig was the capital of the northern kingdom near Loch Ness. Inverness was another Pict kingdom, and Dunbar was the third about 25 miles from Edinburgh. The Picts referred to themselves as the "People of Cruthne"; Cruthne was the man who first came to Pictland in the distant past. By 200 AD, the Picts had experienced immigration and were a mixed ethnic group of Celts. The Picts' began raiding the wealthier southern Roman occupied territory. After defeating Allectus, Constantine I went to fight on the Rhine against German barbarians but returned to Britain in 305 AD, to drive the Picts back beyond the Antonine Wall with his son Constantine the Great. Upon his death at York in 306 AD, his son Constantine the Great was declared Emperor, and he travelled back to Rome. The key to the defense of Britain is the sea.

Over the next 100 years Roman Britain faced foes encroaching from all sides. At this time more and more German and Frankish tribe were taking to the North Sea for piracy and trade; they raided the east coast of Roman

Britain. On the west coast, Scots were raiding Britain from the coast of Northeast Hibernia, from around the area of Antrim Ulaid (Ulster); they were taking land from the Picts in Argyll and starting what would become the Gaelic maritime archipelago of Dal Riata (470-840 AD). In 367 AD, the Picts King began raiding with the Scots and Saxons under a plan devised by the Pict King Gartnait Duberr (370 AD). They overran Hadrians Wall and raided as far south as London throwing the whole province into chaos. Roman military order collapsed, but Imperial rule was reinstated by Theodosius. At the same time, he had coordinated with the Saxons in Jutland and the Frisian islands to attack south across the Rhine into Roman Belgium and Gaul. They almost got to Paris but were driven back across the Rhine. The Scots and the Picts were also driven back. In 384 AD, their raiding continued. The Irish champion Niall of the Nine Hostages, organized raiding expeditions from Ireland against the entire west coast of Britain. Niall took Romans as slaves, along with precious metal and cattle. One of the slaves taken in these raids was a young Roman man named Patrick. Patrick was sold as a slave in Hibernia and spent 6 years there working as a Sheppard slave before escaping on a ship to Brittany. He rejoined his family in Britain, but heard 'the voice of the Irish calling" and returned to Ireland in 432 AD. Patrick was a Christian. He began to battle the Druids for the hearts and souls of the Irish people and was successful in converting Ireland to Christianity. Scots began colonizing northern Wales, and western Caledonia from their home in Hibernia. The Kingdom of Strathclyde, Alt Clut, (450-1093 AD) arose after 430 AD, south of the Clyde-Forth line with its capital of Dumbarton on the River Clyde, in the tribal lands of the Damnonii. The Kingdom of Manau Gododdin rose in the east, south of the Firth of Forth and lasted until the Anglo Saxons kingdom of Northumbria replaced it in 550 AD.

The Roman occupation of Britain was nearing its end. Roman gods were being replaced by Germanic ones like Odin, and the Christian one. Druids were still the priests running Ireland, looking after the Celtic Pantheon in 406 AD. This was a devastating time for any native child born in the peaceful 340's under calm southern Britain. In their old age, in the year 400 AD, looking back on their life, they would have seen an incursion of unfamiliar aliens, and felt dislocation from what they knew, and they would have had to become mobile in their lifestyle to survive. Psychologically everyone must have been devastated. By 500 AD, Britain began to quiet down, in consolidation. After Rome was sacked by a Gothic Germanic tribe in 400 AD, Rome began to withdraw legions from Britain and Gaul, and Rome completely withdrew from Britain by 407 AD. The Western Roman Empire completely collapsed in 476 AD.

In 408 AD, the groups of Germanic tribes that were living north of the Rhine River on the coasts of the northern European plain mounted serious raids into Britain. These groups of Frisians, Saxons, Angles, and Jutes tribes were living on the coasts what we call the low countries of Holland, the Frisian Islands, and Jutland (Denmark). The oceans sea levels were still rising encroaching on lands that they lived on so now their land had become uninhabitable. There were population pressures on them from tribes further to the north and the east of them at the same time. They were stuck between a rock and a hard place. They took to the seas in boats, crossed the southern North Sea, landed, conquered, and colonized eastern Britain. This became an invasion over the next 100 years; the native British male population was displaced to the west and north or killed by the invasion. No sooner had Britain been ridden of one oppressor than another entered the scene.

The western part of Britain was in almost complete anarchy, after the Romans left and the Anglo-Saxons arrived. Some kings and strongmen took over, with names like Vortigern, Aurelianis, and Artorius (Arthur); Arturius was mentioned in Welsh legend, as King Arthur and the Knights of the Round Table. These kingdoms were in central Britain, Wales, Cornwall and Northern Britain in the 5th to 7th Centuries. Many Britons escaped to Armorica, Gaul and settled in what henceforth was called Brittany. British Army's fought in Gaul against the Visigoths and others. The Frank leader Clovis (481-511 AD) united the Frankish tribes into one tribe in Gaul, and expanded the Franks domination throughout Gaul that has lasted until today. In 500 AD, the British won a major battle of Mons Badonicus, the Battle of Badon against the Anglo-Saxons. The Anglo-Saxons were slaughtered and this stopped Anglo-Saxon expansion for a number of years, but by the 580's AD, the Saxons had conquered parts of Wales, like Bath and Gloucester, and as far North as the Firth of Forth.

In 568 AD, the great, great grandson of Niall of the Nine Hostages, Saint Columba (521-597 AD), sailed from Antrim with twelve followers and founded the monastery of Iona. Saint Columba went on to convert the Kingdom of Dal Riata to Christianity and then went on to convert the Picti. In 844 AD, the Kingdom of Alba, was formed combining Dal Riata with the Picts under Kenneth MacAlpine. The Kingdom of Alba went on to become The Kingdom of Scotland. Trade with the Mediterranean Sea continued from the West Coast of Britain and from Erins' isle via the Irish Sea. On the East coast the Anglo-Saxons traded across the English Channel with the Franks in Gaul.

Beginning with Saint Patrick, churches were set up throughout Ireland, but these didn't last. The monastery system began replacing the churches. The monastery system was invented by monks in Christian Egypt and it spread across Christianity. Holy men wishing to remain apart from the world to reflect and contemplate life sought out remote uninhabited places to dwell. This led to the discovery of the uninhabited Faroe Islands, and the discovery of numerous islands north of Scotland. Iceland was discovered by the group of monks called the Papar monks, Papar meaning father, in the 700's AD. They settled there and were discovered still living there in 874 AD by the Vikings when they re-discovered and settled Iceland.

"Noigiallach" is "Niall"; Niall of the Nine Hostages (357 AD – 411 AD). Noigiallach is a given name in Celtic Irish; it means champion, warrior, and passionate in Gaelic. Niall of the Nine hostages was the patriarch of the Ui Neill clan family of Ireland. The Ui Neill family dynasty lasted from the 6th to the 10th centuries in the North of Ireland. Niall had seven sons who ruled over both the northern and southern Kingdoms. In their lifetimes they were all part of the Connachta Dynasty. The Ui Neill names of the dynasties were not used until the time of grandsons and great-grandsons of Niall. Descendants of Ui Neill clan held power in Ulster up until 1603 AD; after the loss of the Nine Years War to the Protestants, they fled for Catholic Europe. "The Flight of the Earls" was what their departure was called, they left from their stronghold in Donegal. The O'Donnell clan was derived from the UI Neill clan. The Trinity College of Dublin reports from DNA Y haplotype testing that 21% of all men from Northwest Ireland have the same haplotype as Niall, 8% of all Irish have the same haplotype as Niall, and 2% of all Irish men in NYC are also descendants of Niall, and the Ui Neill clan. There are 2-3 Million descendants of Niall. Niall was buried outside the Ulster fortress of Navan, where he lies today, after being dug up by Trinity College to get some DNA from his skeletal remains. I hope they put a bottle in with him after they reburied him, and had some sort of ceremony at least.

The Y haplotype DNA for Niall, Ui Neill from family Tree DNA is as follows on a 25 marker test:

DYS 393 - 390 - 19 - 391 - 385a - 385b - 426 - 388 - 439 - 389i - 392 - 389ii - 458

13 25 14 11 11 13 12 12 12 13 14 29 17

DYS 459a - 459b - 455 - 454 - 447 - 437 - 448 - 449 - 464 a, b, c, d.

9 10 11 11 25 15 18 30 15,16,16,17

According to the Family Tree DNA testing lab I am one of the descendants of Niall of the Nine Hostages. My DNA is close enough to be the same considering the 1,700 year, long time period since Niall lived in Northwest Ireland. This means it was my family that enslaved Saint Patrick and put the wheels in motion that resulted in the conversion of Ireland to Christianity. It also means that Saint Columba is one of my fathers' direct ancestors. Saint Columba started the monastery of Iona and brought Christianity to Dal Riata, the Picts in Caledonia, and thus Christianity to Scotland. And I haven't been to church in 30 years, yikes!

My own Y haplotype DNA is as follows: R-M269, R1b1a2

DYS 393 - 390 - 19 - 391 - <u>385a</u> - <u>385b</u> - 426 - 388 - 439 - 389i - <u>392</u> - 389ii - 458

   13   25   14   11   11   13   12   12   12   13   14   29   <u>18</u>

DYS 459a - 459b - 455 - 454 - 447 - 437 - 448 - 449 - <u>464 a, b, c, d.</u>

   9   10   11   11   25   15   <u>18</u>   28   15,16,16,17

What distinguishes Niall's haplotype from the other western European RM-269 haplotypes is the presence of 11 and 13 at DYS 385a and 385b; the presence of 14 at DYS 392; and the 15,16,16,17 at DYS 464 a, b, c, d.

From the time that the first humans settled in Ireland and Britain, up until the time Saint Patrick started preaching, the earth revolved around the sun 6423 times. Cave paintings, fire, fighting, killing, surviving, kissing, loving, stars in the sky, Sun, the man in the moon, seasons, hot, cold, wind, rain, animals, Dust in the Wind. Where am I, what's going on here, where did we come from? Where are we going?

Stars and Dust

Twinkle, twinkle little star, how I wonder what you are,
up above the world so high, like a primate in the sky.

When the blazing sun is gone, when he nothing shines upon,
then you show you little light, twinkle, twinkle all the night.

When the glorious sun has set, and the night with dew is wet,
then you show your little light, and twinkle, twinkle, all the night.

The Sun God of the Greeks, Helios, rode a chariot across the sky and gave us the day. Later, Helios became Apollo for the Greeks. The Romans adopted and called Helios, Sol, Sol became "Sol Invictus", the undefeated Sun God of the Empire. The Sun is not a God it is a star. I am here. I am inside of a living body, which exists on the surface of a circular sphere made of rock and salty water. It is called the Earth, it is round, and it is not flat. This rock, this terra firma, circles around a swirling ball of burning gas called a star, at a straight distance of 93,000,000 miles, or 1 Astronomical Unit, 1 AU, or 491,040,000,000 feet away. One foot is the distance from my toe to my heel. This star is called "The Sun". The sun is 423,976,800 feet, or 80,299 miles in diameter. It's circumference around is 252,139 miles. The sun like the other stars, is a fusion reactor, a thermonuclear furnace, burning at a surface temperature of 10,000 degrees Fahrenheit. The gas of the Sun is mostly Hydrogen gas, along with some Helium and other trace elements. The Hydrogen atoms are fused together in the core of the sphere and the energy that is released by this fusion slowly makes its way to the surface over a 100,000-year period. The Sun is producing 385, 400,000,000,000,000,000,000,000 Watts, or $3.854E26$ Watts of luminous energy, as compared to a 60 Watt light bulb. The sun has a lifespan of 10 Billion years; it is halfway through its fuel supply. In another 5 Billion years it will run out of fuel and its outer surface will expand into Red Dwarf type of star as it begins to collapse into itself. The Earth will be consumed as the sphere expands. Other stars in the sky follow the same routine where they are born, burn through their Hydrogen fuel then extinguish themselves in any number of ways. I am kept warm and alive by this thermonuclear furnace. The Sun is at just the right distance from the planet earth to allow varied life forms to grow. The warmth generated by this close by star is what enables this life to grow with the help of the water on earth and the element Carbon, and Iron that is abundant here. It is a planet full of mysterious things and living beings, almost resembling a General Biology textbook.

Over the past 500,000 and more years, the orbit of the Earth around the Sun has varied from elliptical to circular and back again due to the fluctuating gravitational pull of the Sun and the gravitational waves that are moving through the fabric of space-time. As the Sun orbits the center of the galaxy its orbit brings it into unknown varying gravitational interactions with other stars also orbiting the center of the galaxy. The Sun doesn't just orbit in a straight line; it bobs up and down in a sinusoidal wave fashion as it orbits. The Sun is affected in its own orbit by varying proximities to passing gas fields and stars. Gravitational interactions keep everything in place within the galaxy and the universe, relative to one another and to the black hole.

The general relativity of the positioning of various masses in space like the Sun, moon, Saturn, Jupiter and so forth all effect the movements of one another and the planet earth. Gravitational waves affect light and they affect the metallic molten rock deep within the planet. This helps create earthquakes, volcanic eruptions, and magnetic variations on the surface of the planet. The Sun is situated about 25 light years above the Galactic mid-plane and is traveling at about 30,150 m.p.h. towards the Constellation Hercules; it is also traveling up from the mid plane of the galaxy at 16,200 m.p.h., in an inward trending tangential motion. The vertical velocity component causes the bobbing motion like a sinusoidal wave with a period between wave peaks of 42 million years. The Sun is orbiting at about 492,000 m.p.h. around the center of the galaxy at about the same speed as all the stars in the local neighborhood. These motions also oscillate creating an elliptical rosette shaped orbit around the Black Hole that takes 222 Million years to circumnavigate.

These previously mentioned earthly events, along with the variations in the orbit of the earth about its axis, the earth's precession with a 23,000 year cycle, the earth's eccentricity with a 100,000 year cycle, and the axial tilt with a 41,000 year cycle comprise what is known as the Milankovitch cycles. The Milankovitch cycles, named after the professor Milankovitch, cause alternating Ice Ages and inter-glacial warming as we experience now in this Holocene warm period. In 2015, the orbit of the earth about the sun is mostly circular, like the henges of the sundial called Stonehenge. The tilt of the angle of the axis of the earth varies over time, tilting at various angles, towards and away from the Sun. When tipped away from the Sun, less direct warming radiation allows for Ice Age formation. The Milankovitch cycle takes about 26,000 years to complete one cycle, then starts over again, but to this cycle there are additional variables, that are not completely charted at present. The interactions and the mechanical physics involved in general relativity makes charting and predicting difficult since we don't know exactly where we came from, or what we passed along the way, or even what we will run into along our path. On earth, there are oceanic currents in the oceans that redistribute warm and cold seawater in an attempt to continually come to equilibrium. The change of warming radiation to cooler radiation from the sun on the land and water alters the direction of oceanic currents which resemble a conveyor belt. The Gulf Stream current can be turned southward, leaving a less warmed North Atlantic, which leads to prolonged cooling of oceanic waters, colder land and a colder atmosphere in the Northern hemisphere. The heat of the Sun creates climate and weather; one thing affects another.

My next nearest neighboring star is in a star cluster called Alpha Centauri Triple Star Cluster. Triple means three. It is called Proxima Centauri. It is not visible to the naked eye as are the naked women on Haulover Beach, Florida, who are much closer, but it can be seen with a telescope, a thing which helps me to see things far away. Proxima Centauri was discovered by a Scot named Robert Innes. Proxima Centauri is 4.24 light years away. I am told a light year is the distance that light can travel in 365 days.

One light year is about 6 trillion miles, (6E12 miles). As this rock circles the Sun it also spins around itself on its axis in a period of 24 hours. There are 60 seconds in one minute, 60 minutes in one hour, 24 hours in one day, and 365 days in one year. The speed of light is 186,000 miles per second. In 60 seconds, or 1 minute a sunray can travel 11,160,000 miles. In 60 minutes or in one hour a sunray can travel 669,600,000 miles. In 24 hours or in one day a sunray can travel 16,070,400,000 miles, and in one year, 365.25 days, a sunray can travel 5,869,713,600,000 miles, (5.8697136E12 miles) or about 6 trillion miles. A ray of sunlight can travel from the surface of the sun, continue past the earth, and head out to our next nearest star, Proxima Centauri, and it will arrive there in 1,581 days or in 4 years and 3 months (4.24 years). Proxima Centauri is 25,400,000,000,000 miles away, (2.54E13 miles away). That is 25 trillion, 400 billion miles away. Light is pretty fast, must faster than a 1963 Rambler Classic. At

45 miles per hour in a '63 Rambler it would take a long time to get to Proxima Centauri, about 553,057,459,200 hours, or 23,044,060,800 days, or 63,091,200 years to get there. It would take 63 Million years to drive to Proxima Centauri in a '63 Rambler at 45 m.p.h., if you got on at the on ramp by the Sun. The Sun must appear bright if you are circling Proxima Centauri because Proxima Centauri is a red dwarf type of star. The other two stars in this cluster are Alpha Centauri A and B. Alpha Centauri A is a yellowish color, Alpha Centauri B is bluish in color, Proxima Centauri is a dim ruddy color. The triple star cluster Alpha Centauri is in the Constellation that the Greek philosophers called The Centaur. A Centaur is half horse and half man. It can be seen in the Southern sky, or wandering around the sponge docks in Tarpon Springs, Florida. The Alpha Centauri Star Cluster is about 40 degrees to the right if you are facing the galactic center and looking past the Constellation Sagittarius. There are about 33 stars scattered within 12.5 light years from us here at the Sun. If thought of as a sphere, it would be a sphere around us with a radius of 7 trillion (7,337,142,000,000), (7.337142E12) miles, and a diameter of 14 trillion (14,674,280,000,000), (1.467428E13) miles, containing 33 stars.

The Pole star, or The North Star, Polaris, which is roughly straight up from the North Pole of the axis of the Earth is also a triple star cluster. It is about 330-430 light years, 2,523,976,848,000,000 miles, (2.5 Quadrillion miles, 2.5E15 miles), above us if we are facing the center of the Galaxy. If the center of the galaxy was straight out on an "X" axis, at 26,000 light years, (152 Quadrillion miles), the North star would be straight out on the "Y" axis at 430 light years. The North Star is the tail star in the Constellation Ursula Minor, the little dipper.

Our Sun is one of many stars in a group of stars called a galaxy. Someone called our galaxy the Milky Way Galaxy because it looks milky on dark nights. The sun is one of the brightest stars in the entire Milky Way Galaxy. It is around 85 on a scale of 0-100 with 100 being the brightest. There is also something we call "dark Matter", which makes up the overwhelming percentage of all matter within the galaxy. It is called "dark matter" because it doesn't react to the electromagnetic spectrum instruments we have invented. In the near future we will invent instrumentation that will be able to measure and analyze the "dark matter". The Sun and the Earth and We, all of us are in the Orion arm of the Orion-Cygnus arm within the Milky Way Galaxy.

This arm is 3500 light years across, (2.1E16 miles across, 2,100,000,000,000,000 miles across or 2.1 Quadrillion miles across) and 10,000 light years in length. The Orion arm is named for the Orion Constellation which is also located in the Orion arm. Orion was also named by the Greek philosophers, it means, "The Great Hunter". The Orion arm is located between the Carina-Sagittarius Arm, towards the galactic center, and the Perseus Arm, which is towards the outer universe. The Milky Way Galaxy is 100,000 to 120,000 light years in diameter (5.8697136E17 miles - to - 7.04365632E17 miles) or (586,971,360,000,000,000 miles - to - 704,365,632,000,000,000 miles) in diameter, and it contains well over 100-400 Billion swirling balls of gaseous stars. We all circle around the center of the galaxy at a speed of 492,126 miles per hour. The circumference of the Milky Way Galaxy is 1,844,024,138,360,000,000 miles around. It takes 222,275,887 years to complete one complete revolution about the center, at the suns distance from center. The sun is 26,000 light years away from the center of the galaxy. It is 1.56E17 miles away, (156,000,000,000,000,000 miles away). Our circumference around the center is 9.7968E17 miles, (979,680,000,000,000,000 miles around) at the distance of 156,000,000,000,000,000 miles away.

The galaxy is about 14 Billion years old. The Milky Way is part of a binary galaxy system of giant spiral galaxies. The sister of the Milky Way galaxy is the Andromeda Galaxy. There are also 50 closely bound galaxies called the local group. Two smaller galaxies and a number of dwarf galaxies orbit the milky way. Andromeda is approaching us at 224,000-895,000 miles per hour, in 3-4 Billion years there may be an Andromeda- Milky Way collision. Good thing I have Geico.

Out here in the spiral arms of the Milky Way there is about one star in every 30 cubic light ears. There are about 33 stars scattered within 12.5 light years of the sun. 12.5 light years' distance from the sun is a sphere with a diameter of 15 trillion-mile diameter. If I take a Sunday drive to the center of the galaxy in my '63 Rambler Classic, I first pass Proxima Centauri then after a while I notice the stars are becoming denser and they are packed closer together. At 50 light years from earth there are now about 2000 stars surrounding me. I can turn off my headlights for a while. Continuing on towards the center I reach the edge of the Orion arm which was 3500 light years completely across, the stars become less dense like a desert. I have to cross this desert and get to the other side where the Carina-Sagittarius begins in the far distance. I reach the Carina-Sagittarius arm and I cross it only to reach another desert like expanse that separates the Carina-Sagittarius arm from the Norma Arm of the galaxy. When I am about 10,000 light years (6,000,000,000,000,000 miles) away from the Sun I stop and get out and look up and down. The spiral arms now have converged into a huge spherical bulge or ball. This spherical bulge is about 5,000 light years up and 5,000 light years down and down it looks like its 10,000 light years to the left and to the right. My map says it's another 16,000 light years to the center, so I get back in and go. I am about to enter the bulge. The bulge is the large milky white area seen in the night time sky on earth. The density of the stars here is amazing, there are 300,000 stars per cubic light year within this spherical region. I figure, since there is one light year equals 6 trillion miles, and there are 300,000 stars within each cubic light year, there must be 67 stars every 6 trillion miles in every direction, or 11 stars every trillion miles or one star every 91 billion miles in every direction. Considering that it is 25 trillion miles from the Sun to our closest star Proxima Centauri, and considering the density of the spherical region with 1 star every 91 Billion miles, you could fit 275 stars in between the earth and Proxima Centauri, to achieve the same density. It is very bright here and it reminds me of the light fixture area at Home Depot. I turn the air on and put on my Cool rays. All the stars in this region form a spherical bulge that surround the center.

Continuing on to about 25,500 light years into my trip I open up a Milky Way candy bar and munch down. My cat is stretched out on the dashboard looking up at the stars and contemplating life. The stars are getting piled up even more like rush hour traffic heading for the Holland Tunnel in the morning. Now there are even bigger stars about 100 times as big as the Sun. I am 300 light years out from the center now. There are 300,000 stars within every light year. I have to swerve continuously to continue straight ahead and it's getting denser still. At 100 light years out from center, I am 50 light years away from the "event horizon" there is more than 300,000 stars around me now and a dense molecular nebulosity that is being jostled about by really intense magnetic and gravitational tides and waves. After slowing down and carefully navigating closer to the center, I observe an incredibly dense cluster of stars. Within half a light year of the "event horizon" there are 400 hot, young, massive stars. Some of these stars make complete orbits around the center. One star called SO 16 orbit the center at 90 astronomical units, or 8,370,000,000 miles. By calculating the motion of this star into gravitational mass, astronomers have deduced the size and mass of the center of the galaxy. I have arrived at the center of the Milky Way Galaxy. My cat just stares straight at it with her blue unblinking eyes. She is not purring but her tail is still. I wish I had a Snickers bar.

The center of the Milky Way Galaxy is peculiar and interesting. In the center, is a thing we have called a black hole, not to be confused with a black hoe. The name of this black hole is Sagittarius A, SagA*, Sag A star. The name of the black hoe is Charandra. Unlike Charandra, the black hole is an unknown thing. Chandra is the name of the satellite with the equipment to observe the black hole from earth's orbit. We do know that the black hole has an immense pull, so much gravitational pull that not even light can escape from its grasp. This pull that it has seems to be what holds all the matter in the galaxy in place and revolving. Gravitational force is one of the four basic forces and the least understood. The 4 basic forces we know about are gravitational, electromagnetic, strong nuclear, and weak nuclear forces. The black hole has a mass that is equivalent to 4 Million Solar masses. This is 4 million times the mass of our sun. By using an equation called the Schwarzschild radius equation for a black hole, it is calculated that the radius of the black hole is 7,750,000 miles. It is 15,500,000 miles across in a spherical shape, and it weighs 4 million times what the sun weighs. The sun is 864,576 miles across and the earth is about 8,000 miles across. What happens to everything that falls into the black hole is anyone's guess. It is speculated that everything goes into a singular point called a "Singularity". I think it was named a singularity because it is a singular point.

Could be smaller than this period. (.) From this singular compact point where everything went, or is, or what happens to it, is beyond our space and time and understanding in 2016. It is "undefined" mathematically. At the edge of the black hole is the "event horizon" where stuff starts to fall into it. I am thinking of getting out of the car and walking just around the edge and throwing some flat rocks into it to see if I can skip the rocks off the "event horizon" before they enter it. Damn, I really wish I brought a Snickers bar.

Sagittarius A is 24,000-26,000 light years away from the Sun and the Earth. It is 156,000,000,000,000,000 miles away, or 156 Quadrillion miles away from Earth. It is 805 Quintillion feet away from earth, how far it is from the "event horizon" to the "Singularity" may be infinity.

So, as I am sitting there in my '63 Rambler Classic, in front of the event horizon, and I can't see anything but blackness if I look at it, there is no light at all coming from it, some gas clouds move in towards it and they disappear. I turn on the radio to get a weather report and there are sound waves that are emanating from the black hole. They are 57 octaves below middle C, which is 1.7×10^{-15} Hz. The range of human hearing is 20-20000 Hz. I start to wonder about where all this galaxy came from, did someone make all this and me? Is there a God? I just don't know. I suspect that these subconscious sound waves are the reason I am thinking and wondering about God. I feel this way on earth a lot but I never associated the longing for God with the Black Hole, as if I am being drawn to God subconsciously. Humans must hear these inner sound waves that ride along the dark gravitational matter and gas clouds and misinterpret them as being a God in our primitive primate brain housing groups in much the same way animals can sense earthquakes and other natural phenomenon. I understand now.

And what is producing this sound? I am sure it is a large gorilla like primate sitting behind the veiled shroud of the "event horizon" playing some type of musical instrument. He sits there, all powerful, all knowing, all seeing, playing the sounds we all hear in our deepest soul, eating bananas and looking out on the universe. I'm not sure what he does with the peels, he might throw them at the "Singularity" or he might open the veil and throw them out of the "event horizon. I wait to see if this monkey God sticks his head out or maybe just his fingers like the Michelangelo painting on the ceiling of the Sistine chapel at the Vatican, so I roll down the window, and start to eat my Ham and American cheese sandwich on Rye with mustard. Just as I bite into it a banana peel flies though the open window and lands in the back seat, a sign from the almighty. I have faith, I am one of the faithful now. He exists. My Siamese cat says Me-ow. Driving home always seems faster than going there.

As I return to the solar system, I encounter the moon revolving around the earth. It is really large next to the earth; it just doesn't seem normal.

Swinging on a Star

Would you like to swing on a star,
carry moonbeams home in a jar,
and be better off than you are,
or would you rather be a mule?

A mule is an animal with long funny ears,
kicks up at anything he hears,
his back is brawny but his brain is weak
he's just plain stupid with a stubborn streak,

Raymond Robert Martin

And by the way if you hate to go to school,
you may grow up to be a mule.

Or would you like to swing on a star,
carry moonbeams home in a jar,
and be better off than you are,
Or would you rather be a pig,

A pig is an animal with dirt on his face,
his shoes are a terrible disgrace,
he has no manners when he eats his food,
he's fat and lazy and extremely rude,

But if you don't care a feather or a fig
you may grow up to be a pig.

Or would you like to swing on a star,
carry moonbeams home in a jar
and be better off than you are,
or would you rather be a fish.

A fish won't do anything but swim in a brook,
he can't write his name or read a book,
to fool the people is his only thought,
and though he's slippery he still gets caught

but then if that sort of life is what you wish
you may grow up to be a fish
a new king of jumped up slippery fish.

And all the monkeys aren't in the zoo,
everyday you'll meet quite a few,
so you see it's all up to you,
you could be better than you are,
you could be swinging on a star.

Gods and Truth; Psychopathy, Philosophy, or stepping into a Black Hole

So, what is truth, and what is gobbledygook? What is the concept of God if it is not the Sun, the stars in the galaxy, the earth, or the moon, or the heart of darkness at the center of the galaxy? Is it a large gorilla like primate sitting behind a black veil playing musical notes with his feet while eating bananas?

The word "God" is the Angle tribes word of the Germanic word Odin (Wotan). The idea, the concept of God is an idea, like any other, but it becomes a power greater than me; it is merely a thought but a powerful thought for myself, in my experience. This idea can keep me or make me strong minded, and it evokes intense emotions. Any idea of God may be true or untrue. The idea itself is light, it is consciousness. It is "en-light-en-ment" in a primate. "Let there be light." Consciousness of what? Is it just consciousness or does it have to be consciousness of something else; is it awareness of being? Where does consciousness lead? It makes me aware that I am a single life form, a higher primate, a man; and I am alone here in this body in a vast universe. Oh God, what a thought that is! The thought of being alone in the universe is too much for any primate, who is a social animal. The primate creates another supernatural being to fill in the loneliness. The consciousness is like an empty golden chalice or goblet, a grail, a holy grail. It is truly empty and truly pure, and the primate is free to fill it with whatever true or untrue gobbledygook he or she or someone else makes up. What do I believe; what do I fill the chalice with? Should I just follow the troop? Should I reason, should I love, hate? I need to survive and eat first and foremost.

I have been lucky and am grateful to have been born in the middle of the twentieth century and to live in The United States of America. I am free to think, to reflect, to write about anything I wish to pursue, and I am free to associate with whomever or whatever group I want. I am free to reflect on truth, on God and on whiskey. I was lucky and am grateful that I was taught to read and write by my parents, when I was just a wee little lad because it has given me some ability to understand some science, arts, literature, music and mathematics. The reading and the writing I have learned has allowed me to make some sort of sense of the creation that is the universe around me, and it has allowed me to support myself in this western civilization, without hunting, gathering and fishing for survival.

So I ask myself the question, "What is God, who is God"? My truthful answer is, "I don't have a fucking clue? Sometimes I like to think I understand but when it comes down to it, I don't, and I am old enough now to believe I never will. It is an unanswerable question, without using my imagination. I could associate with a religion but it would be a false association because I really and truly don't believe what these "Prophets" of these religions have made up, or cobbled together.

But what is the meaning of life, if there is one? To survive to reproduce, to die; what is the meaning of that, just a furtherance of the life line until it evolves to a higher more evolved life form? And the meaning in that? To experience life? Where was I before then, and after death, then what? Imagination could fill these questions in, but they would be just imaginary. These types of questions, I think, are what the patriarch Abraham, some of the Prophets, and a lot of primates have asked themselves. Most primates I suspect just let these questions be and followed what the troop surrounding them believed, finding comfort in the easier, softer way of just believing what was already made up for them, and passing it on to their children.

Which belief system is truth? Is that belief system with truth? Is that belief system an aid to my survival, to my reproduction, to my death? A Greek goddess once told the philosopher Parmenides in his poem, "beware of the un-truth of men". "They are lies which do not lead to the path of truth". Good advice concerning religious beliefs and the concept of God. One mans' truth is the untruth to yourself because it is not your truth but another mans' truth; one mans' truth is the untruth of other men.

Survival, belief in a supernatural or natural being is about survival. A whole tribe is kept together by a common belief, they work together or against each other but with this common belief, it keeps them from killing each other because another belief is too foreign to think about, and thus it binds the tribe together as a group. We are complex animals compared to the other animals inhabiting this planet. We have survived for a long time on this planet and we are always at war with each other for survival. It is better to be in a warring group than alone without a group, because there are warring groups all around a lone individual. The lone individual with his or her beliefs is in a distinct minority and either is annihilated by the warring group, defeats the entire warring group, or is forced to submit to the warring groups beliefs to continue to survive. This group belief in religion pits the group against the individual rights of a man outlined in the First Amendment of the Constitution of the United States of America. This previous scenario of submission is the reason that the writers of the Constitution wrote the Second Amendment. The individual has the absolute right to keep and use arms and weapons for his or her survival against the warring group.

A true belief system is one that enhances and puts forward a groups survival and prosperity, either peacefully or not so peacefully. Either way the system is a true belief system because it aids survival. The ones' in the group may not be the fittest, but the group becomes powerful, and the unfit individuals survive collectively. What this leads to could either be extermination and extinction of the group or dominant survival of the primate group, or some gray area in the middle.

I wonder if the Neanderthals prayed to any God, or if the primates walking out Africa prayed or thought about God. Both must have been in awe of the Milky Way and the moon, and faith developed in them together that all was well.

Time goes by, it is eternal time. It takes 222 Million years for the Earth to travel around the center of the galaxy. Earth was formed 4 billion, 500 million years ago. Life on earth began or arrived 4 billion years ago. The Milky Way Galaxy has revolved around itself 18.9166666667 times since Earth began, and 16.6666666667 times since life began on earth. Notice all the 666's. Human life has been short compared to eternal time, and we have invented the idea of God. We go round and round and like days through an hourglass, so go the days of our lives, just a little further along in the circumnavigation of the sun about the Milky Way, to eternity. I don't think about God much, but when I do it's mindboggling. I am that I am and that's all that I am, I'm Popeye the Sailorman. My mind doesn't think about God much but when I do, it's mind boggling. Stay thirsty my friends.

Throw me a rope God

There have been many Gods made up by primates since the last Ice age ended. Mostly all within the last 5,000 years and especially more after primates invented farming. Religions developed out of the common beliefs in Gods, and elaborate rituals came into being to support the majesty of these Gods. Mithra and Zoroastrianism were from Persia, Zeus and the Pantheon of Greek Gods were from southeast Europe, the Celtic Pantheon from Central and Western Europe, Norse Gods from Scandinavia, the God of Abraham and his three offshoot religions, Judaism, Christianity and Islam from the Middle East, African tribal Gods, Inca, Mayan and Aztec Gods, Native American Gods, Pacific Island Gods, desert tribal gods, Arctic primate Gods, Hinduism, Buddhism, Confucianism, Taoism, all arising from tribes of people and an individuals' personal truth. The following paragraphs cover some of these beliefs.

Buddhism, "I am awake"! Buddha, born 563 BC as Siddhartha Gautama in Nepal, turned his back on his wealth, comfort and love, and sought the forest grove's for solitude; he wandered around India for 50 years, and then died of dysentery after eating a wild boar. He had a cool head and a warm heart, he was a silent sage. Buddha contemplated and preached, a no authority religion, devoid of ritual, devoid of tradition, devoid of supernatural, avoidance of speculation, along with intense self-effort, "Tread it". Life is suffering. Life's dislocation is in the self-seeking, we can overcome this selfishness, by following Buddha's eightfold path. The eightfold path is right views, right intent, right speech, right conduct, right livelihood, right effort, right mindfulness, and right concentration, eat one of the other white meats.

Hinduism, you can have what you want; "The beyond is within". Yoga, Intuition, Love, work, people are different so they have to live in a caste system; these are all part of Hinduism. Hinduism is a synthesis of the Iron Age Vedic Brahmanism religion combined with various Indian cultural traditions. Hinduism coalesced around 500-300 BC. The Vedic religion was the religion of the Indo-Aryan peoples in northern India; these Indo-Aryan people were part of Kurgan culture that developed in the steppes south of the Ice Wall. Cows are sacred; no beef allowed and make sure to put a dot on your head.

Sikhs, Guru Nanak dispelled ignorance and darkness. Born in 1469 AD, in 1500, he falls into a river and disappears for 3 days. After climbing out of the river, he follows the path of God, avoiding both Hinduism and Islam. Sikhs worship and seek salvation through a union with God by realizing God deep within them. They have their own chalice of truth; there is nothing supernatural about Sikhism. They are not Rastafarians and are not from Jamaica.

Confucianism, Confucius is Kung Fu-tzu, he is the first teacher. Confucius was born around 551 BC; he died in 479 BC in China. His father died before he was three years old, but he had a loving modest upbringing. He was a politician but failed at it. Before this he set his mind to seeking knowledge, learning, education and then worked in public administration. After this he wandered around China, and saw the need to reform society, to steer it away from social anarchy. Confucius says...........!

Yezidism, Yazidis' are an endogenous ethno-religious group. Yezidism is an ancient Mesopotamian religion of some of the Kurds. Yazidi's are a monotheistic religion that believes in God as the creator. God has appointed seven angels, with the chief angel called the Peacock angel who allows both good and bad to befall primates. This religion is tied to

Mithras, they have four festivals that correspond to the equinoxes. The number seven is sacred. There is a Yazidi belief in seven heavens and a seven level spiritual system.

So many Gods and so little time, or is that men? Put another nickel in, in the Nickelodeon. All I want is love, and music, music, music. When looking at religions, I am dumbfounded at the fact that so many humans have and do follow about seven world religions made up by seven different men. There are billions and billions of people now and in the past, but mostly all just accept the truths of these men. It reminds me of the saying, Monkey see, monkey do. The people of the world just accept these as truth without question or they change to another religion and truth. It is amazing to me, that so many humans have an unquestionable faith in another mans' truth over their very own. No wonder the Neanderthals committed suicide. Mithra, (3000 BC), Zoroaster (1700 BC), Adam and Eve (3760 BC), Abraham (1700 BC), Lao Tzu (604 BC), Buddha (563 BC), Confucius (551 BC), Hinduism (500-300 BC), Mithra, the second one, (272 BC), Jesus of Nazareth, (0), Mohammad (570 AD), Guru Nanak (1500 AD). Mormons (1820 AD), Pastafarianism (2005 AD), Reverend Al Sharptonism (ongoing).

The Celtic Druid Pantheon

The Mystery

I am the wind which breathes upon the sea,
I am the wave of the ocean,
I am the murmur of the billows,
I am the ox of the seven combats,
I am the vulture upon the rocks,
I am a beam of the sun,
I am the fairest of plants,
I am a wild boar in valor,
I am a salmon in the water,
I am a lake in the plain,
I am a word of science,
I am the point of the lance of battle,
I am the God who created in the head fire.
Who is it who throws light into the meeting on the mountain?
Who announces the ages of the moon?
Who teaches the place where couches the sun?

The Celtic Pantheon is difficult if not impossible to understand. The Celtic Culture in Gaul and Albu was conquered by the Roman Empire, many were taken into slavery and sold around the Empire. The druid priests were murdered by Rome for being the knowledgeable leaders of the Celts. Without writings, beliefs were lost for all time. After the subjugation for 400 years, the Romanized Celtic peoples were overrun by Germanic tribes, then finally Western Christianity suppressed any of the Celtic pagan beliefs or merged them in with Roman Catholicism. There are some sources of information about the religion and one is from the Roman leader who conquered the Celts for the Roman Empire, Julius Caesar. He wrote a book called "The Gallic Wars", and recorded some of the religious beliefs of the conquered. Also some of the pre-Christian Myths and legends of Ireland, written by Irish Christian monks mention these Gods, and the stories about them.

In proto-Indo-European, "Kel" means, to protect. Celtic tribes offered protection to Celts. The Celtic tribes are derived from groups called the Cimmerians and the Scythians. These groups lived north of the Caucus Mountains, around the Black Sea, and the Caspian Sea. They were groups that had derived from the hunter-gatherer clans south of the Ice Wall in central Europe and Western Asia. They are mentioned in the old testament of the Hebrew book. Gomer was the son of Noah. Gomer was the leader and patriarch of the Gomerites. The Gomerites are Cimmerians,

Cymmerians', or Cymru, they are also known as Galatians. The Galatians' are Celtic tribes that settled in Turkey after their unsuccessful southerly attack and migration to Greece in 279 BC. The new Testament of the Christian Bible also mentions the Celts; it has a section written by Saint Paul to the Galatians. Gomer was also an ally of Gog, Gog was leader of the MaGog. It is unknown exactly when in time the Celtic tribal waves migrated to Ireland and Britain, but it ranges from 3000 BC until 800 BC. The Scythians are forerunners of the Saxons. The Cimmerians and the Scythians fought against the Assyrian Empire in 675 BC in Upper Mesopotamia and were defeated, then they moved west into Anatolia, and stayed north of the Caucasus'. In 626 BC, both the Scythians and Cimmerians fought against the Persian King Darius I, north of the Bosporus, and north of the Black Sea, but he was unable to subdue them. Further on, Cimmerians and Scythians, fought against the Greeks, then the Romans, when Rome was fighting to subdue the Hellenistic Empire created by Alexander the Great around the Black Sea. Cimmerian and Scythian strongholds were north of the Black Sea and around the Danube River stretching west to the Alps. After the beginning of the rise of the Roman in 800 BC, they all headed west into western Europe and Gaelic tribes settled there and in the British Islands. Turkic like tribes from further east on the steppes of Asia moved west onto the steppes they vacated.

The myths and legends of Ireland, along with some of the old books of Ireland give insight into the gods and the settlement of Ireland. These stories of settlement in Ireland seem to have evolved into stories of Gods and the names of the characters themselves became the names of the Gods. These main Celtic Gods seem to have spread east to Gaul and the continent, or the stories of the invasions of Ireland were about the continental Gods invading Ireland. At any rate, by the time Julius Caesar invaded western Europe, these old Gods were well established throughout Celtic western Europe, with variations in local deities spread out over the lands. The Celts honored the forces of nature and the sacred and divine was intricately interwoven in the rural surroundings of Europe. Celtic mythology and religion is the story of an animist polytheistic religion of Bronze Age and Iron Age Celts, mixed with earlier pre-historic religious beliefs from earlier stone age times. There was a fertile and willing spiritual chaos among the Celts. Animist religion believes there is no separation between the spiritual world and the physical world. The Latin word 'anima' means "breath", "spirit", or "life". Animists believe both human primates and non-human entities possess a spiritual essence. In Celtic beliefs there is no separation between the spiritual and physical world. It is all one. Souls and sacred spirits' existed in human primates, animals, plants, rocks, lakes, springs, groves of trees, mountains, rivers, thunder, wind, shadows, moon, sun, the Milky Way Galaxy, each and every star, and sacred spirits existed in words. There was no separation of the mental and physical world, as in modern religions.

In ancient Irish myth, there were six waves of known immigration to Ireland. They were: first, in 2958 BC, the female leader Banbu and her two sisters, Fodla, and Eriu, along with their three husbands, Mac Cuill, (son of the hazel), Mac Cecht, (son of the plough) and Mac Griene, (son of the Sun). The second wave was by Muintir Partholoin, (The people of Partholoin); when they arrived in 2680 BC, there was no one else there. The Partholoins introduced farming, cattle husbandry, fishing, building, cooking and trade. They may have come from the Iberian Peninsula. They fight against supernatural beings called "The Fomorians" to settle Ireland. The Fomorians represented the destructive forces of nature. The Fomorians lived underground, and under the sea; they represented chaos, disease, darkness, death and blight. The Fomorians won their battles and all the Partholoins died of disease in one week. The third group to settle are the Muintir Nemed, (people of the leader Nemed) arrived in 2350 BC, after setting sail from the Caspian Sea, in 2348 BC. There was no one there when they arrived. The Nemed also battle The Fomorians. Nemed dies in 2341 BC, and the entire Muintir Nemed is destroyed or some flee to Britain or head north by sea, or south to Greece. Ireland now is unoccupied again for 200 plus years. The fourth group to immigrate to and settle in Ireland are the Fir Bolg, in 2111 BC. The Fir bolg, means men of the bag. They are called this because these are the descendants of theMuintir Nemed who escaped to Greece in 2341 BC. They were enslaved by the Greeks for 230 years, and as slaves they were forced to carry bags of earth, giving them the name men of the bags, the Fir bolg. Fir means men, bolg means bag. The Fir bolg escaped from Greece and returned to Ireland in 2111 BC. They divide Ireland into 5 provinces, Ulster, Connacht, Leinster, North Munster, and South Munster. They live and rule there alone for 37 years. In 2074 BC, the fifth group arrives in the north of Ireland, they are the Tuatha De Danaan. Tuatha means tribe, De means God or Goddess, and Danaan means Dana. The "tribe of the Goddess Dana" is the Tuatha De Danaan, the men of Dea. The goddess Dana is also known as Anu, "the mother of all Irish Gods". The Coming of the Tuatha De Danaan, in a book by Lady Augusta Gregory, "Gods and Fighting Men", provides a good poetic description of the tribe of the Goddess Danu.

"It was in a mist the Tuatha de Danaan, the people of the gods of Dana, or as some called them, the men of Dea, came through the air and the high air to Ireland.

It was from the north they came; and in the place they came from they had four cities, where they fought their battle for learning: great Falias, and shining Gorias, and Finias, and rich Murias that lay to the south. And in those citiies they had four wise men to teach their young men skill and knowledge and perfect wisdom: Senias in Murias; and Arias, the fair haired poet, in Finias; and Urias of the noble nature in Gorias; and Morias in falias itself. And they brought from those four cities their four treasures: a Stone of Virtue from Falias, that was called Lia Fail, the Stone of Destiny; and from Gorias they brought a sword; and from Finias a Spear of Victory; and from Murias the fourth treasure, the (Dagdas) Cauldron that no company ever went away from unsatisfied."

The men of the Tuatha de Danaan were Dagda, (This "Sky Father" had a Cauldron no one ever went hungry from), Manannan, (sea god and jokester), Nuada, (king at the time with the Sword of Light), Neit, (god of battle), Ogma, (a chief and a writer), Diancecht, (healer) Credenus, (craftsman) and Goibniu (blacksmith). The women of the Tuatha were the daughters of Dagda, Banda, Fodla, Eire; Eadon, (nurse of poets) Brigit, (a woman of poetry, healing, blacksmithing who made a whistle so each could call the other, she was known as a fiery arrow), and the greatest among the women were Badb, (a battle goddess who causes fear and confusion on a battlefield by screaming like a banshee), Macha, (who fed on the heads of those killed in battle), and Morrigu, (the hooded crow, Corvus cornix, of battle, Morigu is similar to Lilith in the Hebrew Book of Isaiah.); plus, there were many more shadow forms and great queens, and of course Dana was the mother of them all. They arrived on May Day, Beltaine (Bal-tinna). The Tuatha de Danaan were enemies of the Fomorians.

The Fir Bolg only saw mist when the Tuatha came to Ireland, but they knew they were there. The Tuatha de Danaan demanded a portion of Ireland or they would fight for it. The Fir Bolg lost the battles and The Tuatha de Danaan became rulers of the Island, with their seat at Tara. While there a man named Lugh requested entry. He was a child of both the Tuatha De Danaan and a Fomorian mother. He was one man skilled in all of the knowledge that was dispersed among many of the Tuatha. He was admitted to the Tuatha at Tara and was known as Lugh of the Long Hand and he carried a powerful spear, The Spear of Lugh. Lugh became king at Tara. The Tuatha de Danaan became known as the ever living ones.

After a long time passed, and in 1897 BC, the sixth group of immigrants invaded, they were a group of Gaels who had been wandering the world for hundreds of years, the Milesians. They were led by Miles, and it is believed they sailed from the Iberian Peninsula, which was composed of Celtic tribes. The Gaels defeated the Tuatha De Danaan in many battles and took control of Ireland, but the Tuatha would not ever submit. Mannanan hid them all away in different places and put up walls so that human primates could not see them, but they could see out and move in and out of the places. The Tuatha de Danaan occupied the underworld and the Milesians occupied the above world. The Tuatha were now Gods of growth and civilization. The Tuatha live in the otherworld where it is always a happy, summer paradise. The Tuatha are the "Fairies", and "Pixies" Glimpses of the Otherworld can be seen in changes of weather, strange animals, or in an otherworld woman offering a ball of string or an apple. The Otherworld is known as the land of Forever Young, the land of the Living, the delightful plain, and Elysium. It is Paradise. When someone dies they are greeted by

Donn, the king of the dead, who brings them to his house for a while then he brings them to "the Isles of the Blessed", "Elysium Fields", Paradise in the Western Sea.

In the sixth century BC, Hecataeus of Miletus, (550-476 BC), a Greek historian, wrote of the Hyperboreans. The Hyperboreans were a people who lived in the distant north on a large island facing the country of the Celts. On this island, the Hyperboreans built a magnificent circular temple, and worshipped the sun as a God. He is describing Stonehenge on the Salisbury Plain in Britain. The Hyperboreans he is describing are the male haplotype R1b inhabitants of Britain. Stonehenge was already disused when this historical myth was written. Boreas was the God of the north wind. Stonehenge was built in 3100 BC using wood and ditches'. It was rebuilt using stones in 2400-2200 BC. Stonehenge was used to mark time and the seasons. Newgrange in Ireland was built in 3200 BC also out of stone. Mathematics, algebra, metrology and arithmetic were all invented around the same time. The Bronze Age existed from 2100 BC to 600 BC in Pretannia.

Julius Caesar was a Roman general who intervened in Gaul militarily under the pretext of Celtic tribes moving onto Roman Latin lands. His real motive was to make a fortune and further his career. Migrations always caused chaos in the eyes of Rome. Germanic tribes were pushing Celtic tribes west due to increases in populations. He invaded Gaul and ended up conquering all of Gaul, northeast and southeast Europe, then he crossed the English Channel and entered Pretannia. His commentaries on his campaigns gave insight into Celtic peoples. In book 6, "Commentaries on the Gallic War", Julius Caesar correlates the five main Celtic Gods within the territory of Gaul that he conquered, with what he believed was their Roman counterpart. He may be incorrect in his associations, but they are: Esus=Lugh=Odin=God=Mercury. Esus means Lord. Esus is Lugh the God of bright flashing light, like lightning, he is sometimes associated with the sun. Lugh is also god of the arts, oath, and contracts, he was skilled in all knowledge. It was also believed Lugh was a three faced triune god that encompassed Esus, Taranis, and Teutates. Lugh carried the spear of victory. Teutates or Teutatis=Mars. Tuesday is named after Teutates. Teutates mens tribe God. Taranis=Thor=Jupiter=Zeus. Taranis is the thunder god like Thor but carries the solar wheel. Thursday is named after Taranis, Thor, Thorsday. Sunday is Esus, the Lords day. Wednesday was Wotans day. Friday was Frigs day, Saturday is Saturn's (Nimrod's) day. Belenus=Apollo=Helios=Sol=the Sun. The Celtic Gods demanded human sacrifices.

The male deity, the Dagda, meaning "the Good", "the all competent", was the protector of the tribe. He was all embracing and controlled wisdom and warfare. The female counterpart of the Dagda was the Morrigan. She is both fertile and the destructive Phantom Queen warrior goddess. Morrigan becomes aged from one Samhain (Halloween) to the next. The loving coming together and coupling of the good Dagda and the old Morrigan on the fall Samhain festival each year, started the year anew and was similar to our current New Years' Day. Morrigan became young again afterwards and a new year begins. This coupling ensured continuing prosperity for both crop harvests and animal fertility. In 324 AD, Emperor Constantine went to Troy in Anatolia to try to build a new imperial city to replace the malaria ridden pagan-like eternal city of Rome. It was believed the original founders of Rome were refugees from Troy after it fell to Achilles and the Trojan horse Greeks. A dream he had in Troy told him to search elsewhere, so he went to the city of Byzantium on the Bosporus. In Byzantium, on a fall night in 394 AD, he dreamed of an old woman who suddenly became young again, and when he awoke he knew on this spot he would make his capital. Byzantium became Constantinople. The original duet of Dagda and Morrigan was the basis of a pan-European religious belief that sprung the urban Greco-Roman Gods and their associated Pantheons, and this Celtic belief influenced the Roman Emperor in his choice of a capital city, that was about to become the province of Christianity for over a 1000 years.

The coupling of the Dagda and Morrigan produced balance, harmony and productivity and had to be enacted on a regular annual cycle as determined by the seasons. Time was rigorously ordered in Celtic society and religion due to the agrarian and pastoral economics of survival. Charting the passage of time was essential to planting of seeds, harvesting, moving cattle to different pastures. The Celts had a calendar called the Coligny calendar, from a place in Coligny,

France, where an example was found. It tried to reconcile the solar and lunar cycles and was used up until the introduction of the Julian calendar in the 2nd century AD.

There were festivals associated with different times of the year. The four seasons were represented by Taranis solar wheel. Many of the monuments in Britain and Stonehenge are aligned so the date of Samhain can be determined. The start of the New Year was November 1. Samhain fell on this day. It was a dangerous time between the two years. Over the Samhain festival, October 31 until November 1, the Otherworld and the earthly world were connected. The souls of the dead, fairies and spirits from the Otherworld could roam free on the land in this world; they could intermingle with the living. The community all came together on Samhain, having meetings, attending festivities with feasts which included place settings for the dead, performing communal acts for the assembled tribe and performing sacrifices to the Gods. Today, the festival is called Halloween, followed by All Saints Day on November 1, and All Souls Day on November 2. The Roman Catholic church instituted these holy days in order to absorb the pagan festival into Christianity in the 9th century AD. Samhain was the time when the cattle were brought down from summer pastures and slaughtered. Feasts ensued. It also heralded the beginning of the dark half of the year and end of the harvest season. Bonfires were lit as they were on Beltane.

The next Celtic festival, was on February 1, Imbolc. The festival of Imbolc was associated with the Dagda's daughter Brigit, who was the goddess of fertility, learning, healing. Brigit became a saint under the Roman Catholicism and became known as Saint Brigit. Saint Brigit is celebrated on February 1. Imbolc was associated with the lactation of the ewes, when the sheep could be moved to upland pastures in the agrarian, pastoral year.

The next Celtic festival was May 1, Beltane. Beltane is associated with the God of Fire, of the sun, Belenus, Bel. In ancient Mesopotamia, Bel, is associated with the name Marduk and was the leading God of the Babylonians. Belenus, Bel, and Marduk (sun calf) mean about the same thing, the god of the sun. Bel means Lord, like Zeus. Belenus means bright and shining. Belenus was the Sun God, a solar deity. May 1, Mayday is the start of the summer season. Beltane was the occasion when cattle were fumigated before being turned out on summer pastures.

Summer was derived from the Celtic word Samonios, which occurs at the full moon in midsummer. Lugh's celebration is during Samonios. On August 1, the festival of Lugnasadh was held. It was midway between the summer solstice and the autumn equinox. This festival heralded the beginning of the harvest season. Lugh presided over this festival as a god of the summer. This was the day that propitiatory offerings were made to the deities in anticipation of a fruitful harvest. The tribes of the council of Gaul met on this date. These were representatives of all the Celtic tribes in Gaul. There were athletic games, tasting of the harvest produce, feasting, matchmaking, plays, music and visits to holy places like small pilgrimages, hill and mountain climbing. The festival has continued into modern times in what is known as "Garland Sunday" and "Reek Sunday", where people climb Saint Patricks' Hill. Another is "Pucks Fair", or the fair of the He-goat where people climb a mountain, catch a he-goat then put it in a small cage for three days on top of a high platform and crown him with flowers for three days, afterwards he is led back to his home on the mountain.

In 12 BC, Emperor Augustus ordered that this council relocate its yearly festival to Lughdunum (Lyons), and meet at the altar of Rome and Augustus. Lughdunum was an important in Romanized Gaul, eventually having a population of over 200,000 people. Lughdunum was created in 43 BC. By doing this Rome was attempting to show the unity of Gaul and Rome. But it sounds like the mafia moving in on the proceeds of the harvest, or the Prophet Mohammad moving in on the pilgrimage business in Mecca. After the fall of the Empire it slowly turned into Lyon, France.

In this complex Celtic Pantheon there were priests called Druids who understood all the deities, and were scholars, philosophers, judges of civil, criminal matters, and also the overseers of all religious practice. Druids memorized everything over a period of a twenty-year apprenticeship before assuming their roles in society. Druids or "druad" in Gaelic means "knowledge of the oak" or "deep knowledge". Some Druids' were Bards, some were Brehon's, who administered Celtic Brehon Law, historians, physicians, some were priests and some were high priests, "Arch Druids". Druids controlled the sacrifices to the Gods and were mediators between man and god. These druids were also the powerful elite of Celtic culture. When acting as judges in criminal and civil cases, they enforced judgements' by preventing the person from sacrificing to the God, which in turn made them unclean; society would shun them and exclude them from activities as they were unclean, until judgements were satisfied. Not much is known of the actual rites or philosophy, but there were human sacrifices, performed in different ways to satisfy different deities. Burning using the wicker man was the manner or propitiating Taranis, drowning satisfied Teutates, and hanging satisfied Esus. There were sacred places in cleared areas of groves, 'Nemeton" and shrines in the forest called "fidnemed". Druids were assisted by another type of religious individual called a "seer" or "fathi" or as in Latin literature as a "Vates". Seers could divine and see the future, like the Oracle at Delphi. Seers were the actual ones who performed the sacrifice and could divine by examining the entrails of the one who was sacrificed. Both Druids and Seers could see and understand what was invisible, they were learned. Druids had absolute spiritual sway over Celts. Since nothing was written down only they possessed knowledge. There was one Druid who was elected as Supreme Druid and served as this Supreme Druid for life. Caesar purged Celtic Society of the Druids because they were the brains and the organizing power behind Celtic society. Caesar learned that Britain was the source of and center of Druidic power and doctrine, particularly on the island of Anglesey in the Celtic Sea. Caesar and the Roman legions never invaded or conquered Ireland, so the druids and the Celtic Gods continued there for hundreds of more years. Druidism originated in earlier times and continued in Ireland up until the middle 5th century AD. Saint Patrick managed to convert or strip the druids of their spiritual control of the Celts after his arrival in Ireland in 423 AD.

The Celtic Pantheon provided the tribe with orderly direction in order to survive. It was animist, polytheistic, and the Gods demanded blood sacrifice according to the priests, in some of the Celtic tribes, the Pict tribes had animals as Gods and there was no human sacrifice. That threat must have kept people in line, in this warrior society. There were spirits all about them, everywhere, in the forests of western Europe. This abundance of spirits is sort of like standing in an Irish pub on a late Saturday night, and makes as much sense.

THE IRISH PUB SONG

Well you're walking through a city street you could be in Peru and you hear a distant calling and you know it's meant for you, and you drop what you are doing and you join the merry mob, and before you know just where you are you're in an Irish pub.

> They've got one in Honolulu
> they've got one in Moscow to
> they got four of them in Sydney
> and a couple in Katmandu.
> So whether you sing or pull a pint you'll always have a job,
> Cause wherever you go around the world you'll find an Irish Pub.

Now that design is fairly simple, and it usually works the same, you'll have raisin hell in scoring the Ireland England game, and you'll know you're in an Irish pub the minute you're in the door, for a couple of boys with forearms will be muttering Christie Moore.

> They've got one in Honolulu
> they've got one in Moscow to
> they got four of them in Sydney
> and a couple in Katmandu.
> So whether you sing or pull a pint you'll always have a job,
> Cause wherever you go around the world you'll find an Irish Pub.

Now the owner is Norwegian, and the manager comes from Cork, and the lad that's holding up the bar says he just only works, he was born and bred in Bolton but his nanny's from Kildare, and he's gonta make his fortune soon and move to county Clare.

> They've got one in Honolulu
> they've got one in Moscow to
> they got four of them in Sydney
> and a couple in Katmandu.
> So whether you sing or pull a pint you'll always have a job,
> Cause wherever you go around the world you'll find an Irish Pub.

Now it's time for me to go, I have to catch me train, so I'll leave you sitting at the bar and face the wind and rain, but I'll have that pint you owe me, if I'm not gone on the dry, when we meet next week in Frankfurt, in the fields of Athenry.

They've got one in Honolulu
they've got one in Moscow to
they got four of them in Sydney
and a couple in Katmandu.
So whether you sing or pull a pint you'll always have a job,
Cause wherever you go around the world you'll find an Irish Pub.

MITHRA

Mithra (truth) is an ancient Indo-Iranian God who was worshipped in Persia as early as the second millennium BC, starting around 2000 BC, related if not the same as the Vedic Mithra worshipped in India. Mithra pre-dates Zoroastrianism. Mitra was the Indian name of Mithra. Mitra means covenant, treaty, agreement, promise, and oath. In Sanskrit, Mitra means friend. The myths of Mithra are tied in with all the myths of Indo-European peoples.

Mithra----the Lord of vast green pastures----we do praise,
To "First Celestial God" our voices raise.
Before the sun shines from hilltops, indeed,
the everlasting Sun, Mithra will proceed.

It is the first being with ornaments of Gold,
that from mountaintops the earth does behold.

And from there, the powerful Mithra will
Watch the abode of the Magi calm and still.

The ancient Persian yashts are liturgical hymns and poems. The name Mithra has three meanings; **"Love, Sun, Friend"**. Mithra can be summoned by repeating the three words, love, sun, friend. The divinity is the sun, or the light of the sun, but not the sun itself. Mithra is also an unconditional love that emanates regardless of our existence or thoughts. Most importantly, Mithra is a friend who walks beside us, side by side in fellowship. He is the protector of the Aryan nations, a friend to humanity in this life and a protector against evil in the next.

The ancient polytheistic religions were reformed between 1200 BC and 600 BC. A man was born called Zarathustra, (Zoroaster), he lived around 1700-1300 BC. Zoroaster was born by a miraculous birth; his mother conceived when she was visited by a shaft of light. Zoroaster's teachings led to the first monotheistic religion. The deity was of the Zoroastrian religion (650 BC-650 AD), was Ahura Mazda, the creator. All the previous polytheistic Gods were demoted including Mithra under Mazda. The Zoroastrian was monotheistic dualism; Mazda represented light and was in opposition to Ahriman, who represented dark. Ahriman used the symbol of the snake, and he was called the great lie. Good versus evil, and light versus dark, truth versus lie, these are the elements of this dualistic belief system. Zoroaster preached about "The Golden Rule", and believed in the earth, fire, air, water and quintessence. These classical elements are the same as the states of matter, solid, plasma, gas and liquid. The fifth element, quintessence, the scientists are still working on through projects like LIGO, the light Interferometer Gravitational-Wave Observatory. The Avesta is the Zoroastrian holy book. The Zoroastrians were the first "People of the Book". Mithra held a special place as the warrior of light to combat dark, he was also able to mediate between Mazda and Ahriman, so his truth lies in the gray middle way between this dualism. He is the liberated third way, the 3% solution. He was worshipped in the Zoroastrian fire temple also called the court of Mithra. The Zoroastrian religion was the official religion of Persia from 650 BC until 650 AD, when Mohammad's Islam overran Persia and abolished it.

The Golden Rule

Do unto others as you would like them to do unto you.

The ancient myths, legends and history become blurred regarding Mithras as time goes by. Another Mithras comes into existence in 272 BC. On the night of the 24th to the 25th of December, 272 BC, a savior was born to a virgin female by Immaculate Conception, somewhere near Lake Hamun, Helmand province. He lived for 64 years among men, died and ascended to his father Ahura Mazda in 208 BC. In Armenia, the last stronghold of the religion of Mithra, it was reported that the Lord Mithra, the savior, was born of a virgin human primate mother and he was the Son of God. The virgin birth of Jesus Christ was based on this model.

An oversimplified time line for Mithra is as follows:

2000 BC	I.	Indo-European Mithra, and then Mithra absorbed into Zoroastrianism
272 BC- 208 BC	II.	Mithra the savior, humans are saved by Mithra shedding his blood
200 BC- 400 AD	III.	Roman Mithras, a very popular religious cult of the Roman Empire
35 AD- 67 AD	IV.	Saint Paul the Apostle gets a brilliant idea and begins to merge the Judaism of Jesus of Nazareth with the Roman Cult of Mithras, after his Epiphany on the road to Damascus.
381 AD	V.	The cult of Mithras is absorbed into Christianity; worship of Mithras outlawed by Emperor.
Middle Ages	VI.	Rise of secret western European Mithratic societies, Freemasons, Rosicrucian's, Knights Templar
1870- present	VII.	Revival of Mithratic Mysteries, U.S. President Garfield addressed the Mithras Lodge of Sorrow in Washington DC in 1881. In 1990, the Lodge of Sorrow opened an offshoot Mithras Lodge

The Roman secret cult of Mithras was adopted by the Roman legions fighting against the Parthian Empire in Mesopotamia, and mixed with the Greek cult of Perseus. The cult of Perseus originated in Tarsus. After this combination the secret Roman cult of Mithras became the most sophisticated in the Roman World. It was at the forefront of astronomy and philosophical thought. All were equal in the Cult, from the Emperor to the slave. It was the last pagan state religion and was the main competitor of early Christianity. The Roman Mithras was the "Invincible Sun God" of the Roman Legions from 50 BC until 381 AD. There were temples scattered all over Europe and Asia Minor. Some of the temples are still visible, including along Hadrian's Wall in northern Britain. The cult of Mithras had all the same mysteries of Christianity, which frightened the Christians because it meant all the Christian mysteries were known before the birth of Christ, and before the formation of early Christian religious dogma. Mithras evolved over the centuries from the god of green land, wild pastures and solar light to that of the Invincible Sun God who slays the Constellation of Taurus in order to move the cosmos.

Christianity assimilated Mithras (381 AD) but both religions lost something when this occurred. Christianity was peace-loving before the assimilation, but became more warlike afterwards. Mithras was a warrior religion before assimilation into Christianity, but afterwards it ceased to exist and the peacefulness of Christians made the adherents of Mithras more peace like. The best aspects of each were lost. Paul of Tarsus, (Saint Paul) grew up as an observant Jew in the town of Tarsus, which was a hotbed of Mithraism and Perseus worship. He was influence by all these ideologies, Yahweh, Perseus, Mithras and he heard of the story of Jesus Christ. He was trying to make sense of it all, but in many of his writings he writes like a warrior of Mithras, at other times like a Jew, and at others like a Christian. He was instrumental in starting to pull together the Christian narrative, which may not have continued without his Epiphany on the road to Damascus. December 25th was made Jesus Christs birthday in the 4th Century, 350 AD. The winter solstice was the nativity, the birth of the Sun, Mithras was identified by his worshippers with the sun. Gospels say nothing of when Christ was born. On December 25, 274 AD, Emperor Aurelian declared the Sun God to be the principle patron of the Roman Empire. Catholicism preserved some of the outer forms of Mithras.

Mithras	**Christianity**
December 25, birth	December 25, birth
born of virgin by Immaculate Conception	born of virgin by Immaculate Conception
Celibate	Celibate
savior God, saved by shedding his own blood	savior God, saved by shedding his own blood
created water and bread by slaying the Bull,	turned bread and wine into the
and thus created the universe and life on earth.	Body and blood of Christ.
Equidistant cross was symbol of the Sun	Crucifix cross as a symbol of Son of God
worshippers were baptized	worshippers were baptized
worshippers viewed wine as sacrificial blood	worshippers view wine as sacrificial blood
Sunday was sacred	Sunday is sacred
ate bread marked with a cross; hot cross buns	Hot Cross Buns
called themselves "brothers"	call themselves "brothers in Christ"
Mithra	the "Mitre" adopted as a sign of office; the word "mitre' is the Greek word for 'Mithra"
leader of Mithras ceremonies wore red cap, ring, and carried a Sheppard's staff	Head Christian, "pope" wears a red cap, ring, and carries a Sheppard's staff
Sun crown, halo, on Mithras	Sun Crown, halo, on Jesus Christ
Mithraism Liturgy, Greek Magical papyri	Book of Revelations are the same story
Mithras Temples	Vatican Hill sits on top of an old Mithras Temple

In 381 AD, the Roman-Byzantine Empire declared Christianity to be the official state religion, and the Mithras cult was outlawed along with all other pagan religious practice. December 25, 381 became the holiday celebrating the birth of the Son of God, instead of the birth of the sun. The same day was still celebrated; the Emperor just changed the "u" in "sun", to an "o" in "son" as in Son of God. Clever these Chinese.

Silent Night

Silent night, holy night,
all is calm, all is bright,
round yon virgin, mother and child,

holy infant, so tender and mild,
sleep in heavenly peace
sleep in heavenly peace

Mithraism, "the ancient cattle rustling religion". Saint Paul what were you thinking, when Lugh's bright shining spear of light got you on the Road to Damascus. Paul you got some splainin' to do, about all this plagiarism.

Judaism

Judaism. Judaism began when Abrams and Carol or Sarai (princess) stole some gold in Mesopotamia and lighted out of town, out of the country and out of the whole countryside. Changing names to Abraham and Sarah along the way, they could be heard singing while moseying their camels along, "We got Jews that jingle, jangle, jingle as we walk merrily along." Finally, they came upon some unsuspecting saps in a place called Canaan, where they met Moe, Larry and Curly. Thus began the fine history of Judaism.

Judaism is one of the three Abrahamic religions. The Abrahamic religions include first, Judaism; second, Christianity; and thirdly, Islam. They are monotheistic religions each with the God of Abraham as the deity. All three religions have a history of killing each other, because of the off shooting doctrines of each. The Abrahamic religions do not associate with astronomy, physical science, farming, weather, or pastoralism. They are not animistic to a great extent. The religion originated in The Levant, thousands of years ago. The originators of the Abrahamic religions were Semites, some became Jews, some Christians and some Muslims, before each religion expanded worldwide. The Hebrews followed Abraham and the records of the tribe were eventually written into a book. They became known as the Israelites and "The People of the Book". Semites are male haplotype J, which was the predominant haplotype in the Middle East area.

Oral traditions were passed down through the ages by word of mouth. There were different Mesopotamian Genesis stories told. The history of the Jews of Israel originated there in Mesopotamia, and many of the stories in the Old Testament mirror previously established fragmented stories. Genesis stories were not put on paper until the later part of the monarchy period in Judaic history, this was around 500 BC. Genesis stories were made up and borrowed from, then adapted to Jews by Jews, for Jews and anyone who wanted to listen. The Jewish elders picked up foreign epic material and transformed it into their own religious narrative, with two goals in mind. One, they wanted to portray Yahweh as sovereign, without challenge and transcendent over all of creation. Secondly, they presented the origin of a relationship with Yahweh, which led to a covenant (a bargain) with Abram, (Genesis 15). The bible used genealogies of Hebrew tribesmen, and stories explaining origin and causation. The Judaic God was one, transcendent, and consistent (as opposed to Islamic Allah who is inconsistent). There is an absence of other deities competing for the number one spot, Yahweh is without challenge. Yahweh is a universal God operating outside space and time and outside human political systems. Yahweh is independent of humanity or human beings, but at the same time, Yahweh, the God of Abraham was created and used by one tribe, the Israelites, just like the many other surrounding tribes that had created their own Gods. One tribes God is better than everyone else's God.

The Genesis story starts in Mesopotamia with Abram and Sari, in the city of Ur, in the Sumer region. When written, the people who lived in Ur were Chaldeans, an ethnic term that applies to the neo-Babylonian people there in 625 BC-540 BC. This date gives us the date of the final editing of the story but not where Abram actually lived. Yahweh tells Abram to leave and go to Canaan, through Harran. He and Sari then take the caravan route through Palmyra, Damascus and south along the coast to Canaan. Abraham is a stranger in a strange land. Abraham thinks Yahweh is testing his loyalty at some point in time and he offers to sacrifice his son Isaac to show God he means it. The altar of his sacrifice is the foundation stone which is built into the Jewish temple in Jerusalem. This stone is where the "Well of Souls" is and where the "Holy of Holies" was. The Muslims of Islam built the "Dome of the Rock" mosque over the top of this foundation stone, when they conquered Jerusalem in their Islamic conquests in 691 AD. Jerusalem was the capital city of the Kingdom of Judah, Israel.

The auld testament was an oral tradition up until 1000 BC. The time period after 1000 BC was the start of the Monarchy period in Jewish history, and there was nationalistic fervor over the Hebrews which was sweeping the land of the Israelites. Around 1000 BC, the oral tradition was first starting to be written down, writing systems started to be common around that time, and added to the nationalistic fervor.

Writing systems started to be used around 3500 BC in Egypt and Mesopotamia and were very difficult to understand. Cuneiform was developed around 1600 BC to 1200 BC along the coast near Syria and Turkey for merchants. Another alphabet was developed in Canaan and Sinai around 1600 BC by Semites. The Semite group known as the Phoenicians' perfected an alphabet around 1100 BC. From 1000 BC until 200 BC, the Hebrew oral tradition was written down into texts, on scrolls.

The "Book" of the "People of the Book" was divided into different sections. The five books, the five chapters at the beginning of the bible make up what is known as the Torah. The word Torah means Law. It is the Pentateuch. These 5 books of the Torah are composed of Genesis, Exodus, Leviticus, Numbers, and Deuteronomy (from the Greek, spoken words, or second law). The old testament contains historical chapters that tell the story of Israel as a nation before its destruction and exile and then continues Israel's' story following exile. The Historical Books and chapters of the Old Testament are divided into major divisions as follows, Wisdom, Liturgy, Songs. Six works are concerned with Wisdom, and worship. They are Job, Psalms, Proverbs, Ecclesiastes, Song of Songs, (Song of Solomon) and Lamentations.

There are also six Deuteronomy Histories. These six books and chapters are concerned with the history of Israel from their conquest to the end of their independence as a nation. The Deuteronomy Histories are Joshua, Judges, 1-2 Samuel, and 1-2 Kings. Then there are post-exile histories. These books tell the Israeli story from those of the viewpoint of those who returned from exile. The post-exile stories are 1-2 Chronicles, Ezra, and Nehemiah. Then there are popular histories which are role models. They are Ruth, Daniel, Esther, Adam Sandler, and Seinfeld.

Prophets. There are 15 books associated with named prophets from the 8th century BC (800 BC- 700 BC). A prophet is a primate who has been contacted by a supernatural entity who wants to say something to everyone through the prophet. The words of the supernatural being, speaking through the prophet, are called the prophecy. This time period was around the starting period of Rome by Romulus (733 BC), before it became an Empire and was also when the rise of the city-states of Greece began. The major prophets were Isaiah, Jeremiah, Aunt Jemima, and Ezekiel. Minor prophets were Hosea, Joel, Amos, Obadiah, Jonah, Micah, Nahum, Habakkuk, Zephaniah, Haggis, Zechariah, Malachi, and Captain Ahab.

There were additional books composed during the second temple, (500 BC-100 BC). They are not included in the Judaic Canon, but they are included in the Christian Bibles, the Deuteron-canonical or Apocrypha books. These included 1-2 Maccabees, and additions to Esther and Daniel. These books were included in Christian Bibles because they provide insight into the period leading up to the birth of Christianity. The Latin translation of the Bible is called the Vulgate, the church says Miley Cyrus is vulgar.

Chronicum Holocenum Dated Timeline I

The following timeline briefly outlines Judaic primate history mixed with certain European and Eastern Mediterranean historical events. It was thrown at me by Bigfoot while I was hiking on the Appalachian Trail.

Dated Timeline

40000 BC	Neanderthal populations invite Mesopotamian, migrant Homo sapiens into Europe, because of conflict in the Middle East; this proves to be a mistake as the Homo sapiens begin to rape the Neanderthal culture. The Neanderthals commit cultural suicide and become extinct.
20000 BC	The Glacial Maximum occurs, the ice wall is 5280 feet high, extending from the North Pole to the Alps and all is frozen around the top of the planet down to 40 degree's north latitude.
10000 BC	Slavery is rare in Hunter-gatherer societies'; slavery does not arise until there is surplus food supplies; The Late Glacial Ice Age is ending, ice retreats north followed by growth of old growth forests, and rise in sea levels, lakes, rivers. Hunter-gatherer tribes move through the forests hunting food, clothing and taking shelter in caves.
9400 BC	Melted ice in North America is dumped into the Atlantic and Arctic Oceans, sea levels rise 9 feet in a 36-hour period sending the world back into another cold period called "The Younger Dryas". This cold period lasts for 1000 years until about 8400 BC. 9000 BC In Britain, the population was about 1100-1200 people; farming was invented around this time in Mesopotamia; female haplotype J as in Jasmine arises at the same time and place and the invention of farming is attributed to this bloodline.
8400 BC	End of the cold Younger Dryas
8000 BC	In Mesopotamia, small baked clay tokens are used to keep account; the Saber Tooth tiger and the Wooly Mammoth become extinct; slavery begins to develop and parallels closely the rise of farming and populations due to surplus food supply. In Britain the population was about 1500 to 2000 people.
7400 BC	Bond Event Cooling, glacier expansion in Norway
6500 BC	Doggerland breaks off from Europe and Britain sinking beneath the North Sea; Britain becomes an Island.
6500 BC	The Black Sea was a fresh water lake from 10,000 BC until 6500-5500 BC; five rivers to its north emptied into it, including the Danube, Dniester, and the Dnieper

Rivers, as the ice melted. The Bosporus channel is 213 feet deep. The sea level of the Mediterranean like the rest of the world's oceans was about 450 feet lower than it is today. The area within the Bosporus channel had become filled with silt over time as the water from the lake spilled over the falls into sea water which was lower than the lake level. Eventually the sea level of the Mediterranean Sea rose through the Dardanelles, and began to eat away at the silted wall of earth. As the river runoff slowed, the lake level became lower and the rising sea level higher. One day in the time around 6500 BC, the silt dam gave way and the Mediterranean Sea poured into the lake like Niagara Falls making it the Black Sea. An area of 63,000 square miles, the size of Austria, became flooded around its shores within a few months. This could have been the inspiration for the story of Noah, along with the flooding of the Persian Gulf in Mesopotamia.

6200 BC	8.2 kiloyear event, and a Bond Event Cooling period starts, lasting 200- 400 years; this was a climate cooling event that was milder than the "Younger Dryas", but more severe than the "Little Ice Age" (1300 -1850 AD); the two events happened to begin at the same time; the cause of this was the final melt of the Laurentian Ice Sheet in North America, which in turn upset the North Atlantic Gulf Stream; this 200-400 year long event produced a cool, dry climate that in turn caused aridification of soil.
5300 BC	Neolithic writing in Romania and Greece according too archeological records
5000 BC	In Britain, the population was about 5000 people
4000 BC	In Britain, the population was about 100,000 people due to immigration and farming; Horses domesticated around this time.
3900 BC	a 5.9 kiloyear event, and a "Bond Event Cooling" starts, again the two events coincided. There was a period of cooling and dry aridification; the Sahara Desert came into being, and people migrated to the Nile Valley, which led to the emergence of complex, organized society. There was also desertification in the Middle East and Mesopotamia leading to the development of polarized societies with elite classes and underclasses.
3800 BC	City-State of Ur, Sumer founded in Mesopotamia, the God of Ur is the Moon, called Nanna, or also known as Sin, it is a male deity. Lunar deities are the enemy of the Sun deity, whether either one is male or female. Nanna, or Sin represents "Wisdom", especially in astronomy, the priest tracks the cycles of the moon
3600 BC	Mesopotamia, first cuneiform writing developed.
3400 BC	"The Mound of the Hostages", Dumha na nGiall, was constructed on Temhair, the Hill of Tara, in county Meath, Leinster, Ireland. This neo-lithic passage tomb was built so the entrance doorway to the tomb is aligned with the rays of the sun on only two days of the year, Samhain, (November 1), and Imbolc, (February 1). It is one many Neolithic constructions built on the Hill of Tara, that preceded the invasions of The Sons of Mil. It was used by the Tuatha De Dannan and the Fir Bolg before the Sons of Mil, and afterwards by the High Kings of Ireland. The "Stone of Destiny", Lia Fail, is also located near the Mound of Hostages on Tara;

it is an upright stone that was said to scream aloud only when a rightful king of Ireland laid his hand on it. The scream could be held throughout the island. In 1798, 400 Irish rebels opposed the British on the Hill of Tara, and were killed by the "Redcoats" there. The Stone of Destiny was moved and placed on their common grave there.

3180 BC	Skara Brae (3180-2500 BC) was started in and occupied in the Orkney Islands of northern Scotland. Climate got colder after 2500 BC, causing people to leave and move south to a warmer climate, leaving Skara Brae abandoned.
3100 BC	Egypt begins: Egypt had canals dug that connected the Nile River to the Red Sea, so there could be ship passage from the Mediterranean to the red Sea, but they silted up and the Egyptians found that the sea water would contaminate the fertile farming fields.
2750-2500 BC	Epic of Gilgamesh written King of Ur, Sumer, Mesopotamia
2580-2560 BC	Great Pyramid of Giza built
2400 BC	Bronze Age Canaanite "City of Peace", Urusalima founded (Jerusalem)
2200 BC	4.2 kilo-year event, and Bond Event Cooling starts; again the two events were coincidental; this event lasted for 100 years; it was cold and dry with continued aridification across the Middle East and the Sahara; this produced famine in the Nile Valley and led to the collapse of the Old Egyptian civilization.
2000 BC	population of Britain and Ireland 300,000 people
1897 BC	Celtic tribes invade Ireland, and Alba; The Parrthalon group of migrations to Hibernia
1500 BC	Phoenicia (1500- 539 BC) begins, a Canaanite Semitic maritime coastal culture, credited with the invention of the rowing, sailing ship called a "bireme"; geographically encompassing the coast of the Levant, and trading as far as Iberia, Morocco, and Cornwall; they had a monopoly on murex purple dye.

Phoenicia's Canaanite culture invented the Alphabet that we use today. The capital city was Byblos. Sailing ships began covering the entire Mediterranean Sea and the Eastern Atlantic Ocean as far as Cornwall and Ireland for trade.

Dated Timeline	**Old Testament**	**Pre-Monarchy Period**
date uncertain		Creation, a myth from Sumerian legends
5454 – 3760 BC	Primeval Period	Adam and Eve, Able, Cain, Adam to Noah is ten generations; Between 5500 and 2500 BC the oceans sea levels rose 21 feet, due to melting ice from glaciations
3000-2804 BC		Noah and his ark, flood epics occurred about midpoint in the period between the 5.9 and 4.2 kilo year Bond Cooling Events, in the year 2804 BC or earlier. Noah had a whole zoo, and a family.
		Noah had three sons. The sons of Noah were **Shem, Ham**, and **Japheth**. Japheth had

seven sons. The sons of **Japheth** were **Gomer, Magog, Madai, Javan, Tubal, Meshech, and Tiras.** Gomer had three sons. Gomer is associated with the group known as the Cimmerians, the Gomerites; Magog means Russia; Magog is the land of present day Russia, Magog settled there. Madai moved south of the Caspian Sea into what in now northern Iran, Madai is associated with the Medes in Iran; Javan was associated with the Greeks; Tubal was associated with the clan that headed northeast and settled in Tobol-ski, on the River Tobol, in Russia, where the Kurgan culture arose; Meshech is another name for Moscow, Meshech settled around the Moscow area.

The three sons of **Gomer** were **Ashkenaz, Riphath, and Togarmah.** The descendant's' of Japheth sprang the maritime nations, in their respective lands, each with its own language and each with its own clan, within its own nation. These sons of Gomer settled on land around the Black and the Caspian Seas, in the areas of modern day Turkey, the Caucasus's, and Greece. **Ashkenaz is associated with the Scythians, haplotype R1a; Riphath**, or Ibath, **is associated with the Celts, the Cimmerians, haplotype R1b**; and **Togarmah is associated with the Adyghe, who became the Khazars,** they lived on the north-east shore of the Black Sea around the Crimean Peninsula in present day Russia and Ukraine. The Cimmerians and the Scythians became very large nomadic horse tribes that rode the Eurasian steppes eastward and westward, grazing their herds, living in tents, and burying their dead in Kurgans (burial mounds) on the steppes, before the Viking Rus arrived. Some of the Gomerites are, The Galatians, the tribe of the son Riphath.

The descendants of Japheths older brother, **Shem**, were Elam, Asshur, Arpachashad, Lud, and Aram. Arpachashad was the father of Shelah. Shelah was the father of Eber. Eber was the father of Peleg. Peleg was the father of Reu. Reu was the father of Serug. Serug was the father of Nahor. Nahor was the father of Terah. Terah was the father of **Abram, (Abraham)**, Nahor, and Haran. Haran had a son called Lot, a daughter named Milcah, and Iscah. Nahor married his brothers' daughter Milcah, and Abraham married Sarai. They were all living in Ur, Sumer, Mesopotamia. Haran died in Ur. Terah took Abram, Sarai, and his grandson Lot out of Ur and moved with the goal of settling in Canaan. Moving up the Euphrates River, they got as far as Harran, in what is now southeastern Turkey, where they settled. Harran was the spiritual center of the Moon God, named "Sin"; the main deity in Mesopotamia. Terah died in Harran, but after a certain time Abram, Sarai, and Lot continued on to Canaan, after God rang him up on the telephone. Abram was advised to go to Canaan, and run his shit there. It could actually have been "Sin", the Moon God calling, but we are not sure. I requested the telephone records, but they said they couldn't release them because they were private.

The descendants of **Shem** are called **Shemites** or in today's common usage, **Semites**. The story of Abraham will be continued later under the Judaism section. The bible doesn't accurately portray time well. Some of the people who wrote the Bible, I think, were drinking Mogen David wine, they have some characters living 950 years, but then it is the Middle east and anything can happen there.

Ham had four sons. The descendants' of Noah's son **Ham** were Cush, Mizraim, Put, and Canaan. Canaan became the Patriarch of the Canaanites, and settled in Sidon, Gerar near Gaza, Admah, Zemolim, near Lasha and in Sodom and Gomorrah. Ham was also associated with Swiss on Rye with Mustard, which is why Semites don't eat pork and sodomy is a "sin" of the moon god.

Noah also had a grandson called Nimrod, who ruled in Uruk, Sumer, Mesopotamia, where

Babel was located, Nimrod built the "Tower of Babel".

Around this time, after the flood, and when Abraham was 60 years old, according to the Chronicum Scotorum: "The Parrthalon arrived in Hibernia. The Parrthalon was the first who occupied Erin after the flood. On Tuesday the 14th of May he arrived, his companions being eight in number; four men and four women. They multiplied afterwards until they were in the number of 4,050 men and 1,000 women. There were four plains cleared in Erinn by Parrthalon; Magh Tuiredh, or nEdars in Connacht; and Magh Ita in Laighen; and Magh Latrainn in Dal Araidhe; and Leemagh in Ui Mac Uais between Bir and Camus. Seven years after the occupation of Erinn by Parrthalon, the first man of his people died; -Fea was his name. In Magh Fea he was buried; from him, therefore, it has been named.

There were seven lake eruptions through the land in the reign of the Parrthalon; -Loch Meeca and Loch Decet, Loch Laighline, Loch Rudhraides, Loch Echtra, and the sea inundation at Brena and Loch Con. Three years afterwards occurred the first battle which Parrthalon gained, in the Slemains, (smooth places or plains) of Magh Itha, over the Fomorians'; - they were demons, truly, in the guise of men; men with one hand and one leg each.

The Parrthalon lived for 400-500 years in Hibernia, then they all died because of plague. Erinn laid waste for thirty years after the death of Parrthalon. From the plague of Parrthalon's people the Tamhleachda, (plague graves) of the men of Erinn are called."

The Parrthalon died off around 1500 BC, they were followed by the Fir Bolg, then by the Tuatha De Danaan, then the invasion by the Celts of the Sons of Mil of Espania between 1000 BC and 537 BC, in Ireland.

2000-1864 BC	Ancestral Period	

Abram or Abraham moved to Canaan from Harran, Upper Mesopotamia. Abraham sought God and finds the God of Abraham, who he makes a covenant with; God tells Abraham to go out for a pass, and throws the football to him. He has a son called Ismael with his slave girl Hagar. Then he has a son with his wife Sarah, called Isaac. Ismael and Hager are driven out and away after Sarah gives birth. At some point in time he offers his son Isaac up to his God as proof of his allegiance, and places Isaac on the Foundation Stone as an altar, but an Angel interrupts him, and he offers a sheep instead. In Mecca 2500 years later, the Prophet Mohammad thinks he and his tribe the Quraysh are direct descendants of Ismael, Hagar and Abraham. Abraham bought a cave for burial from the Canaanites, called the Cave of the Patriarchs. The Muslims, in Saladins time built the Ibrahimi mosque on top of it, where it stands today in Hebron, Israel. Circumcision is the mark of the covenant with the God of Abraham, so after trying to slit Isaacs throat, he just cuts the foreskin off his Peter.

1750-1570 BC

Isaac had twin sons with a woman named Rebecca, Esau and Jacob God chose Jacob even though Jacob was a less than an ideal character. Jacob was the first born of the twins, and it was said they fought in the womb. When Esau was born he was all "red", so he was named Esau. Jacob gave Esau a bowl of red berries in compensation for not being "chosen" by God and this started a never ending fight between the two. Jacob changed his name to Israel, and Esau changed his name to Edom. Jacobs tribe became the "chosen people of Israel", and Edoms tribe became the Edomites. The Edomite Kingdom was south of the dead sea, Israel, and Moab in what is now Jordan or trans-Jordan. Jacob had a few sons, one was named Joseph; Joseph moved the tribe into Egypt, which was then being run by the Hykos; when Egypt expelled the Hykos, all non- Egyptian people were enslaved in Egypt.

Edom was not enslaved, but flourished. Like his grandfather Abraham, Joseph wandered, but eventually ended up in a living hell.

The word "Hebrews" was a word that was used to describe a low class of society, a people who were landless and wandered in search of work as a means of survival. The word "Israel", Is-ra-el, is a word made up of three different names. "Is" is from "Isis" the virgin mother Goddess of Egypt; "-ra" is from "Ra" the Sun God of Egypt; and "-el" is from "El", a universal "moon god" who was, "the father of the gods', the "father of man". "El" is also known as "Saturn", "El" is the singular of "Elohim", the "deity". The virgin goddess, of the sun, and the moon deity. There is an "el" in "elite" and in "spell". When someone writes a word they "spell" it; when a witch casts a "spell", a human becomes "spellbound". When a story is told a primate becomes "spellbound' by the story. The "El" in Elohim is the father of the gods.

1550-1226 BC	Exodus

Moses, Charlton Heston, Aaron, Ramses II, Yul Brenner; Moses lead an exodus of enslaved Hebrews from Egypt. He parts the Red Sea, discovers "manna" from heaven. The patriarch Moses gets a renewed covenant with Yahweh; God chisels out the Ten Commandments in stone that he wants the Hebrews to live by. Moses constructs the portable Tabernacle of Moses, a dwelling place, which had an inner sanctuary called the Holy of Holies, shrouded by a veil in which the ark of the Covenant was kept. The Ark of the Covenant contained the stone tablets of the commandments, and was a portable throne for Yahweh's invisible presence; they carried this around with them in front of them followed by Bob Marley singing Exodus. Moses and his people wandered around in the Sinai desert for many generations.

The Ten Commandments of Yahweh to Moses

I am the Lord your God, who brought you out of the land of Egypt, out of the house of bondage. You shall have no other Gods before me. You shall not make for yourself a graven image, or any likeness of anything that is in heaven above, or that is in the Earth beneath, or that is in water under the earth; you shall not bow down to them or serve them; for I, the Lord your God, am a jealous God, visiting the iniquity of the fathers upon the children to the third and fourth generation of those who hate me, but showing steadfast love to thousands of those who love me and keep my commandments.

You shall not take the name of the Lord your God in vain; for the Lord will not hold him guiltless who takes his name in vain.

Remember the Sabbath Day, to keep it holy, six days you shall labor, and do all your work; but the seventh day is a Sabbath to the Lord your God; in it you shall not do any work, you, or your son, or your daughter, your manservant, or maidservant (slaves), or your cattle, or the sojourner who is within your gates; for in six days the Lord made heaven and earth, the sea, and all that is in them, and rested on the seventh day, therefore the Lord blessed the Sabbath day and hallowed it.

Honor your father and your mother that all your days may be long in the land which the Lord your God gives you.

You shall not kill.

You shall not commit adultery.

You shall not steal.

You shall not bear false witness against your neighbor.

You shall not covet your neighbors' house, you shall not covet your neighbors' wife, or his manservant, or maidservant (slaves), or his ox, or his ass, or anything that is your neighbors.

| 1250 – 1100 BC | Settlement | Moses transmitted the oral law to Joshua; Joshua infiltrated Canaan and slowly took over in a determined way. In those days, the group taking over territory killed all the inhabitants of the defeated tribes, or sold the children and females into slavery. Hebrew villages became interspersed with the Canaanite ones. Joshua transmitted the oral law to 70 elders, who in turn passed it on to the prophets, to the synagogue, and then to rabbi's. |
| 1200 – 1020 BC | Judges | When a military threat arose, the Hebrew Israelites looked to someone who could lead them, and this person was called a "judge". Philistine threat occurred during this time period. The Philistines were remnants of Greeks who had unsuccessfully tried to conquer Egypt, and settled on the coast of Canaan. In this time period the Philistines moved from their coastal city-states inland to Canaan due to seaborne invasion by the Sea Peoples in 1177 BC. The Judges of Israel were Gideon, Jephtheh, and the last judge Samuel, who appointed Saul as King Saul of the United Kingdom of Israel. |

There is no archeological evidence to support any of the previous Hebrew biblical stories, there is archeological evidence to support the writings of The Old testament starting with the Monarchy Period, when The United Kingdom of Israel came into existence. The following are more peripheral historical events and Hebrew history.

Dated Timeline

3200-1050 BC	Bronze Age Greece
1200 BC	According to the "Chronicum Scotorum", "Milidh, son of Bile, proceeded then from Spain to Scythia, and from Scythia to Egypt, after the slaying of Reflor, son of Neman; and understand not that it was soon after the death of Nel in Egypt, but many years indeed, after it that Milidh departed from Scythia, after the slaying of Reflor, contending for the sovereignty of Scythia. His great fleet consisted of 100 ships, as the vellum relates from which this copy has been drawn; fifteen families in each ship, and soldiers without wives in it besides. They remained three months in the island of Taprobane, (Ceylon or Cyprus). Three months more also they were on the Red Sea, until they came to Pharaoh, the King of Egypt. They learned the arts of that country. They remained eight years with Pharaoh in Egypt, where they propagated their various arts and their various actions. Scots, Pharaoh's daughter, married Milidh, son of Bile. After that, Milidh went with his host on the Great Sea (Mediterranean), (and Scots, Pharaohs daughter, along with him went.) past the island of Taprobane, in which they stayed a month. They rowed afterwards round Scythia to the "Inbher" (estuary), (there are rivers that extend inland from the Black Sea towards the Caspian Sea, and there are rivers which extend westwards from the Caspian Sea towards the Black Sea). of the Caspian Sea. They remained three nomada, (undefined period of time, possibly nine days and nights), motionless on the Caspian Sea, through the chanting of mermaids, until Caicher, the druid, rescued them. They voyaged afterwards past the point of Sliabh Rife, from the north, until they landed in Dacia, (the land surrounding the mouth of the Danube River, where it meets the Black Sea.) They stayed there a month. On Thursday, the Kalends of May, (May Day, May 1, Beltane), on the seventeenth of the moon, the fleet of the Sons of Milidh occupied Erinn at Inbher Sgene, and the wife of Aimergin Giuingil, Sgene Davilsir, died there, and her grave was made there; hence it was called Inbher Sgena. Erennan's grave was placed on the other side. The third day after the occupation of Erinn by the sons of Miledh, they fought the battle of Sliabh Mis against demons, (Tuathe De Danaan) and Fomorians, and the sons of Milidh gained it, and they assumed the sovereignty of Erinn very soon afterwards." This invasion of Erin occurred around the time of King David and Solomon, (1200-537 BC).
1194-1184 BC	Trojan War, Achilles
1177 BC	The Collapse of Civilization in the Eastern Mediterranean Sea; the "Sea Peoples" invasions of the region; possibly related to Bronze Age weapons versus Iron Age weapons; or there was a climate change and drought further north possibly prompting migrations, south. All of the Levant and Egypt were invaded, leading to collapse.
1100- 800 BC	Greek Dark Ages; this is also known as the Homeric Age when Homer wrote Iliad and Odyssey. Homer (1102 BC-850 BC); Homer mentioned, 'The Cimmerians' in his book called "The Odyssey of Homer"; he said they lived as inhabitants of the opposite side of the Oceanus River surrounding the earth, a country forever

deprived of sunshine, thus at the entrance to the kingdom of Hades; toward which Odysseus sails to obtain an oracle from the soul of the seer Teiresias.

1000 BC	Population of Brettania was about 2,000,000-2,300,000 inhabitants.
850-760 BC	Climate starts to get colder, causes migrations of humans from Scandinavia and Baltic areas south, "Bond Effect Cooling"
800 BC	Cimmerian tribes moved west from Pontic steppe into and up Danube River Valley, across Hungarian plain, into the Alps and continued westwards on both the north and south sides of the Alps, to Gaul, and the Atlantic Ocean; this culture became known as the Hallstat culture, (750-450 BC). Trade begins to exist between Greece and the Celtic cultures.
800-480 BC	Archaic Greece, rise of city-states
600 BC	Greek colony of Massila, (Marseilles) founded in southern Gaul
574 BC	Phoenicia defeated and occupied by Babylonian Empire
500-323 BC	Classical Greece, Athens, Sparta, Persian Invasions, Alexander the Great (356-323 BC), philosophy; Aristotle (384-322 BC), Aristotle wrote Meta physics, which is investigation of "truth"; he said no one person can ascertain the truth adequately but with everyone contributing a little bit a vast amount of insights into truth can be amassed. Aristotle started the Lyceum gymnasium school which lasted until around 125 AD. Aristotle mentioned two islands called Albion (Alba) and Ierne or Iwerne, occupied by Iwernians in his book, "On the Cosmos". The Romans later called the Iwernians, Hibernians; they also called Ierne, Scotia and some of its inhabitants Scoti, (Scots). Albu is the old Celtic, Indo-European name for the islands. "Albu" means "white", because of the white chalk cliffs at Dover. These are the islands of Britain and Ireland. Hippocrates (460-370 BC), lived in this period he was is considered the "Father of Western Medicine". Plato, (428-348 BC), another Greek philosopher started a school called Plato's Academy that lasted for 900 years from (387 BC – 529 AD). Plato's Retreat was a swingers' sex club founded in 1977 by Al Goldsteins friend, Larry Levenson in the Ansonia Hotel in NYC. It replaced a homosexual sex club called the Continental Baths, at the same location on Broadway and West 73rd Street. The Continental Baths hosted Bette Midler, and other musicians until being taken over by Plato's Retreat. Plato's retreat was shut down by Mayor Ed, (Don't let Koch grab your Crouch) Koch in 1985, during the AIDS crises in NYC. Plato's Retreat then moved to Fort Lauderdale, Florida, where it operated as a heterosexual swing club, on Sunrise Boulevard, from 1985 until 2006. From 2006, until the present it went back to being a homosexual sex club at the same location.
430 BC	**Plague of Athens**, (430-426 BC), an unknown cause; possibly viral hemorrhagic fever like Ebola or Marburg virus, or HTLV I, II, III, or Human Immunodeficiency Virus. Ashzenazi Jews exhibit a protective allele in their autosomal DNA that protects against some diseases like HIV, rheumatoid arthritis, and smallpox, and possibly other diseases as well. This CCR5 gene mutation, CCR5-Delta 32 allele, could possibly be derived from the intermarriage of the Ashkenazi Jews with the inhabitants of Khazaria, the Khazars. The mutation to the gene occurred between

	the years 800 and 1000 AD, just after the Khazar peoples converted to Judaism. It occurs in about 20% of Ashkenazi people tested. The Khazars may have contributed this allele; Khazarian territory on the Black Sea is about 750 miles across the sea to Athens.
430 BC	Celtic La Tene culture developed in western Gaul and areas north of and in Alps. This culture was an elite aristocratic war like Celtic culture. Celtic migrations south, west and east began around this time also; a large number migrated south across the Alps into the Po Valley in northern Italy and settled there, coming into conflict with the local Etruscan, the Veneti, (around present day Venice), and the Ligures, (around Genoa), indigenous tribes of the Italian Peninsula. Some of these Celtic tribes were the Insubres, the Libicii, the Cenomanii, the Lingones, the Boii, and the Senones, eventually being absorbed into the Roman Empire. Celts also moved south down into the Balkans towards Greece.
323-146 BC	Hellenistic Greece, Alexander the Great conquered and spread Greek culture as far as India, Persia, Egypt, the Levant, Anatolia and Italy.
310 BC	Aristarchus of Samos (310-230 BC), born, a mathematician and astronomer who puts forth the theory of heliocentric solar system in opposition to Aristotle's and Socrates geocentric solar system and geocentric universe; this theory was ignored then lost until Copernicus figured it out again in 1543 AD.
300 BC	Euclid works with geometry, the science of space; geodesy means earth in Greek; geometry is measuring the earth.
850-300 BC	Europe, beginning of Volkwanderung, folk wanderings by Germanic tribes mostly to the south and west due to colder climates further north.

This pushed the Celtic tribes south of the Alps and they start settlements like Milan, Verona, and Narbonne; some move south into Greece then Anatolia. These Germanic tribes eventually federated and coalesced into the Alemanii, Franks, Saxons, Frisians and Thuringians. (The Thuringians went on to found The House of Hesse, like in Hessians, in Germany 1500 years later.)

According to the "Lebor Gabala Erenn", "The Book of the Taking of Ireland", between the years of King David, Solomon and the Babylonian captivity (1200 BC-537 BC), the Sons of Mil of Celtic Iberia migrated to Ireland, and fought with the Tuatha De Dannan, a previously settled Celtic tribe, for domination of the island.

Hism chetramad amsir in doman tancatar Gaedil in hErinn, .i. in amsir Duida meic Iase, diar triallad Tempul Solmon;"

"In the Fourth Age of the World the Gaedil came into Ireland, that is, in the age of David son of Isa; by whom The Temple of Solomon was projected;" "and in the twentieth year of the princedom imperu regis Assyriorum On Thursday, as regards the day of the week, on the Kalends (first day of any month) of May, as regards the day of the solar month, Thineus was King of the World in the time of David, Dercylas, moreover, was prince when the temple of Solomon was projected. Thus Dercylas and Solomon were contemporaries of the Sons of Mil. Battle is joined in Tailtu between the Sons of Mil and the Tuatha De Dannan, till the three kings of the Tuatha de Dannan fell there, with their three queens. MacCecht fell at the hands of Erimon, MacGuill of Eber, MacGreine of Amorgen, eriu of Suirge, Banba of Caicher, Fotla of Etan."

There is archeological evidence in Israel to the support the Old Testament starting with the monarchy period. The following date line outlines major events in that time.

Dated Timeline	Old Testament	Monarchy Period (1020-587 BC)
1020 – 1000 BC		Early Monarchy King Saul, was ordered by Yahweh to exterminate the Edomites, but he ignored Yahweh's order; Saul was subsequently killed by the Philistines in battle.
1000 - 922 BC	United Kingdom	David killed the Philistine giant Goliath and after Sauls death, the Hebrew elders then asked David to become King Solomon; David's personal army captured the Jebusite Canaanite city of Jebus or Urusalima which means the "City of Peace". Urusalima also means the "foundation stone", or "cornerstone", of the Bronze Canaanite god Shalem, who was the god of the dusk. The word "Shalem" became the word "Shalom" meaning peace. Gihon spring is a nearby spring from which all the water in the Urusalima, "Jerusalem" area was derived and was situated below the "Fortress of Zion", a Bronze age hill fort also called Metsudat Zion, or Mount Zion by the Jebusite Canaanites. After the capture by David's army it was given to David as his personal property. He renamed it the "Fortress of David" and the "City of David". David entered a new covenant with God in which the Southern Kingdom of Judah would forever be the property of David's descendants without the "if" clauses of the covenant with Moses. Jerusalem lay on the border between the Northern and Southern Kingdoms of Israel. David chose this city to be his capital city. Jerusalem was established. Solomon was a good administrator but an inept soldier, he divided tribal boundaries with his land divisions, but increased prosperity through his commercial transactions. Israel became wealthy but lost territory as a result. The first temple was built based on a Phoenician model. The First temple of Solomon was built and it housed the Holy of Holies (Well of Souls) beneath the Foundation Stone where the Ark of the Covenant rested with the ten

Commandments. (957 BC). The Foundation Stone is also the spot where Abraham was going to sacrifice his son Isaac. Abrahams gravesite is in the nearby Cave of the Patriarchs. Abraham purchased the cave of the Patriarchs from the Jebusite Canaanites as a crypt. Jerusalem with the Foundation Stone became the center of Judaism.

922 -587 BC   Divided Monarchy   The Northern Israeli tribes seceded from the United Kingdom of Israel and Judah, into the Kingdom of Israel and the Kingdom of Judah.

In 735 BC, the northern Kingdom of Israel and the capital of Aramea (Damascus), invaded Judah to try to force Judah to come in on their side in the coming war with the Assyrian Empire. The prophet Isaiah urged Judah to trust in God, and not rely on foreign nations to oppose the Israelite invasion of the Jewish Hebrews of Judah, but Judah embraced Assyria in opposition to the northern tribes of Israel. The Northern Kingdom of Israel survived until 722 BC, then the Assyrians conquered it and deported the northern tribes to parts unknown. The southern kingdom of Judah survived until the Babylonian invasion of 586 BC.

The twelve tribes of Israel were:
Northern tribes: Asher, Dan, Ephraim, Gad, Issachar, Manasseh, Naphtali, Reuben, Simeon

Southern tribes: Judah, Benjamin

722 BC   Divided Monarchy   Assyrian invasion, deportation of Jews, this deportation created the 10 Lost Tribes of Israel; the Northern Kingdom of Israel was obliterated.

650 BC   Start of Zoroastrian religion (650 BC- 650 AD), in Persia

587 BC   Divided Monarchy   Babylonians conquer the Assyrian Empire and the Kingdom of Judah; the Babylonians destroy Solomon's temple, the Ark of the Covenant disappears, possibly taken to Babylon or possibly hidden somewhere in the temple somewhere. This was normal tribal city state behavior. The conqueror steals the god of the conquered and brings it back home to its own temples, except it got lost this time. Judah's inhabitants were exiled by Nebuchadnezzar to Babylon, but Judah was not repopulated by any other peoples, except Edomites took over parts of southern Judah. Some Jews escaped to Arabian oasis.

Dated Timeline	**Old Testament**	**Exile and Persian Period**
(596 - 332 BC)		
599 BC – 201 BC		Celtic Expansion in Europe
596 BC – 539 BC	Babylonian Period	Persian Empire under Cyrus begins, Achaemenid Empire, (First Persian Empire 550 BC-330 BC)
537 BC		Babylonian Empire falls, Babylonian exile of Judah ends; Jews return to their promised homeland after 50 year exile, some stay in Babylon and establish a Jewish community there. Cyrus offers to pay for temple reconstruction.
539 BC – 332 BC	Persian Period	Cyrus, Darius, Xerces; Darius re- digs the first Suez Canal from the Nile to the Red Sea, difference in water levels and salinity eventually cause it to silt over.
520 BC – 515 BC		Second Temple is built in Jerusalem. The foundation rock or stone on the top has an opening that leads to a cave below that is the "Well of Souls". This is Holy of Holies. Jews face this when they are praying.
484 BC		Greek historian Herodotus (484- 425 BC) is born. Herodotus documented the Seven Wonders of the World

The Seven Wonders of the World
The Great Pyramid of Giza
The Statue of Zeus at Olympia
The Hanging Gardens of Babylon
The Temple of Artemis at Ephesus
The Mausoleum of Halicarnassus
The Colossus of Rhodes
The Lighthouse of Alexandria

Dated Timeline	**Old Testament**	**Exile and Persian Period**
480 BC		Xerxes battles the 300 Spartans at the Hot Gates of Thermopylae as Persians expand into Europa
479 BC		Xerxes I driven out of Greece and Macedonia
445 BC		Walls of Jerusalem rebuilt, Ezra Nehemiah
430 BC		**Plague of Athens** affects entire Eastern Mediterranean
400 BC		Belinus, brother of Brennius, starts to build where city of London will eventually be on the Thames River.

Dated Timeline	Old Testament	Hellenistic and Roman Period
		(336 BC-324 AD)
390 BC		Brennius, a Brythonic Celt from Britain, leads an army of Celts against Italy and Rome, he slaughters the Roman army, and conquers Rome, he killed the Roman Senate, and seized all the wealth and riches from Rome before he left
335 AD		Celts meet Alexander the Great at the Danube
334 BC		Alexander the Great, (356 BC-323 BC), attacks the Persian Empire at 22 years old.
333 BC		Alexander of Macedon, "Alexander the Great", conquers the Levant, Jerusalem and Egypt.
331 BC		Alexander breaks up the Persian Empire, burns Persepolis the capital city, and breaks up the Persian control of the Near East. He implements Greek culture into the Near East of the ancient world. Greek philosophy, arts and reason are introduced.
330 BC		Greek City of Alexandria founded at the mouth of the Nile River
326 BC		Alexander starts to conquer India but is reasoned with to stop at the Indus River
325 BC		Pytheas of Massila (350-285 BC), voyaged to Albion and recorded the existence of the Hyperboreans, Thule, Orkney, the midnight sun; he recorded the connection between the moon and the tides; polar ice, and frigid zones in his book "Periplus".
324 BC		Alexander plans to conquer Arabia, but his plan is never put into action.
323 BC		Alexander dies; he is 33 years old; two of his generals, Ptolemy and Seleucus gain control over Egypt (Ptolemy) and Persia (Seleucus) creating the Ptolemy's (323 -30 BC) and Seleucid (323-60 BC) Hellenistic cultures that will dominate until Islam arrives.
323 BC		Judah is ruled by Ptolemy's (323-198 BC), of Egypt until 198 BC, then by Seleucids after
309 BC		Ptolemy II, (309-246 BC) is born. Ptolemy II builds the Musaeum in Alexandria; it is comparable to a 21st century university, containing the library of Alexandria, and an astronomical observatory. It was dedicated to the "Muses", and

it stored ancient scholarly texts, it was a major seat of learning similar to Plato's Academy and Aristotles' gymnasium.

298 BC Celts invade Thrace, but are defeated at Mt. Haemus

279 BC Another Brennus, also a Celt, moves his tribes south into Illyria, Macedonia, Thrace, and onto Thessaly; he passes the Hot Gates of Thermopylae, and he attacked the Oracle at Delphi in Greece. He was defeated by Greek armies and was forced to retreat out of Greece. He continued his advance in the opposite direction into Anatolia, (278-277 BC), and settled in Anatolia with his tribes of Celts. He established Galatia, and the people were known as Galatians. 400 years later, Saint Paul, wrote a letter to the Galatians in the New Testament and told them how fucked up they really are.

272 BC Mithra the Savior (272- 208 BC) is born around Lake Hamud in Helmand province.

264 BC The start of the Punic Wars (264-146 BC); Latin Rome wars against Carthage in North Africa; Punic means they were ancestors of the Semite Phoenicians

250 BC Ptolemy's and Seleucids intensely compete for control over Syria and Palestine area. Some Jews support the one side; some support the other side.

240 BC Antioch was made capital of Seleucid Empire.

247 BC Parthian Empire (247 BC – 224 AD) begins in Persia; the eastern portion of the Hellenistic Seleucid Empire is conquered and becomes the Parthian Empire; the religion of the Parthian Empire is Zoroastrianism mixed with Greek deities, and Mesopotamian gods; the language of the Parthian Empire is Aramaic, Greek and Farsi, Persian language.

233 BC Greek armies under Attalus I, (241-197 BC) defeated a Celt army at the Springs of Kaikos, (The river Kaikos in western Anatolia empties into the Aegean Sea near the town of Foca, Izmir province, Gulf of Smyrna, Turkey; the river starts as a spring in the mountains of Temnos), and he

celebrated this victory by creating a monument on the acropolis of Pergamum. Part of the monument survives today in Roman copies, "The Dying Gaul". Celts were used as mercenaries by the Seleucid and Ptolemaic empires.

227 BC	Celtic tribes were living in Gallipoli
218 BC	Hannibal crosses the Alps with 3 dozen war elephants, and attacks Italy. After his defeat and his return to Carthage he fought with the Hellenistic Seleucids against Romans in Asia minor. He poisoned himself after the Seleucids signed a peace treaty with Rome in 188 BC, and he was to be turned over to Rome. The Jews in the Levant supported Hannibal.
214 BC	Start of the Roman-Macedonian Wars (214-148 BC), The Seleucid War is considered part of the Roman Wars against Greek culture.
210 BC	Chinese "Han Dynasty" started building the "Great Wall of China", (210 BC- 220 AD), to protect trade and the countryside from the "steppe nomadic tribes" like the Turks, and the Mongols. The "Silk Road", (150 BC-1450 AD) ran east-west, south of the wall, then out of the protection of the Han Dynasty Wall, as it wound its way west. The Silk Road ran from Chang-an, Wonei, the Jade Gate, Kaschgar, Andijon, Kokand, Samarkand, Buchara, Merw, Meschhed, Nischhpur, Emamshar, and Tehran, then eventually on to Babylon, Baghdad, Palmyra, and the Mediterranean Sea, carrying all manner of trade goods, in both directions by camel caravans strung out in long lines like freight trains. It was controlled by the Chinese, the Turk nomads, the Scythians, the Arabs, the Greeks, the Romans, and the Persians. The silk road ended in the 1450's AD, when the Ottoman Empire restricted trade to Christian Europe over its loss of its Islamic hold on the Iberian Peninsula, the fragmentation of the Mongol Empire, the rise of mercantilism, and the voyages of exploration by Europe and China around the Dark Continent, Africa.
206 BC	Romans capture Cadiz, Iberia

200 BC	Loyalties of most Jews in the Levant shift to the Seleucids after 200 BC, when Seleucid General Antiochus III won the battle of Panion in the upper Galilee region, thus giving Seleucid Empire control over Jerusalem and the Levant area. The high priest Simon II transferred Israelite allegiance to the Seleucids and advocated strict adherence to Jewish tradition over Hellenization. Antiochus III forbids gentiles from entering the Jewish Temple and eliminates taxes for the priesthood council of Elders, who were called the Sanhedrin. These promises of religious freedom and no taxes evaporate in the new fight against the Romans. The Jews support the Seleucids against the Romans.
198 BC	After defeats of Ptolemaic territory to Seleucids, the Ptolemy's ally themselves with Rome; this lasts from 198 BC until 30 BC. Egypt supplies grain to Rome.
198 BC.	Greek culture becomes popular within Jewish population.
189 BC	Romans defeat Celts at Olympus.
188 BC	Seleucids signed a peace treaty with Rome, ceding European and Asia minor territory to Rome. Jewish priests and politicians shifted loyalty of the Jewish people back to the Ptolemys', but some Jewish rabbis and politicians bought back the high priest position. There was murder, embezzling, and corruption in Judah. This is actually a Jewish civil war starting between Hellenized Jews and traditional Jews.
187 BC	Mattathias ben Johannan, (died 165 BC) was a "Cohen", a high priest. He had a number of sons; Judah or Judas Maccabee, who became known as "The Hammer", Jonathan Maccabee, Simon Thassi, John Gatti, and Eleazar Avaron. One son called Jonathan, was appointed High priest of Israel, in 161 BC. Jonathan like the other religious Maccabees wanted to rid Israel of Hellenistic influence. Judah Maccabee, "The Hammer" ruled Israel and led the revolt from 167 until 160 BC. Jonathan ruled Israel from 161 until 143 BC. Simon Thassi Maccabee was

the founder of The Hasmonean Dynasty of Israel and ruled from 142 until 135 BC.

169 BC   Seleucid Antiochus IV sent in the Syrian Seleucid army and slaughtered the Jews, they looted the temple and garrisoned Seleucid troops in Jerusalem.

167 BC   Antiochus IV allows the temple in Jerusalem to be dedicated to the "Lord", Ba'al (Zeus), Baal meaning Lord was the God of the Phoenicians, and the Philistines. Jews were forced to renounce Judaism and become loyal to the Seleucids, thus forcing Hellenization again. Swine were sacrificed in the Temple, shrines and altars were defiled; circumcision was banned and eliminated.

167 BC   In response to Seleucid actions Jews started a guerrilla war with Seleucids. The Hasmoneans, are also known as the (Maccabees). The Maccabees were joined by the Hasidians, (the holy ones), they both started attacking the Seleucid Greek occupiers, in a war that lasted from 167-160 AD.

166 BC   Judah Maccabee, (died 160 BC) "The Hammer" took over the revolt until 160 BC.

164 BC   Jerusalem was recaptured from the Seleucids by Judah Maccabee, "The Hammer"; Chanukah is the Jewish festival of lights or feast to commemorate this recapture and re-purification of the Temple, it was led by Adam Sandler It occurred in the third year of a seven-year war to rid Israel of the Greek Seleucids Empire. The conqueror was Judah Maccabeus. Afterwards, Judas Maccabeus was approached by Seleucids to rule Judea as a secular ruler of a vassal state of the Seleucid Empire.

160 BC   The Seleucids sent an even larger army to Judea and killed Judah Maccabee at the Battle of Elasa, they overran Jerusalem again; but Jonathan Maccabee and his remaining brothers continued the revolt against the Seleucids.

143 BC   The Seleucids kidnapped Jonathan and when extortion was not paid by Israel, they publicly executed him. The Jews proclaimed Jonathans brother Simon Thassi Maccabeus to be the high priest and leader forever until a trustworthy

Prophet arises. The guerilla war with the Seleucids continued until 140 BC when the Seleucid rule was broken. Simon ruled from 140-135 BC, he was the founder of the Hasmonean Dynasty within Israel.

148 BC   End of Roman-Macedonian Wars (214-148 BC), Rome was victorious.

140 BC   The Greek Seleucid Empire is broken in Judea, The Jewish Hasmoneans have won, and rule semi-autonomously from 140 BC until 110 BC.

135 BC   The Hasmoneans ruled Judah (134-37 BC), they looted David's tomb to pay off the Seleucids, then they sought official recognition from the Roman Senate. They attacked and destroyed the Samaritans, and expanded the territory of Israel. Many of the Jews had been Hellenized over the centuries, and many Jews were traditional Jews. The Sadducees were wealthier land owners and wealthier merchants in Judea. The Sadducees controlled the membership in the priesthood. They were more Hellenized in their interpretation of the Torah; they believed in elitism. The beliefs of the Sadducees encompassed the Hellenized belief that "there was no life after death", "there was no hereafter, there was no reward and there was no punishment after death", there was no such thing as the Oral tradition, it was invented by the Rabbi's, and every generation of Rabbi's had a right to interpret or re-interpret the Oral Tradition, infinitely. The Sadducees believed in "free will", eat, drink, and be merry for tomorrow we die. The Pharisees on the other hand were traditional non-Hellenized Jews, they believed in the afterlife and that God would judge everyone, dealing out reward and punishment. The Jewish community was torn by these different ideological feuds. The written Torah became the most re-interpreted book in the history of primates for Jews, then for Christians, and then for Moslems. The Maccabees were traditional Pharisees, but the Sadducees worked on him in conniving ways until Hyrcannus became a Sadducee himself. The goal of the Sadducees was to undermine

the Sanhedrin. The Sanhedrin were essentially courts that were set up in every town and city of Israel, with complete authority over the inhabitants so as to ensure the Laws of Moses were followed. The Sadducees had to undermine the Sanhedrin to gain control, to establish elitism in the Rabbinical community. The philosophical differences between the sects were similar to philosophical differences between the philosophers Plato and Aristotle. Aristotle believed that no "one" person can ascertain the "truth", but many people's truths can get a more complete and accurate "truth" of what is. The philosophical differences led to "sects" of religious belief, with law enacted to support any sect in power, a prescription for never ending warfare.

134 BC   John Hyrcannus, son of Simon Thassi Maccabeus ruled (134 –104 BC) Judah at this time.

134 BC   The "Book of Maccabees", the first book, part of Torah, was written after this time period, about 100 BC, the second book about the same time; some of it describes the wars between the Seleucids and the Ptolemy Empires, with Judah and the people of Israel in between.

134-63 BC   Lengthy wars over control of Anatolia and access to the Black Sea; Roman wars with Mithridates of Pontus.

126 BC   John Hyrcannus, (as ruler and high priest of Judah, conquers Dora, Marissa and the Edomites, Idumeans. The Edomite tribe, living near Aqaba and Petra, south of the Dead Sea had taken some of the land in Judah, when the Jews went into exile. They had assisted in the exile, and were the sworn enemies of Israel, and visa versa. The other main enemy of Israel and one which they continually feared were the tribes of the North. These were the Tribes north of and around the Black Sea, and Caspian Sea in the land of the Magog. The tribes of the sons of Japheth, Magog, Meshech, Tubal, and Gomer, along with Gomers sons' tribes, the Ashkenaz, Riphath, and Togarmah. The Edomite's were also known as the Amaleks tribe, or the Amalekites. Agag and

Gog mean the same thing, they mean the "King". Thus any given king of the Edomite tribe was **Gog**. When Judah conquered the Amalekites, or the Edomite's or the Idumeans (Greek word for Edomite's), they offered them a chance to convert to Judaism, or be slaughtered entirely. The Edomite tribe converted to Judaism from paganism. From this point on the Edomite tribe was never heard of again, they were absorbed into Judaism. If you ever wonder where **Gog** is, he is the "gog" in the "syna **gog** ue", synagogue. The hatred between the twin brothers, Jacob, ("Israel") and Esau, ("Edom", "Red"), were now both incorporated into the same household of Judah, Israel. Oy veh! The prophet Ezekial continually warned of the Edomites and Gog in his prophecies', along with the Prophet Obadiah, Gog will be the ruler of Rosh, Meshech, Tubal, and the Magog, but maybe the Maccabees needed the Edomite and Gog for something at the time. The DNA of these groups were the same male haplotype J1, J2, Semites, from Shem. Shem is not the same as Shemp from the Three Stooges, although the three stooges were all Semites.

104 BC	Aristobulus I, ruled the Hasmonean Dynasty from 104 until 103 BC.
103 BC	Alexander Janus ruled The Hasmonean Dynasty from 103 until 76 BC.
100 BC	The Seleucid Empire was almost completely collapsed; its capital city Antioch and a few cities in Syria were all that was left of it. Antioch had been the capital city of the Seleucid Empire from 240 BC until 63 BC, when Roman General Pompey finished conquering the Seleucid Empire on the Mediterranean Coast. The Parthian Empire began in 247 BC and lasted until 224 AD. The Parthian Empire, (Persian Empire) was inland from the Mediterranean coastline, and consisted of Mesopotamia, Iran, and parts of what is today Eastern Turkey, it had taken over what was originally had been the Seleucid Empires eastern areas. The Parthian Empire controlled the Silk Road in the west in conjunction with the Han

	Dynasty in China in the East, which made it a target for the Roman Empires economic expansion, to the east.
92 BC	Start of the Roman-Parthian Wars (92 BC- 285 AD)
88 BC	Mithrades IV slaughters the leaders of the Celts, in his territory in Anatolia
76 BC	Alexander Janus' wife Salome Alexander makes peace with the Pharisees; she appoints her older son as high priest and King, called King Hyrcannus II. When she dies her second son Aristobulus II contested his brothers rule and started a civil war to gain the throne, king of the Jews.
73 BC	Herod the Great (73 - 4 BC) is born, he is an Edomite within Judah; he eventually becomes King of Judea (37 – 4 BC), and the Edomite King of the Jews.
63 BC	As a continuation of the Roman-Mithrades and Roman-Parthian wars, Roman General Pompey enters Damascus and Jerusalem. Pompey side-swith the older brother, King Hyrcannus II and Aristobulus is shipped off to Rome in chains. Pompey delegates administration to his second Gabancius; Syria is created; Armenia is left to rule itself; and Judea is divided into 5 districts. They are Jerusalem, Jericho, Sepphorus (Galilee), Amathus (east of the Jordan River), and Gazara (Gezer, Gaza strip).
60 BC	Hellenistic Seleucid Empire is finally destroyed by Rome.
58-50 BC	Gallic Wars (58-50 BC); Julius Caesar pays off his enormous debts and furthers his political career by conquering Celtic Gaul (France and Belgium). After the battle of Alesia, (52 BC), Celtic leader Vercingetorix loses and lays down his arms to Julius Caesar. The Celts were militarily just as strong as the Latins of Rome but they lost because their tribes had divided allegiance. Gaul came under Roman control. After Gaul, Caesar invaded Britain and withdrew after surveying southern area.

49-44 BC	Gaius Julius Caesar is the dictator of Rome, until his assassination. Hail Caesar; Kaiser. Julius Caesar had a son by Cleopatra, named Caesarian (47- 30 BC). This solidified Caesars rule over Ptolemy Empire, in Egypt.
44 BC	Julius Caesar is murdered in the Roman Senate, all the Senators stab him to death; Cleopatra aligns herself with Marc Anthony, in opposition to Octavian (Augustus), who was Julius Caesars legal heir.
37 BC	Herod the Great ruled Judea; he is the start of the Herodian Dynasty of Israel; "massacre of the Innocents", he massacres all males around Bethlehem, because 3 Magi came looking for the new born king from Parthia; an angel told the Magi not to report back to Herod after they found the baby, so they left and went back to Zoroastrian lands; Herod slaughtered all males around Jesus Christs age, because he was afraid of the Messiah rumors in Judaism; a Messiah would save them from the continuous carnage in Judaism, that they had endured for centuries. Herod built the fortress of Masada, Herodium, which is a 2,500-foot hill fort and palace with a small town, seven and a half miles south of Jerusalem, the port of Caesarea Maritima, (25- 13 BC), a colony for Roman veterans, about half way between Haifa and Tel Aviv, and he expanded the second temple in Jerusalem. Herod had 5 wives, and they all had children, one wife, the 4th one, Malthus, was the mother of Herod Antipas; another wife, the 2nd wife, Mariamme I, or Miriam was the mother of Aristobulus IV. Aristobulus IV married Bernice and had a son called Herod V, also known as Herod of Chalcis. Herod V married his cousin another Miriam and had a son called Aristobulus of Chalcis. Aristobulus of Chalcis married a woman called Salome and they had three sons, Moe, Larry and Aristobulus. This last Aristobulus became a Christian missionary accompanying Saint Barnabus and Saint Andrew; he became known as Aristobulus of Britannia. Aristobulus of Britannia

is the one responsible for bringing the "light of Christ" to Britain during the Roman occupation. He preached to the remaining Celt-Iberians in the Iberian Peninsula on his way to Britain. He died in Glastonbury in 99 AD. He was saluted by Saint Paul in Romans 16:10.

30 BC	End of Ptolemaic Kingdom (323-30 BC), Alexandria was the capital city; Cleopatra VII is the last leader of the Ptolemy. After the loss of Marc Anthony to General Augustus, Marc Anthony and Cleopatra committed suicide. The child of Julius Caesar and Cleopatra, Caesarian, was put to death by Caesar Augustus.
27 BC	Start of Roman Empire, Caesar Augustus is first Roman Emperor
20 BC	King Herod Antipas (20 BC- 39 AD) is born; Edomite king.
20 BC	King Herod the Great renovates the temple and then it is known as Herod's Temple
5 BC	John the Baptist is born
4 BC	King Herod Antipas (20 BC-39 AD) becomes King (4 BC- 39 AD) at the death of his King Herod the Great (73 -4 BC). Herod the Great died in 4 BC, so Jesus was born shortly before this date or in this year.
1 BC	10% of the population of the Roman Empire was of the Jewish Religion
0	Jesus of Nazareth, (4 BC – 33 AD), the Christ, was born in Bethlehem by Immaculate Conception to Mary, with Joseph of as father. Joseph was a Jewish carpenter. Both Joseph and Mary were observant Jews who lived in the town of Nazareth, but went to Bethlehem for Roman census to be recorded and stayed till the Magi warned them, so the story goes.
5 AD	Saul of Tarsus (5-67 AD) is born, also known as Paul the Apostle. Rome was conducting another census of Judea to ascertain the wealth there for taxation purposes. This created rebellion against Rome by the zealots and Pharisees. Israel was slowly being ripped apart by Roman occupation and Roman, Greek beliefs. The brief Hasmonean independence was gone. Jews must have been

crazy living through all these occupations and beliefs systems, and Paul was born into it. The area of Tarsus, Antioch, Chalcis, Aleppo was the cradle of Hellenistic Judaism and Christianity. These areas surround the Gulf of Alexandretta, also known as the Gulf of Iskkenderon, or the Gulf of Issus, a gulf of the Levantine Sea in the Eastern Mediterranean Sea. The Euphrates River is about 100 miles east of the Gulf of Alexandretta, which was the birthplace of farming, in 8000 BC

14 AD   Tiberius Caesar becomes second Emperor of Rome (14-37 AD). Roman Census records 5 million people in Roman Empire.

19 AD   4,000 Jews expelled and deported from Sicily by Tiberius Caesar.

30 AD   God tells his son to go out for a pass, then throws the football to him. The summation of Jesus Christs teachings are in the gospel of Matthew 4:17, "Repent, for the Kingdom of Heaven is at hand". Jesus Christ, the Blessed Prophet, the son of God taught the teachings of God to both the Jews and the pagan Gentiles at "The Sermon on the Mount" in Galilee. The Sermon on the Mount gave us "the Beatitudes". The Beatitudes means the supreme blessedness, ecstasy, grace, exaltation, and extreme happiness. The beatitudes were meant to be used in conjunction with The Ten Commandments.

The Beatitudes

Blessed are the poor in spirit, for theirs is the kingdom of heaven.
Blessed are those that mourn, for they shall be comforted.
Blessed are the meek, for they shall inherit the earth.
Blessed are those who hunger and thirst for righteousness,
    for they shall be satisfied.
Blessed are the merciful, for they shall obtain mercy.
Blessed are the pure in heart, for they shall see God.
Blessed are the peacemakers, for they shall be called the sons of God.
Blessed are those who are persecuted for righteousness sake, for theirs
    is the kingdom of heaven.
Blessed are you when men revile against you and persecute you and
    utter all kinds of evil against you falsely on my account,
Rejoice and be glad, for your reward is great in heaven.

31 AD	John the Baptist is killed by Edomite Judaic King Herod Antipas
32 AD	Jesus predicts the destruction of the second temple, he compares his physical body to the temple; it will be torn down and then raised again on the third day. The temple is the body of Christ. He says the first temple was destroyed due to idol worship, licentious behavior, and murder; the second temple will be destroyed because of gratuitous hatred. Jesus commented on the taxation of Jews by Roman authority in his native Aramaic language;

"Render unto Caesar the things that are Caesars and render unto God the things that are Gods"

This attitude pissed off a lot of Jews, and he ended up before the Roman governor Pontius Pilate. This also led to the early Christian view of separation of belief in God and the state, which was in sync with pagan Rome's belief system philosophy. Jesus also commented on the Ten Commandments;

"You shall love the Lord your God with all your heart and all your soul, and all your mind. You shall love your neighbor as yourself."

Jesus also gave us the Lords' prayer when asked how to pray;

<u>The Lord's Prayer</u>
Our father who art in heaven, hallowed be thy name, thy kingdom come, thy will be done, on earth as it is in heaven. Give us this day our daily bread and forgive us our trespasses, as we forgive those who trespass against us, and lead us not into temptation, but deliver us from evil.

Jesus was crucified by Roman soldiers to satisfy demands of the Jews in Jerusalem, and so the Roman governor could maintain order by pacifying the Jewish hierarchy. Jesus died in 3 hours on the cross on what is known as Good Friday. He died and was buried by his mother and Mary Magdalene his girlfriend. On Sunday morning, when they went to check on the grave, the large stone was rolled back, and an Angel of the God of Abraham announced that Jesus Christ, the son of God had rose from the dead and was alive. Jesus appeared to others for 40 days on earth, then he ascended into heaven to be with his father, and of his kingdom there is no end in everlasting life. Jesus and his followers were both a threat to the Hebrews and to the order of the Roman Empire.

33 AD	Jesus Christ was crucified by Edomite Judaic King Herod Antipasto, and Roman governor Punchy Pilate.
36 AD	Paul was a Jewish Pharisee, and a Roman citizen, he zealously persecuted the followers of Jesus as

heretics; while on the road to Damascus, he was struck blind and heard a voice asking him "why he persecuted my followers". He was taken to a house and a man called Ananias came to him, on a "Street called Straight" in old Damascus, he restored his sight and he was baptized as a Christian on January 25, between 33 and 36 AD. Afterwards Paul was a zealous Christian follower of Jesus, and wrote down the Gospels of the New testament.

37-41 AD	Emperor Caligula is the third Roman Emperor, Christian persecutions increase.
41-54 AD	Emperor Claudius is the fourth Roman Emperor, he adds to the Musaeum in Alexandria and invades Britain in force.
43 AD	Roman legions invade Britain
54 AD	Emperor Nero (54-68 AD) is fifth Roman Emperor; he burns Rome while playing his fiddle, then blames Christians for doing it.
60 AD	Romans in Britain attack the Druid sanctuary on the island of Anglesey, Wales and cause a rebellion led by Queen Boudicca of the Iceni tribe in Norfolk, Britain. Britain rebels (60-61 AD), against Roman rule and slaughters legion, legionary pensioners, and burns port of Londinium, among other Roman cities and towns. She is defeated but Roman expansion in Britain comes to a halt for more than ten years.
67 AD	Paul of Tarsus, the apostle (5-67 AD) dies, Paul established several churches in Asia Minor, and preached to Galatians; Nero had him beheaded in Rome and crucified Saint Peter, his trial was held as he was a Roman Jewish citizen, and the presiding judge was Herod Agrippa II. Paul wrote most of the New testament during his lifetime, the Epistles of Saint Paul; both of these men were Jews and Rome was fighting Jewish revolts in Judea at the time.
67 AD	Aristobulus of Britannia, also a Jewish Christian convert, began preaching Christianity in Britain around this time.
66-69 AD	First Jewish Revolt, (66-69 AD), Masada is taken by Roman legions, defenders commit suicide before capture.

68-69 AD	Emperors Galba, Otho, and Vitillus
69 AD	Emperor Vespasian (69-79 AD), ninth Emperor
70 AD	Emperor Vespasian's son Titus puts down First Jewish revolt and destroys the second temple in Jerusalem, leaving only the Wailing wall.
71 AD	Roman Legions arrive at the border of Scotland for the first time, after subjugating tribes in the south of Britain.
79 AD	Mount Vesuvius erupts, destroys the city of Pompeii and Herculaneum
79-81 AD	Emperor Titus, tenth Roman Emperor runs all the Jews out of Jerusalem
81-96 AD	Emperor Domitian, 11th Emperor
96-98 AD	Emperor Nerva, 12th Emperor
98-117 AD	Emperor Trajan, 13th Emperor, Emperor Trajan devalues Roman Currency in 107 AD
99 AD	Aristobulus of Britannia died in Glastonbury, Britain after introducing Christianity to Britain

And did those feet in ancient times,
Walk upon Anglands mountains green,
And was the Holy lamb of God,
On Anglands pleasant pasture seen.

And did the continent divide,
Shine forth upon our clouded hills?
And was Jerusalem builded here,
among these dark satanic mills?

115-117 AD	2nd Jewish Revolt against Rome, called the "Kitos War", the Jews in Judea throw in with the Parthian Empire (Persians) against Rome; the Jews are defeated again.
117 AD	Emperor Hadrian, 14th Emperor, (117-138 AD), continues building the wall and other structures for the Empire, after the currency was devalued in 107 AD, ten years earlier.
122 AD	Emperor Hadrian built a wall across Britain, essentially walling off Scotland, 50 years after arriving there; Romanized Britain developed on the southern side of the wall. On the Northern side of wall there is freedom from slavery.

129 AD	Galen, (129-200 AD) born; Galen was a Greek working in the Roman Empire, He is the "father of Anatomy"; he observed and described the major systems of the Human and animal anatomies; he also described the progression of the Antonine Plague, the plague of Galen, suspected smallpox.
130 AD	From Jesus' life and preaching and death until 130 AD, oral tradition is what kept Christian beliefs going, after oral beliefs were written down, as many as 20 Gospels existed, until 4 were agreed upon.
132 AD	3rd Jewish Revolt against Rome, called the "Bar Kokhba" revolt, (132- 136 AD). Jews massacre Christians, gentiles for siding with Romans instead of Parthia; Roman legions annihilate Judean population; Romans make peace with Parthia, Jews permanently banned from Jerusalem, but allowed to visit; they are allowed to live in Galilee. Romans destroyed all the Judaic records.

This is the beginning of the **Jewish Diaspora**. Third time is a charm, three Jewish revolts against Rome in a seventy-year period; "What a revolting development"; Jewish culture becomes centered in Babylon, Baghdad area again., These Babylon Jews eventually became the Ashkenazi Jews hundreds of years later, after Islam occupied Baghdad. The diaspora moved to the desert oasis' in Arabia, as well as Yemen, Anatolia, Egypt, then some went onto North Africa and Iberia becoming Sephardic Jews. Some Jews went to Rome and tried to blend in, then into Europe, anywhere but Judea and the Levant. These Babylon Jews eventually moved to Khazaria on the Black Sea. The absorbed Edomites and the Israelites become one people in Babylon. All the records were destroyed by the Romans. After a few generations no one really remembered the teachings. The Jews in Babylon codified the Talmud, which then took precedence over the Torah (Old Testament). The Romans renamed Judea; Syria-Palestrina or Syria-Philistina. Palestrina is a corrupted form of the word Philistina, after the Philistines natural habitat.

After the Diaspora began, the Rabbi's realized the oral law was being lost, so they collected all the lists and charts and made a book called the Mischnah, a secondary law. The Mischnah is the foundation and the principal part of the whole Talmud. It was expounded on in Babylon where many of the Diaspora migrated to, and in parts of Palestine, away from Jerusalem. The other part of the Talmud is the Gemarah; the Gemarah is the interpretation of the Mischnah. It was interpreted in two places, one in Palestine and one in Babylon, so there are two Gemarahs, the Jerusalem Gemarah and the Babylonian Gemarah. There is a third part of the Talmud called the Tosephoth. The Babylonian Gemara is the teaching held in the highest esteem of the two versions. The complete Talmud contains 63 books in 524 chapters. Because the Talmud is so voluminous and disordered, a compendium was written in 1032 AD, to facilitate study. This is a shorter Talmud called the Constitutions or the Halakhoth, it was edited in the year 1340 AD. The Talmud contains some very vile descriptions of Christians and some strange language; it was banned during the days of the Christian Empires, up until almost the present centuries. It is similar to the Qur'an in its teachings, or the Qur'an is similar to it. There was, is, something else going on in that area of the world where these "religious" books were written.

136 AD	The Mischnah, part of the Talmud, is an interpretation of the law. It was written during this time period in Galilee, (136- 230 AD).
138 AD	Emperor Antoninus (86-161 AD), becomes 15th Roman Emperor (138- 161 AD) at Hadrians death.
140 AD	The People of the Book presented the world with a **singular** deity called Yahweh. The people of the book entered into an everlasting covenant with the God of Abraham for all eternity. The tribe of Abraham is tied to Jerusalem where the Foundation stone is. The tribe has stayed together for thousands of years under their God and it has helped them to become healthy, wealthy and wise as a whole, with many trials and tribulations. The word "Israel" means "God rules". The chalice of the Judaic religion is filled with an everlasting covenant of faith, hope and wisdom, along with all the failings of human nature. Judaism is a way of life to stay close to a belief in one God, whatever that is.

Dated Timeline

Roman/Byzantine/European/Syria-Palestrina Timeline

140 AD

Scotland, Nessie is swimming freely in Loch Ness; Roman Legions have built Hadrians Wall to keep out the people living in Caledonia, the Caledonians, the Picts. It cuts Britain in half from east to west. Romans are starting to build the Antonine Wall, to wall off the area north of the Clyde to the Firth of Forth, but give up and fall back to Hadrians Wall. Vanduara is the Roman name for Paisley, it is populated by a people called the Damnonii tribe, who reside in the Strathclyde area just south of the Antonine Wall. The Damnonii tribe was recorded in Ptolemys (100-170 AD) "Geography." The Damanonii people inhabited southern Scotland from the North Sea to the Irish Sea, from Firth of Forth to the Firth of Clyde including what is now Renfrewshire, Lanarkshire, Ayrshire, Stirling, Glasgow, Loch Lomond, and south to what is Northumbria. The towns of the Damnonii were Vanduara, Colania, Coria, Alauna, Lindum, and Victoria. These may be the Roman military forts set up in Damnonii territory near populations. The Iwerni peoples were the pre-Roman, pre-Celtic aboriginal people settled in the islands prior to the immigration of the Celts into the islands. The Romans linguistically distorted the name Ierne, Iwerni, Iwernians into Hibernians, notice the similarity in Hibernian to Iberian, and recall the son of Gomer Ibath, Riphath. There was a territory, a Kingdom, between the Black and Caspian Seas in the lands of Gomer that also had the name Iberia, Gomers children made up the maritime nations according to Genesis. These Iwernians were Celts like the

Gomerites, Cimmerians, Galatians. Iberia was a Celtic Peninsula before the arrival of the Greeks. The Iwernians referred to the Gaels (Goidels) as Feini (Fenians). The word Feini means "wagon men". Gaels made splendid chariots of bronze. The Fenians are wagon men, many became "Teamsters", driving teams of horses. The Iwernians are related to the Erainn and Dairine of Ulster and Down. The second wave of Celtic migration was by the Brythons (Britons) from Gaul. These migrations occurred more than 1000 years before the Romans arrived. The Damnonii are ancestors of the second wave of migrations, the Brythons. Further North in what is now Scotland there were even older tribes of Celts, who had been there for thousands of years before the Celtic Brythons and the Celtic Gaels arrived, they were eventually called the Picts. In Vanduara, a great Christian abbey, Paisley Abbey, will be built in 1000 years. William Wallace will receive some of his education there, and the Kings of Scotia buried there.

150 AD	Ptolemy (100-170 AD), comes up with the idea, that the earth is flat and there is a big dome covering it with the stars attached to the dome. There is an "above" and "below". This 'world view' existed from this date until 1543 AD, and eventually fit nicely with the transcendental God of Abraham concept.
161 AD	Emperor Antoninus dies
161 AD	Emperor Marcus Aurelius (121-180 AD) became co-Roman Emperor Marcus Aurelius (161-180 AD), writes his Stoic philosophy called the "Meditations of Marcus Aurelius", and he continued plans for the Empire laid out by Hadrian. Emperor Marcus Aurelius, ruled as a co-Emperor with his adopted brother Lucius Aurelius Commodus (130-169 AD), from 161 AD until 169 AD, then by himself from 169 AD until 177 AD. Marcus Aurelius had a biological son also called Commodus (161-192 AD). In 177 AD, the son Commodus ruled as co-Emperor with Marcus Aurelius until the death of Marcus Aurelius in 180 AD.
180 AD	Emperor Commodus (180-192 AD), was sole Emperor until 192 AD when Commodus was strangled by his wrestling partner in the bath.
165-180 AD	**Antonine Plague** (165-180 AD), (Plague of Galen), unknown plague, suspected Smallpox pandemic brought back to Roman Empire by troops returning from fighting in the Middle-East; population declines over Roman Empire from 70 Million to 40 Million people; there is much infanticide, abortion, people cannot support themselves and neither can the Empire support itself. The Christian religion begins to blossom.
177 AD	Emperor Commodus (161-192 AD) was a weak Emperor and given into others wishes, he succumbed to vices and eventually came to think of himself as a God, like Hercules. He devalued the currency by reducing the amount of precious metal in each coin. He fought in the Gladiatorial games, and had enemies continually murdered. He made the empire regard him as a God. He was murdered by his wrestling partner in the public bath in 192 AD. This started the drastic decline in the Roman Empire.
192 AD	Emperor Pertinax lasted for three months; he was killed by his Praetorian guards after trying to reform them. The Praetorian guards then auctioned off the Emperors

position to the highest bidder, who was Didius Julianus. This started a civil war, and Julianus was killed and replaced by Emperor Severus. The Praetorians were defeated and executed for treason.

193 AD	Emperor Severus (145-211 AD), was emperor from 193 AD until 211 AD; he was born in Tripoli, Libya, he married a Syrian Arab woman, Julia Domna, he had two sons Caracalla and Geta, fought in Parthia in 197 AD, fought battles around Carthage in 202 AD, and then fought against the Caledonians in 208 AD, with 40,000 troops. He moved through northern Britain into the Highlands, but could not counter the guerilla tactics of the Caledonians; he withdrew to behinds Hadrian's Wall, and died in York in 210 AD, from a fatal illness. His wife despised Caledonian women calling them all whores for the way Caledonian culture is or was. Severus issued orders to kill every man woman and child they encounter, including pregnant Caledonian women.
198 AD	Emperor Caracalla (188-217 AD) becomes emperor at the death of his father; he ruled from 198 AD until 217 AD; he was responsible for many massacres in the empire. Caracalla was of mixed Arab Syrian and Berber descent. He was nicknamed Caracalla because of the Gallic hooded tunic he always wore, called a Caracalla, which became fashionable. He assassinated his brother, Geta at a reconciliation meeting arranged by his mother, and he died in his mothers' arms. He devalued the currency again. He spent the rest of his life in the eastern part of the empire. He massacred 20,000 Roman citizens in Alexandria who had assembled in Alexandria to pay tribute to him and then he sacked the city, over a slight. He gave Roman citizenship to all freemen within the Empire, "The Latin Right" and all freewomen had the same status as Roman Latin women, before this only free Italians were Roman citizens, this extended the tax base for him.
200 AD	First written New testament comes into being, most writings are of Saint Paul that existed before his death in 67 AD
200 AD	First Scots begin to migrate to western Pictland around Argyll, Scotland, from Northwest Hibernia.
218 AD	Emperor Elagabalus (218-222 AD) was Roman Emperor from 218-222 AD, he was involved in many sex scandals and religious scandals including prostituting himself in the Palace, having many homosexual lovers whom he lavished expensive gifts on. He was married and divorced five times. He devalued the silver currency from 58% to 46% pure silver. He and his mother were murdered by the Praetorian guards in 222 AD. He was 18 years old at his death, born in 203 AD, murdered 222 AD.
222 AD	Emperor Severus Alexander (222-235 AD), good ruler, relative peace for 13 years; murdered by rebellious legions under Maximus of Thrace
224 AD	Sassanid Empire (224-651 AD), starts after Parthian Empire (247 BC- 224 AD) defeated; Parthian Empire was dissolved.
235 AD	Emperor Maximus Thrax (235-238 AD), from Thrace, a Goth (173 - 238 AD).
235-284 AD	Imperial Crises, economic depression, civil war, legions in rebellion, invasion, plague; half of the population is dead; same as in Persian lands.

238 AD	Emperor Gordian I, Gordian II, and Gordian III, (238-244 AD) from Africa
244 AD	Emperor Philip the Arab (244-249 AD)
249 AD	Emperor Decius (249-251 AD)
250 AD	**Plague of Cyprian** (250-270 AD), smallpox, 30% mortality; also brought back to empire from Sassanid-Parthian Wars; Plague of Cyprian was after Saint Cyprian who witnessed and documented the plague.
251 AD	Emperor Gallus (251-253 AD)
253 AD	Emperor Vallerian (253-260 AD)
260 AD	Emperor Gallienus (260-268 AD)
268 AD	Emperor Claudius II Gothicus (268-270 AD) died of plague of Cyprian
260 AD	Gallic Empire (260-274 AD) established; a breakaway independent empire in Gaul Germania, Britain, due to Imperial crises and invasions of Germans and Franks into Gaul.
270 AD	Emperor Aurelian (270-275 AD), He helped stabilize the Empire during the crises and after.
274 AD	Emperor Aurelius declares the Sun God, Sol Invictus, Mithras, to be the patron God of Roman Empire; Mithras the Savior of the Roman Empire; Mithras was the God of the Roman legions and he needed the legions to be unified and loyal to the Emperor; religious belief held people together in their mutual beliefs.
275 AD	Emperor Tacitus (275-276 AD)
285 AD	Emperor Diocletian (284-305 AD), partitioned the Empire into two halves because one is too "unmanageable". East and West Empires started.
296 AD	Emperor Constantius I, retakes Britain after the Gallic Empire was brought back under Imperial Control
300 AD	Slavic tribes moved west into Central Europe (300-500 AD), and again Germanic tribes wander to Italy (Goths), France (Franks), and Iberia (Visigoths), Constantius I fights the invaders.
300 AD	Population of Caledonia (Pictland), is 400,000; after 300 AD, the population rises to over a million due to the introduction of terraced farming by the Scots from Hibernia.
300 AD	Only 2% of Latin Western Roman Empire is Christian; Greeks in East are Christian
305 AD	Constantius I returned to Britain to fight Caledonians and Picts; drives them back to north of Antonine Wall then retreats to behind Hadrian's Wall and dies at York in 306 AD. His so Constantine becomes Emperor Constantine the Great, also known as Constantine I, and Saint Constantine.
306 AD	Emperor Constantine I (272-337 AD), becomes Roman Emperor (306- 337 AD). Population of the Roman Empire about 56 million. Jews and Christians reproduced at a faster rate than pagans. Rome needed manpower for its legions and for taxpayers.
312 AD	While advancing across Italy from Gaul, Constantine I had a dream and a vision of fighting under the protection of Christ; he witnessed a "Sun Dog", which is when the sun has a cross emblazoned on it, and he directed the armies to put the

"Chi-Rho", the first two letters of Christs name on their shields, and made standards and banners of Chi-Rho fight under. Crosses were put on shields from this time forward.

313 AD   Emperor Constantine I (272-337 AD) issues an "Edict of Toleration", in which he promises under the authority of Rome, that everyone, can have freedom of worship to the God or Gods of their own choosing; this amounted to freedom of speech with regards to religion. Constantine I then issued "The Edict of Milan" (313 AD), which de-criminalizes Christianity.

315 AD   Edict put out by Constantine I, "Judaism prohibited from seeking converts within Roman Empire"; Jews would buy slaves and convert them to Judaism; and the Jews would marry "gentile" women and the women would convert to Judaism. The problem of people converting to Judaism was a problem that continued in Western European Christianity well into the late Middle ages; many laws were drawn up against converting to Judaism and were punishable by state confiscation of property, with the converts being burnt at the stake. The Jewish slave converts wouldn't work on the Sabbath, Saturn's' day, and Rome was forced to pay overtime and holiday pay, which took a toll on the accountants; then nobody worked on Sunday because it was the Christian Sabbath, complicating best accounting practices even further.

324 AD   It was believed Rome began when the defeated Trojans of Troy, fled Achilles and the Greek armies and settled in Rome in the year 1184 BC. By 324 AD, the city of Rome was falling apart, a lot of the empire's business was being conducted in Milan. In 324 AD, Constantine I sought out a new area where he could build a new capital city. He travelled to Troy to survey the area, thinking to return to the place where Rome's founders originally came from. In a dream, while in Troy, he is told to look elsewhere, so he travelled to the old city of Byzantium on the Bosporus straits near the Black Sea. There, in Byzantium, on a late fall night in 324 AD he had another dream of an old woman who was made young again, the Dagda and Morrigan from Celtic mythology, on Samhain. This dream was from his knowledge of the Druids and the Celtic faith that he acquired while accompanying his father in Britain. Constantine I's mother was a Christian. Constantine decided to build the new capital city in Byzantium and it was called Constantinople after him.

325 AD   In 325 AD, Constantine I convened a council of Christian religious leaders in order to bring some sort of coherent doctrine to Christianity. Over the 300 years from the death of Christ, the Christian community was perplexed about what his life meant and what he actually was; Christians came up with many imaginative beliefs and dogmas. They actually killed each other over the diversity of ideas about Jesus of Nazareth. Constantine I as Roman Emperor could not have religious fighting within the Empire, so he convened the "Council of Nicaea" in 325 AD to hash out the differences of dogma into one coherent belief for Christians. In the end, most of the Christian religious leaders cobbled together and agreed upon the doctrine known as "The Nicene Creed". Crucifixion was abolished,

gladiatorial games were ended, slavery was reduced, the Gold "Solidus" was introduced as currency. The "Solidus" was a 24 carat gold coin weighing 4.5 grams of solid gold. Constantine I instituted government reforms and separated civil and military government functions. He built "The Church of the Holy Sepulcher" in Jerusalem, which contains both Golgotha (Calvary) and the tomb of Joseph of Arimathea, where Christ was entombed after crucifixion, before his Resurrection. Constantine I also built the original Saint Peters Basilica in Rome on top of a temple of Mithras, on Vatican Hill.

325 AD

The Nicene Creed

We believe in One God, the Father, the Almighty, the maker of heaven and earth, of all that is, seen and unseen. We believe in one Lord, Jesus Christ, the only son of God eternally begotten of the father, God from God, Light from Light, true God from true God, begotten, not made one in being with the father. Through Him all things were made. For us men and our salvation he came down from heaven: by the power of the Holy Spirit he was born of the Virgin Mary and became man. For our sake he was crucified under Pontius Pilate; he suffered died and was buried. One the third day he rose again in fulfillment of the scriptures; he ascended into heaven and ids seated at the right hand of the father. He will come again in glory to judge the living and the dead, and his kingdom will have no end. We believe in the Holy Spirit, the Lord, the giver of life, who proceeds from the Father and the Son. With the Father and the Son, He is worshipped and glorified. He has spoken through the Prophets. We believe in one Holy Catholic and apostolic church. We acknowledge one baptism for the forgiveness of sins. We look for the resurrection of the dead and the life of the world to come. Amen.

326 AD — The Old Testament, the Torah, was not added to but Jewish scholarship continued, The Babylonian Gemarah was begun around this time, one rabbi worked on it for 60 years, then in 427 AD another rabbi continued working on it, it was completed around the year 500 AD by a third rabbi.

340 AD — Scots from Hibernia have now settled one quarter of Pict territory on the West Coast of Caledonia, from the Northern Hebrides to the Clyde River Forth.

342 AD — Emperor Constans (323-350 AD) is the third son of Constantine I, he reigns as Roman Emperor from (337-350 AD). The empire was divided up by Constantine I, giving parts of each to his four sons, who fought over boundaries. In 342 AD, he travels to Hadrian's Wall because Picts of Caledonia are raiding the Romanized tribes living adjacent to the Wall. He beefs up forts and coastline defenses' in Romanized Britain. He employed barbarians as personal guards for his own safety.

350 AD — The Gemara, part of the Talmud was written in Galilee, Palestine, between 350 and 400 AD, the Gemara were writings about disputes about the meaning of the Mischnah and doctrinal rulings that were made about the disputes over time.

350 AD — Goths are fighting with Roman legions to get into Roman territory. They are being driven by the Huns. Many Roman citizens start immigrating to Palestine where it is safer.

351 AD	There is a Jewish revolt in Galilee against the Christians, Samaritans, and Greeks; the non-Hebrew was increasing drastically with a lot of emigration from Italy and the Balkan regions. The Roman Legions crushed the Jewish revolt in Galilee, and further dispersed Jews to the south.
353 AD	Patrick is born in Britannia; he would go on in life to become Saint Patrick.
357 AD	Niall of the Nine Hostages was born in Tara, Hibernia, to King Eochad Mugmeddin (357-365 AD) and second wife Caireen, daughter of Saxon King Sachel Balb. Niall is taken from Tara to be raised by Druid Torna Eices.
363 AD	Emperor Julian dies and Emperor Valentian (363-378 AD) takes over the Western Empire, and his brother Valenten (363-376 AD) takes over the Eastern Roman Empire. Valentens in the Eastern Empire and his legions are completely annihilated by Gothic immigrants in Romania. Rome then suffers a defeat to the Sassanid Empire and loses some border provinces on the opposite side of Eastern Empire.
364 AD	Patrick is taken captive by a Hibernian raiding party from the west coast of Britain and is made a slave in Hibernia.
365 AD	At the Samhain festival in Tara, first wife Mongfinn MacFidaig, of Hibernian King Eochad Mugmeddin, poisons her husband to try to ensure her sons and not Niall will eventually come to the throne. Her brother becomes King of Hibernia then; but when he goes off on a raiding party to Britain, she stirs up mutiny in Hibernia. When he returns he puts down mutiny; then at a festival she poisons both him and herself before he can take retribution on her sons. It is recorded that after she poisoned her brother, she offered another poison cup to Niall but he suspected her and he switched the cups, then she drank the poisoned wine.
369 AD	According to Chronicum Scotorum, Patrick escaped from Hibernia and went to the coast of Brittany Germanus; he was released by an angel.
376 AD	Scots, Picts and Saxons, attack Roman Britain and cross the frontiers of the Rhine in a coordinated attack on the Roman Empire. The Scots and the Picts each had a large navy and could raid the coastlines, while troops poured across Hadrian's wall in hordes bypassing Roman forts, but attacking Londinium. After the initial attacks they split up and pillaged the Romanized villas. The Romans under Theodosus drove them back and restored Roman order, first on the Rhine, then in Britain.
378 AD	Huns reached the borders of the Roman Empire
379 AD	Niall of the Nine Hostages is made High King at Tara. He is 22 years old. Emperor Gratian is Western Emperor.
380 AD	Emperor Theodosius (380-387 AD) becomes Emperor of Eastern Roman Empire.
381 AD	Constantinople; The Rise of Faith and the Fall of Reason; Nicene Creed rewritten, called the Constantinople Creed, it is about the same writing. Emperor Theodosius issues an Epistle, which is a formal letter announcing that the only acceptable religious belief of Roman subjects is the Nicene Creed, Constantinople Creed. Most forms of pagan worship were now legally forbidden. The majority of the Empires subjects were pagans. The Cult of Mithras was suppressed and for the most part completely absorbed into Christianity. Legions were then Christianized

and fought under the Cross. This was a pivotal moment in European history, this epistle put an end to free thought and free reasoning which was the basis for the rise of classical civilization and classical history. The epistula closed the western mind to reasonable thought processes until the age of enlightenment and the Gutenberg press in the 1500's. From this point forward Christianity was the Law of the Land, no more Live and Let Live.

381 AD	At the request of the Pictish Kings, the Scots under Niall and the Picts attack Hadrian's Wall again. The Romans drive them back again. Niall did not lose any men in this attack.
382 AD	The Pictish Kings and their troops attack the Scots living in the fledgling Dal Riata settlements' in western Caledonia. Niall pulls together his 30,000 troops, crosses over to Caledonia in his Navy and arrived at the Scots fortress of Dunadd. The Picts had 50,000 troops amassed. Niall invited the Pictish Kings to a feast before battle in the Celtic tradition. They obliged him and sat down to feast with their entire families and Niall. After the meal, Nialls men rushed in and took all the families of the Pictish Kings hostage. He demanded tribute in accordance with Brehon law. There were Druids present and this was all in accord with Celtic society. The Pictish Kings agreed and Paid tribute each year to Niall in Tara; the hostages were kept in Tara and they were not hurt as per custom, and the troops all left without anyone killing and dyeing. Niall gained control over Pictland for the Scots. This was the first of the legends of Niall and the Nine Hostages.
384 AD	Caledonia; Picts and Scots attack Roman Britain again; Scots begin settling in northern Wales and on west coast of Roman Britain. Scots put up Ogham stones too demarcate Hibernian territory. Ogham was written language developed by the Druids shortly after contact with Roman writings of Roman merchant traders.
395 AD	Roman Empire was formally partitioned into two halves, East and West Empires; Eastern Empire spoke Greek, Western Empire spoke Latin. Many Christians emigrate into Palestrina-Prima, reducing further the percentage of the Jewish population in the area. Hebrews are spread out in Arabia, Babylon, and the Parthian Empire; Jews only compromise 10-15% of the population that is now known as Israel. 85% of the population was Christian, in the area.
395 AD	With the partitioning, this marked the start of the Byzantine Empire (395 AD-1453 AD), in the Eastern Mediterranean.
400 AD	Goths sack Rome; Jewish scholars finish writing the Gemara in Galilee.
401 AD	There are two Roman Legions remaining in Britannia
405 AD	Niall organizes more raiding parties against Roman Britain from Irish Sea, then for two years he declares a stand down and his troops do not engage in warfare. He returned to Tara and started preparing for an invasion of Gaul.
406 AD	Roman General Stilicho strips legions from the Rhine River garrisons, and pulls back to the Alps to defend Rome from Alaric and the Gothic German tribes. Roman Emperor Honorus fled to Constantinople. 100's of thousands of Germans crossed the frozen Rhine River, descended on and advanced south into Romanized Gaul. In Britain, Roman General Constantine III, is ordered to take the remaining

	two legions out of west Britain and go to Iberia to take command of the remaining Roman forces there and drive out the German barbarians arriving over the Pyrenees.
407 AD	Constantine III withdrew and landed in Gaul, then moved south, picking up straggling legions from Gaul while on route to Iberia. When he arrived at the Pyrenees Mountains he ran into the Visigoth hordes and the Romans were all annihilated.
408 AD	Niall finished his two-year invasion preparation plan. Niall leads an invasion force of Scots, Picts, and British tribes to Brittany; the force has over 500 ships and 50,000 warriors. They seize Brittany and Brittany becomes an independent Celtic Kingdom for the next 300 years, then they moved up the coast towards Calais where they ran into the Saxon horde. Further east of Brittany the Frankish horde was moving and settling from the Rhine River to the Pyrenees Mountains. None of the Germanic tribes encroached on Brittany for 300 years or so, the original Celtic tribes of the Romanized Veneti, Osismi, Coriosolites, integrated with the new Scots migrants, and were eventually integrated with Brythonic tribes that escaped from Britain when it was overrun by Anglo-Saxons in 441 AD.

The Nine Hostages of Niall of the Nine Hostages

Ancient Celtic Brehon law spoke of the rule of Hostage taking, if one tribe took a leading hostage of another tribe that tribe would become politically subservient to the hostage taking tribe. It would have to pay yearly tribute, and provide warriors for the cause of the hostage taking tribe. This avoided massive bloodletting, and the hostages were to be kept, not harmed, and they would live a good life in their over lords' kingdom. Niall succeeded in taking nine hostages and creating an Irish Empire between 379 AD and 411 AD, building on the foundation that his father Ard Ri King Eochad Mugmeddin started. The nine hostage tribes were:

1. The Picts in Caledonia, 382 AD, which leads to the Kingdom of Dal-Riata, then the Kingdom of Alba, then the Kingdom of Scotland, then the country and nation of Scotland.

2. The Northumbrian tribes, 380 AD, the Damnonii, Novantee, Selgovae, Votadini, (north of Hadrians Wall, in Roman Valentia), and the Brigantes, (Roman Dux Britannianum, south of Hadrians wall and west of the Pennine Mountains.)

3. Gwenyd, (Northwest Wales, Roman Britannia Secunda), including the island of Anglesey, 380-397 AD, The Brythonic Celt Ordovice tribe; Scots from Hibernia migrated there and by 397 AD, the entire area was taken over by Scots; the Ogham stones were put down as the markers of Scots territory; the capital city of this area was Caernarfon.

4. Dyfed, (Southwest Wales, Roman Britannia Secunda), 391 AD, the Brythonic Celt Demetea tribe; Niall takes this area, and over the next 10 years Scots migrate from Hibernia and settle there. Ogham stones were put down as markers; there are still hundreds of Ogham stones scattered throughout the areas of the Scots Empire.

5. The Dumoni Brythonic Celt tribal areas in Cornwall peninsula, (Britannia Prima), 380 AD; with this conquest Niall has secured all the ports in Britain that are engaged in trade with the outside world; Cardiff, Tintagel, and Isca (Chester), he allows foreign trade to continue, even though he is in full command of the Irish Sea.

6. Cornovii, 405 AD, another Brythonic Celt tribe in modern Cornwall

7. The Saxons, north of Brittany, 408 AD, surrender a hostage to Niall, near Calais, and this establishes the northern boundary of Niall's Brittany.

8. Niall puts down a revolt of the Romanized Celts in Brittany in 411 AD. The three Celtic tribes of Britttany that Julius Caesar conquered in his conquest of Gaul, the Osismi, the Coriosolites, and the Veneti, rebel against Niall and the Scots and try to restore their free independence again. Niall suppresses the revolt and hostages are offered up in Celtic tradition. Ogham stones are again placed in Brittany as markers of Scot territory.

9. The Franks, south of Brittany around the Loire River, 411 AD surrender a hostage to the Scots after they are defeated by the Celtic Scots in Brittany. Niall was assassinated just before this by another Scot, of the Leinster Kingdom, but the Scots rallied and defeated the Franks. This last ninth hostage was a attributed to Niall by the Scots, and ensured Brittany would remain an independent Celtic nation, Brittany.

411 AD	Niall of Nine Hostages wounded by Eochaidh, son of Enna Cennsealach at the Ictian Sea. Niall dies in second assassination attempt by Eochaidh, Niall died in Brittany, his body was brought back to Tara, and was buried in a plot just west of the Ulster Fortress of Navan. He was succeeded on the throne by Dathi, a competent, capable leader. The Irish Empire, based in Tara, encompassed all of Ireland, all of Pictland, (modern day Scotland), the west coast of Britain from the Pennine Mountain Range to the Irish Sea, Wales, Cornwall, the Irish Sea, and Brittany. Between the Pict and Scots Navy, he had 1,000 seaworthy ships at his disposal.
430 AD	Celtic Druid High Priests, priests, Brehon's, and Bards still the elite, scholarly, philosophically knowledgeable leaders running Scots Hibernia.
431 AD	The book, "The Annals of Ulster" begins chronology in this year; it is a history of Ireland (Hibernia). According to the "Annals of Ulster", the world began 5885 years earlier in 5454 BC. This date just about coincides with the first inhabitants' arrival into Ireland after the "Younger Dryas" and the time Doggerland Island had finally gone under the North Sea. This is the same when the English Channel opened and Britain was no longer part of Continental Europe.
432 AD	Patrick arrived in Erin (Hibernia) and starts to convert the Celtic population to Christianity. If he wins his battles with the Druid he will gain control over the spiritual Celtic society, for Christian Rome.
434 AD	First Saxon depredation in Hibernia
441 AD	Angle, Saxon and Jute tribes invade Eastern Britain; now call it Angle-land (England), they speak Angl-ish (English); Beowolf becomes part of English history, and the Anglo-Saxon Chronicles records their history. Roman Britain is burned from one end to the other and its inhabitants are slaughtered. Britons that are left move west and begin to reform their tribal societies. Romanized Britain came to an end.
450 AD	**Kingdom of Strathclyde** (450-1093 AD) begins in Clyde River Valley. The northern limit of this Kingdom was at the "Rock of the Britons" on the north end of Loch Lomond, the eastern limit was in the marshes at Bannockburn and Stirling; the western limit was along the coast in Ayrshire, Renfrewshire, and Lanarkshire. This was a Brythonic Kingdom which fought against the Pictish Scots tribes who

were further north and northwest. The language spoken in this kingdom was Cumbric.

451 AD	Attila the Hun and his Hunnic Empire of vassal tribes were still driving other Germanic tribes westward; Attila and the Huns attack Italy but are defeated; they are driven back eastwards after a battle in north central Gaul called the Battle of Chalons. After their defeat at the hands of a combined Roman, Saxon, Visigoth, Burgundian, and a Frankish barbarian tribe led by the barbarian leader Merovech, the Romans make Merovech king of a Frankish Empire which evolves into the Merovingian Frankish Empire, the forerunner of France. The Huns and the Hunnic Empire started to fall apart and the Germanic tribes dismantled it after The Battle of Nedao in 454 AD, fought in Pannonia, (eastern Austria and Hungary). After another battle in 469 AD, the Huns were no longer heard of in Eastern and Central Europe.
470 AD	Saint Patrick passed away after converting Erin (Hibernia) to Christianity. The Celtic Druid Pantheon of Gods is suppressed by the teachings of Christianity.
470 AD	**Over Kingdom of Dal-Riata** (470-840 AD) began; The Gaelic maritime archipelago over kingdom of Dal-Riata began; it encompassed the people and western lands in what is now Scotland, primarily in Argyll, and up the coast and around the north of present day Scotland. It also included the North of Erin, like Antrim and Ulster, and was part of a growing Irish Empire governed from Tara in Erin. The capital of Dal-Riata was Dunadd in Argyll. Dal-Riata lasted until the Viking Age when it merged with the Pict Kingdoms and became the Kingdom of Alba, (900-1286 AD).
476 AD	The Western Roman Empire (27 BC -476 AD) ended. The Byzantine, (Eastern Roman Empire), (395 AD-1453 AD) continued.
480 AD	Saint Benedict of Nursia establishes Monte Cassino in Italy; he writes the "Rule of Benedict", describing the rules that need to be followed in a monastery; He founded the Benedictine Order.
481 AD	Warlord and leader Clovis united all the Frankish tribes of Gaul.
482 AD	Emperor Justinian, (485 AD-565 AD), wrote the "Justinian Code" of Law; European law is based on this law.
500 AD	Radhanite Jews take over the old Roman Empires trade routes, and continue the trade route from the far east into Europe from 500 AD until the year 1000 AD. These trade routes continued to carry white European slaves that were exported to the Middle-East, the Far East, and Africa. These Radhanite Jewish merchants acted as middlemen up until the time of the Mongol invasions. At the same time the Babylonian Talmud was written in Babylon, and the Passover Haggadah was written in Galilee.
500 AD	The Merovingian Empire (500-750 AD) was established in Gaul,
508 AD	Clovis established Paris as the capital city of the Merovingian Empire. The Merovingian bloodline seeded the royal houses of Europe, some of which were The House of Saxe-Coburg-Gatha, which went on to become the House of Windsor in England. The fleur-de-lis was the symbol of the Merovingian Empire.

527 AD	Yemen, a Jewish convert, came to power within the Jewish tribes there; he slaughtered 20,000 Christian men, women, and children when they refused to convert to Judaism. This created a geo-political response from the Christian Byzantine Empire, which led to the conquering of Yemen by Christian Abyssinia, and Byzantine plans being drawn up to Christianize all the tribes on the West Coast of Arabia in the Hejaz area adjacent to the Red Sea, including Mecca.
535-536 AD	**Extreme Cold Weather Event** due to unknown reason; possibly volcanic or a collision with a celestial object like a comet or asteroid somewhere on planet; it was reported there was snow in summer, and a dry, cold fog that encompassed the planet or the entire known world; there were massive crop failures, hunger, starvation, resulting in massive population death.
535 AD	According to "The Annals of Ulster", there was famine this year, no bread.
537 AD	The Hagia Sophia church was built in Constantinople by the Byzantine Empire.
538 AD	According to "The Annals of Ulster", there was famine this year, no bread.
541 AD	**Justinian Plague,** (541-548 AD), after the massive crop failures and resulting deaths the rat population exploded, each carrying fleas containing the bacteria, Yersinia pestis, (the Black Plague), 20-50 Million people died of plague in the Eastern Mediterranean area; there was a 40% death rate among the population; almost half the population died in a short period of time. The Persian Sassanid Empire was also affected in the same way, half the population died. The plague came and went from this time forward until around the year 800 AD. The rat population with fleas, must have exploded with all the dead corpses from the Extreme Cold Weather events aftermath.
544 AD	As recorded in "The Annals of Ulster", a disease called "Blefed" caused the mortality of Mobi Clarainech.
548 AD	As recorded in "The Annals of Ulster", there was great mortality this year from disease.
555 AD	As recorded in "The Annals of Ulster", there was a great mortality caused by the "cron-conaill", and the "buidhe-conaill", some kind of yellow jaundice, the same disease as in 548 AD.
570 AD	Merlin stays at Alt Clut, Dumbarton Castle, across the Clyde River from Renfrewshire. Mohammad, (570- 632 AD), the future Prophet of Islam is born in Mecca, into the Quraysh tribe, a supposed descendent of Ishmael, first son of Abraham the Hebrew Patriarch. This year is known as the "Year of the Elephant" in Islamic culture; it is the year the Christian armies of Byzantine march north from Yemen intent on conquering and Christianizing the pagan tribes and Judaic tribes of western Arabia, as a consequence of the 527 AD massacre of Christians in Yemen by Jewish fanatics. As they advance on Mecca and engage, a "smallpox" epidemic defeats them and they retreat back to Yemen in disarray. Western Turkish Empire rules over Khazars.

According to "The Annals of Ulster", Saint Patrick died 100 years earlier.

Arabia and the Desert

The vast expanse of the Middle East is desert. It was never invaded by Alexander the Great, nor was it by the Roman Empire. The Roman Empire used its Limes system south of Syria and Palestrina as a line of demarcation. The people of the desert were nomadic tribesmen wandering from waterhole to waterhole, since they first left Africa back in 70,000 BC. Some left the desert to greener pastures, some came or were driven to the desert and existed there. The people of the Arabian Desert were warring clannish Semite tribes, Hebrews and pagans, moving about in search of water and shifting oasis, farming in lands with stable water aquifers. Before the Romans, there were extensive caravan routes that crossed through parts of Arabia from East to West and North to South, from Yemen to the Mediterranean Sea. Frankincense, Myrrh, and other incense and spices travelled over these routes. Frankincense and Myrrh were used in pagan religious rituals and originated in Yemen. The caravans travelled from oasis to oasis, up and down the breadth of the Arabian landscape. Warring, pillaging tribesmen would plunder the armed caravans in a fight for economic survival. After the Roman Navy with its sea legions, cleared the Red Sea of pirates, Rome used this Red Sea waterway as a trade route bypassing the caravan routes. This enabled Rome to trade with Indian ports and the ports in Yemen. This led to the demise of north, south and overland trade in Arabia. It also caused a demise in the economics of the warring clannish tribes of the desert, there were less caravans to plunder now. Mecca was never recorded in any of the extensive ancient records of caravan trade and did not exist up until about the year 100 AD, before that, Mecca was an uninhabited wilderness.

The people of Arabia, like the Celts and many other peoples were very much different in their thinking compared to modern humans. They believed there were gods everywhere and genies (jinn) behind every rock, possessing people and animals, in mountains, water and so forth. The people of the desert sat around at night watching the night sky show in the galaxy. The meteors they saw were the Gods hurling darts at the jinn. The Gods were good, and the jinn were bad. One time a meteor came down and crashed behind a mountain that was very close by. The next day some of the Bedouins' looked for it and found it in a valley. They thought it was a gift from the gods' and it was a sure sign the valley was sacred. They cried out to the gods' "we are here, we are at your service", and waited for an answer. After a short period of silence, they all looked at each other and the ground, then they asked each other what should we do with the rock? They placed it atop other stones and this place eventually became known as "the Sanctuary", Mecca. This year was about 100 AD. Sanctuaries existed around Arabia as "safe spaces" and "safe places", where no blood feuds or violence could occur; otherwise it would infuriate the Gods. So Mecca became another "sanctuary city", or sanctuary town. The Bedouins walked seven times around the stone to imitate the stars. The Arab Bedouins also had four holy months within each year. One month was in the spring and then three consecutive months in the autumn. During these times people could travel unmolested in Arabia. The crescent moon with the star, marks the sign of the holy month. This symbol is displayed on many flags of Islamic countries today. In the present age, this holy month was modified; it is now the ninth month of the Islamic lunar calendar, called Ramadan, and shows up at various times of year because it is based on a lunar cycle, instead of a solar cycle.

The Islamic religion has the year revolving around them, instead of revolving around the year, like the earth revolves around the sun. They revolve around the sun but the focus is on the moon revolving around the earth before the earth revolves around the sun. Ramadan starts when the crescent moon is first observed, and it lasts for the following 30 days. It used to be in the desert the hottest month of the year where fasting during daylight would keep a human alive and well in the heat of summer.

Some tribes started to settle near the stone and built a rectangular temple with the black meteorite stone at one corner as a "foundation stone." Mecca became a rising star of pilgrimage sites. Allah was the deity worshipped in the Temple. Allah was a name that the Jews, pagans, and Christians used for the "One" deity. Other tribes would conquer and drive out or absorb the people living there, over and over again. One tribe, the Khuzas, formally dedicated the temple to the worship, by importing the Nabataea God Hubal from southern Jordan. Hubal was a God of manly virtues of valor and war and chivalry in victory, and of course of "rain". Hubal regulated time, and at the same time held the secrets of the future, which you could learn if you paid the priest for divining it. Hubal had diving arrows both for the future predictions and to divine for water. Al-uzza, (a goddess), Manat, (a goddess), and Allat (goddess Aphrodite), were goddesses in the haram of Hubal. Hubal was a warrior, rain, spirit god, and he remained in the Kaaba with his haram until Mohammad the Prophet took over, threw them all out and introduced his Mohammadanism.

A man named Qusay took over Mecca at some point in time. He was a small town man with big ideas, and he was both wily, and ruthless enough to realize them. Qusay was Mohammad's 4th great grandfather. Qusay was Mohammad's great, great, great, great, grandfather. Mohammad was born in 570 AD, so Qusay was born about 440 AD? Qusay ousted the Khuzas tribe and started a little bustling town with a temple as the economic pillar of Mecca. Qusays father Kilab was from Mecca but lived in Syria with his wife, Kilab died before Qusay was born. His mother remarried and moved to Qudah territory with her husband and became part of her new husbands' tribe, the Qudahs. The Qudahs' traced their ancestry back to overcrowded Yemen. When Qusay learned of Kilab, and that he was actually from Mecca with noble lineage also going back to Yemen, he set out for Mecca. Qusay married the daughter of the Khubal leader of Mecca. He was ambitious. After the death of his father-in-law he took over Mecca, and ousted his wife's' and deceased father-in laws tribe.

There were two distinct pilgrimages at the temple in Mecca; one the Sun pilgrimage, the other the moon pilgrimage. During the Sun pilgrimage the pilgrims would start out twelve miles east of the valley of Mecca, where they stood in reverence of the sun until it disappeared below the horizon. Then they would chase the sun west until they reached a mount called Muzdalifa, a two-hour hoof on foot. There they remained overnight and celebrated the rise of the sun in the morning. Then they walked further west to Mina, a valley adjacent to the valley of Mecca. Here they stoned pillars of stacked rocks representing the devilish jinn. This was like the gods throwing meteor darts at the jinn. Why they were acting godlike is probably inherited primate behavior. After this there was a celebration and the slaughter of sacrificial animals. This ended the Sun pilgrimage; afterwards some would come to Mecca to worship the moon god, Hubal in the temple. Qusay ignored the idea of the holy month and sanctuary and slaughtered the tribe running the Sun pilgrimage, then drove out the Khuzas tribe from Mecca. He formulated a new tribe and called them the Quraysh.

Qusay altered the sun pilgrimage having it now terminate at the temple, and having the pilgrims walk seven times around the Kaaba; finishing by kissing the black meteorite at the corner. He put a lock on the door of the Kaaba so that someone would have to pay him to get inside and sacrifice or pray to Hubal, the moon god. He supplied food and water for the pilgrims, sold miniature Hubal gods to take home and administered very well for 40 years until he passed away. He re-introduced caravan trade and imported food from the Jewish agricultural oasis settlements of Yathrib and Khaybar and the walled off city of Taif.

Early pagan civilizations like Egypt, Greece, Persia, and pagan Rome used aromatics in their religious ceremonies. These aromatics were made in Yemen and sold for gold to these civilizations. Yemen became very wealthy and overpopulated, as these aromatics were shipped by caravan from Yemen to all over the known world. With the birth of Christianity in the Roman Empire, in the 1st through 4th centuries this trade dropped off causing a depression in overpopulated Yemen. The populations dispersed to survive. Christianity did not use aromatics until the 5th century.

In the 5th and 6th centuries, the Roman Empire was in decline but the caravan trade was inclining again in Arabia. Mecca was in on this trade as a stopover point on the routes. Qusay had four sons. One was named Moonface, he was a servant of the goddess Manf. Moonface had four sons. One was named Hashim. It was these sons of Moonface that brought Mecca into prominence in trade, (insert missing 28 classified pages of 911 report here). Hashim was Mohammads great grandfather. Hashim means provider of bread. Hashim became the leader of Mecca. When his leadership was challenged, his enemies dipped their hands in a bowl of blood at the Kaaba temple. The supporters of Hashim dipped their hands in a bowl of perfume and were called the Perfumed ones, the opposition was called the Blood lickers. They were going to do battle but reached a peaceful compromise through reorganization of Meccan administration. Hashim turned Mecca into an export rather than import town. Hashim was out on a caravan when he stopped in Yathrib. There he met Salma a divorcee who was living there. Here he fathered Mohammad's grandfather Abdul Muttalib. Hashim died in Gaza before he could pick her and the child up again. At ten years old Abdul Muttalib was picked up by one of Hashims brothers called Muttalib and brought to Mecca to be part of the Quraysh tribe. Abdul Muttalib could not take over Hashims previous role without outside support from Yathrib. He got that support and took over where Hashim had left off.

Abdul Muttalib was born in 497 AD. He led during a time of geo-political turmoil. The turmoil was in Yemen, there were a succession of coups. In 527 AD, a Jewish convert staged a coup to rid Yemen of Christians. 20,000 Christians were slaughters when they refused to convert to Judaism. This led to Byzantine intervention via Christian Abyssinia. When the Abyssinian Christians troops took over Yemen they began to devise plans to Christianize all of the tribal lands of western Arabia. They planned to build a cathedral where the Kaaba was in Mecca, and abolish pagan worship, as had been done in the Empire. Then they figured the pilgrims would come to the Cathedral and worship Jesus Christ in the sanctuary city. The Abyssinians invaded Mecca with their Elephants in 570 AD, but they could not acquire the Kaaba, a smallpox epidemic broke out and the diseased troops retreated back to Yemen. This year is known as the Year of the Elephant in Islamic texts, the year 570 AD. Abdul Muttalib had ten sons and six daughters. Mohammads father was the youngest of Abdul Muttalibs sons. Mohammads father was named Abdullah Muttalib, (553-570 AD). Abdullah married Amina in an arranged marriage and Mohammad was (Qathem) Muttalib was born. Abdullah Muttalib went on a caravan trip to Syria in 569 AD, after impregnating his wife, and never returned. He died in Syria of disease at 17 years old. He left Amina with five camels, an Abyssinian Christian slave girl, a flock of sheep, and the future Prophet of Islam, Mohammad. Topsy-Turvy world begins.

AMORE

When the moon hits your eye like a big pizza pie
    that's Amore.
When the world seems to shine like you've had too much wine,
    that's Amore.
Bells will ring, ting a ling a ling, ting a ling a ling, and you'll sing
    Vita Bella.
Hearts will play, tippy tippy te, tippy tippy te
    like a gay Tarandella,
when the stars make you drool justa like pastafazul
    that's Amore.
When you dance down the street with a cloud at your feet
    you're in love
when you walk in a dream but you know you're not dreaming Senioree
    Scuzza me, but you see back in old Napoli
    that's Amore.
When the moon hits your eye like a bigga pizza pie, that's Amore.

THE MOON

Before the Prophet Mohammad was born and forcibly converted everyone to his religion, the Bedouins in the Saudi Arabian desert worshipped the moon as their god, they called him Allah, "Elohim". Abraham, the Jewish patriarch also worshipped the moon god, called Nanna, or Sin, in the city of Ur, in Sumer, Mesopotamia, before he thought up his own God. Some people believe the moon is made of green cheese and smiles at us with a loving face. A rock smaller than the Earth, and made of some different type of rock, revolves around our bigger rock, Earth, we call it The Moon.

The Moon is 2,160 miles in diameter, or 11,104,800 feet in diameter. The diameter of the moon is the same as the distance from Stonehenge, England to Antioch, Turkey. The moon has a circumference of 6,780 miles. Someone could drive around the circumference of the moon and it would be like driving from Boston to Los Angeles and back again. The diameter of the earth is 7,926 miles. The diameter of the earth is 3.67 times larger than the diameter of the moon. The moon is 1/4 the size of the earth. A 1/100 scale model of a B-767 airplane has a wingspan of 21 inches and a length of 24 inches. A full size B-767 has a wingspan of 171 feet and a length of 201 feet, for relative comparison. The mass of the moon is 1/81 that of the earth. Density is mass per unit volume. The moon is less dense that the density of the earth. If the earth has a density of 1, the moon is only .6 of that, just over less than half the density of earth. The escape velocity to take off from the moon is 1.5 miles per second, 90 miles per minute, or 5,400 miles per hour. The escape velocity of the earth is 25,020 miles per hour, meaning it requires a lot less thrust to take off from the moon, than from the earth. It also means gas molecules can escape into space resulting in there being no atmosphere, and no weather on the moon.

The moon revolves around the earth in an elliptical orbit, while at the same time it rotates on its axis. If you were looking down on the North Pole from the North Star Polaris, you would see the moon revolving counterclockwise around the earth, and the earth revolving counterclockwise around the sun. The rotation of the moon about its axis is also counterclockwise, and the rotation of the earth about its axis is the same, counterclockwise. The revolution of the moon about earth is just so that only one side of the moon is visible to the planet earth. The moon is in a "synchronous rotation" with the earth. This is very strange when you think about it. What are the chances of that placement so that only one side is visible to earthlings?

The moon is 220,000 miles to 252,000 miles away from the earth depending on its position in its elliptical orbit, and it is traveling at 2,287 miles per hour around us or 38 miles per minute around us. The moon completes one full elliptical orbit around the earth in 27.322 days. This time, a "sidereal month" is relative to the celestial stars in the distance in the galaxy. The "full moon" occurs when the moon is said to be in "opposition"; at this time, the Sun, then the Earth, then the moon, are in a straight line, with the earth in the middle; the moon is in opposition, it is opposite, to where the sun is. When all three are in a precise line and directly lined up a lunar eclipse occurs, this is called a "Blood Moon". The "Blood Moon" occurs because the shadow of the earth blocks the rays of the sun from hitting the moon, and from earth we only see the reflection of scattered light hitting the moon, the moon appears red like blood, like a red sky at sunset. The "New Moon" occurs when the moon is said to be in "conjunction". At this time, the Sun, the Moon, and the earth are in a straight line, with the moon in the middle; the moon is in "conjunction", it is in a "combination" or a "union", to where the sun is, as we look up at them both. During this time, the moon appears dark to us here on earth because the rays of the sun are hitting the back side of the moon, it is a "new moon", it is dark looking. When all three are in a precise line and directly lined up a solar eclipse occurs. The solar eclipse by the moon blocks out the sun, the sun goes dark as we watch the moon pass in front of the Sun during daylight hours. After the new moon occurs the moon begins "waxing" towards full. The "crescent moon" first appears and grows towards full, then "wanes" from full towards the next new moon. This entire process takes on average 29.530 days, called a "Synodic month".

When the moon and the earth and another celestial body line up in a plane it is called "syzygy"; when the further object, the one in the distance, appears to move behind the moon it is called "occultation", it is hidden, it is "occult". The moon and the planets transit the sky in the "plane of the ecliptic". Some of the stars out in the galaxy are also situated in the "plane of the ecliptic", so as the moon transits the sky, as it revolves around the earth, it will pass in front of some of these celestial objects, creating an "occultation". The crescent moon and the star are an example of this. The star or planet could be on either side of the moon as we view it, and it changes from month to month as the earth, moon, planets and stars revolve in their orbits. For instance, on September 12, 2001, at about 7 a.m., I climbed up the hill in Hoboken, New Jersey to where Stevens Institute of Technology is and I looked out at the burning heap of twisted metal that used to be the world trade center buildings. It smelled like Auschwitz when the crematoriums were operating. From that view I looked up in the sky and saw the crescent shaped moon with a star behind it, close to the convex side of the crescent, not like the Islamic flag symbol, but with the star on the other side. That star was the planet Jupiter appearing to be in syzygy and it was about to move behind the crescent moon in an example of occultation. The moon passed in front of that star Jupiter and it became the more familiar crescent and star configuration, like the Islamic flag.

Back in the past, the ancient civilizations observed the moon in all its phases, with its occultation's. Not knowing what was actually happening with their primitive primate brain housing groups, they imagined, and then decided that the moon was a god and it was either being attacked, when it turned red, a "Blood Moon"; or it was harmonizing, as with some other goddess, whenever the "occultation" in the sky appeared. They eventually realized that the moon was being attacked or smoozing regularly, and made up charts and calendars to keep track. In the Hebrew Talmud it is said that Yahweh on Mount Sinai, told Moses about the moon and he described to Moses the length of the "sidereal month". This oral law was passed down from Moses, after his conversation with Yahweh, by word of mouth to the Jewish sages and to the Rabbi's through the ages. Talmud, tractate Rosh Hashanah, Chapter Two, Mishna V and VI, Rabbi Gamliel explains the time to wait until the start of the new lunar month. "The consecration of the moon cannot take place at a period less than twenty-nine and a half days, two thirds and 0.0052, (seventy-three Halaqim) of an hour." When this is multiplied and divided out the Talmud comes up with a period of time equal to 29.530359 days. This Talmud information is the same as the observations made by the ancient Babylonians, the astronomers of "Sin" the Moon God. The Sin astronomers came up with one day being equal to 360 degrees, or a fraction of 72/72. They further subdivided the degrees into increments of time that they called "Barleycorns". One Barleycorn equaled 1/72 of the day, it equaled 5 degrees. 72/72 equaled 25,920 Barleycorns, (72 times 360 = 25,920). At some point in time after the Nicene Creed was written, and the dates of the Christian feasts were trying to be calculated, the Barleycorns started to be converted into hours. 25,920 Barleycorns equals 24 hours. 1,080 Barleycorns equaled one hour, and equates to 3/72 of a day. 180 barleycorns equaled 10 minutes, 360 Barleycorns equals 20 minutes, 540 Barleycorns equals 30 minutes, and 720 Barleycorns equals 40 minutes, 900 Barleycorns equals 50 minutes. Further calculation led me to figure one Barleycorn equals approximately 3.333333 seconds. Barleycorns cannot be subdivided into partial Barleycorns, but I figured 1 second equals 0.03 Barleycorns. When I did the calculations I ran into strings of numbers with 666 666 666 666. The devil is in the details. The Jews changed the name of the Barleycorn to a Halaqim, so they are one and the same thing. In the 1970's NASA placed a prism on the moon during one of their Apollo exploratory missions there; from earth they focused a laser beam on the prism and with powerful telescopes connected to an automatic clock they computed the accurate length of the "sidereal month". The period of time that NASA measured 29.530388 days. A difference of 0.000029 of a day. The Talmud was written in Babylon after the Diaspora began in order to record the Oral Tradition. The Rabbi's and sages that had not been crucified were afraid the knowledge of the sages would be lost forever if it was only passed down orally. It was written over the centuries beginning in 136 AD. There was great precision and accuracy in their observations and calculations in Babylon or they were just copied from the Sin records.

The Crescent Moon with the Star, was representative of the male God "Sin" or "Nanna", with the female Goddess "Venus", as the star. The Crescent represented the "male", and the Star represented "fertility", the "female". The "FERTILE CRESCENT". This symbol of the star and concave crescent was also the symbol of the God Mithra beforehand. It really is one of the prettiest things in the sky along with the Milky Way. The symbol was the Emblem of the Bosporan Kingdom, around the Crimean Peninsula, the Sea of Azov, near the Caucasus, the land originally settled by the Cimmerians, and the Kurgan culture. It was used in Persia, and by all the kings called Mithridates in Anatolia, especially on coins. Later in time the star and the crescent made its way to the Levant and the Arabian desert, the Moab tribe near the Dead Sea in Israel adopted it and it existed in Babylon. It is now the symbol of Islam displayed on Islamic flags. The actual symbol represents Mithra; and "Sin", "Nanna" the moon God of Sumer, Mesopotamia. The god "Sin" is where the Semite word for sin came from. The spiritual capital of "Sin" or "Nanna" was in Harran, which is in Urfa Province, Turkey, on the border with Syria, near Kobani, Syria, where ISIS has been sinning since 2015. In Harran, there are ancient domed huts all lined up in a row, similar to the domed enclosures found in the aerial photographs that are on the moon. The design of these huts in Harran has been the same for 5000 years. Urfa Province is also home to prehistoric Gobekli Tepe archeological site, dating back to the year 9,000 BC. Gobekli Tepe is built similar to Stonehenge in Salisbury, England. All the civilizations in that area used the symbol of the fertile crescent for thousands of years, western civilization not that much due to cloud cover and weather.

The gravitational attraction of the moon causes the oceans' tides to come in and go out every 6 hours, as it moves along at 38 miles per minute. This attraction also affects electrolytes in living animals, as does the changes in distance caused by its elliptical orbit. Where did the moon come from? No one knows. All the theories fall through, it has different percentages of types of minerals from earth so it didn't originate from earth; if it came in as an Asteroid it would have impacted the earth and destroyed both itself and the earth, and what are the chances of it coming in as an asteroid, then going into an elliptical orbit around earth at 220,000 miles, so that only one side is visible, more than astronomical? It could have been parked there by someone or something along time ago. But why?

The National Aeronautics and Space Administration, N.A.S.A, has been studying it along with the Russian space agency, the Roscosmos State Corporation, for about 60 years. NASA sent many orbiters and landers to the moon, with Astronauts walking and driving there doing scientific experiments. There are seismographs there that measure geological activity below the surface. After World War II, when the U.S. was at loggerheads with the Communist Bolsheviks in the USSR, the US Army drew up plans to place US troops on the Moon in a permanent base. The operation was called "Project Horizon". It was headed up by the ex- SS Nazi aerospace engineer Werner von Braun. Werner von Braun was the Nazi who invented the German V-2 rocket missiles that were used to bombard Great Britain during the war. He was brilliant, after the war, the OSS and the US Army, picked him up along with his fellow Nazi scientists in "Operation Paperclip", and ushered them off to the U.S. to employment with the U.S. Army Ballistic Missile Agency, then the National Aeronautics and Space Administration. He kept working on perfecting rocket technology and eventually built the Saturn V rockets that launched astronauts to the moon. The Ranger, Luna, and Surveyor programs were launched with numerous missions to take pictures and land on the moon. The Apollo manned program landed two men on the moon in 1969 on the Apollo 11 mission. Apollo 12-17 followed, then the program was cancelled in 1972, the three remaining missions never were attempted, Apollo 18,19, and 20 were scrubbed. Geological samples were brought back and analyzed. In 2009, NASA launched the LRO, Lunar Reconnaissance Orbiter, which orbits the moon performing reconnaissance work.

There have been many explained and unexplained observations that exist on the surface of the moon. The side of the moon we can see from earth has a vast smooth oceanic appearing surface, while the North, the South, and the far Side of the Moon, look like they have been completely bombarded, and pot-marked. There are unexplained tracks in the photographs, and in some photographs there appear to be engineered structures, there are giant gears, and other strange structures in some craters. Some craters appear to have been worked by machinery of some sort, with gigantic moon moving equipment, one aerial photo shows a large piece of machinery that appears to have partially exploded with the gears scattered about. Another photo shows domed enclosures, some of which are not magma domes. Considering there is no atmosphere, with no wind erosion, this is kind of amazing stuff. There appears in places what can only be described as stiches, like as in sewing stiches, covering areas of the ground, as if holding it together. There are also lights that appear then disappear, there are what appear to be glyphs in the bottom of craters, and stones that have left trails behind them rolling, except they rolled up the side of the crater. Strange stuff. When the moon is hit or impacted it rings like a church bell, according to one scientist from Notre Dame University. He said it rang one time for half an hour, which would indicate it is partially hollow. Strange stuff, maybe that is why the last 3 Apollo missions were cancelled. Last mission the astronauts reported light that they could see even light with their eyes shut, as if they were being scanned. Only way to find out if it was hollow would be to return and drill through it, 1,080 miles to the center, then send down a robotic camera. It's not that dense, only half as dense as the earth is. Also, as primates we should send teams to investigate the ancient machinery in the photographs.

The moon is part of the Islamic and Hebrew Calendars', it was important to the Babylonians in Babylon. The important religious holy dates revolve around the lunar "sidereal" month. Why? When the moon hits your eye like a big pizza pie, that's Amore.

ISLAM

Mohammad the Prophet of Islam (570-632 AD) was born Qathem, in Mecca, in the year 570 AD, to a widow woman named Amina. "Allah" means "the deity"; "Al" is "the", and "ilah" means "deity". In Hebrew, Allah is Elohim. Elohim is "the God" of the Bible. Elohim is the God of Abraham, it is the God in Genesis, "In the beginning God…….". Mohammad's father was named Abdullah, Abd-Allah, which means "slave of Allah", "slave of the deity". Abdullah died while Mohammad was gestating inside his primate host Amina. Primates worshipping Mohammad and belonging to the Mohammadanism religion do not eat Ham and Swiss on Rye with mustard.

The child who would be known as Mohammad was born to a widowed woman named Amina. This was her only child. Mohammad was given the name Qathem by his uncle Abd-al-Mu'taleb. The name Qathem means "the damaged one", or "the rotten one" because Abd-al-Mu'taleb had lost his own son Qathem three years earlier. Qathem changed his name to Mohammad when he was older, either at thirty years old, or when he fled to Medina. The word Mohammad means "the praised one". There was plague, smallpox, and other assorted communicable diseases prevalent in Arabia and Mecca in 570 AD. The caravan routes to the Empires and Africa were a source of transmission. Qathem was given over to a Bedouin nurse, named Halima; she raised him away from Mecca. Halima recounted years later about how Mohammad was a solitary child who lived in an imaginary world with imaginary friends. Halima took Qathem back to Amina in Mecca when he was 5 years old; she told Amina she thought Qathem had had a stroke, and feared a demon possessed him. Qathem lived with his mother in Mecca for a year until he was six, then she died. His grandfather, Abdul Muttalib took care of him, along with a nurse called Baracka. Qathem was allowed to sit on the carpet with his grandfather at the "moon temple" Kaaba, and received preferential treatment from him. Mohammad later in life would say his grandfather would admonish Baracka by saying, "Beware Baracka, lest you let him fall into the hands of the Jews and Christians, for they are looking for him, and would injure him. He has a great destiny, and will inherit a kingdom. After two years, when Qathem was eight, his grandfather died and his uncle Abu Talib took over caring for him. Abu Talib also cared for young Mohammad very well until Qathem was an adult. Mohammad suffered from a fear of abandonment. Abu Talib took him on a caravan business trip to Syria. Qathem was an orphan, a loner, loveless, and lonely in childhood; he grew up and became a recluse, distant from others, timid and insecure. Qathem did not pick up any profession or occupation. At times, he would tend a flock of sheep, mostly girls or women did this task back then and there. Abu Talib got Qathem a job at 25, (595 AD) as a trustee for a wealthy merchant business woman named Khadija who was 40 years old, twice widowed. He took a caravan to Syria for her and on his successful return, she proposed marriage to him. They were married (595-622 AD) and it worked for each of them, it was a marriage literally made in heaven. She was a co-dependent daughter of an alcoholic father, "daddy's girl", and he was a man needing of attention, and afraid of being abandoned. He still had his imaginary world that he could retreat to for comfort and solitude. Khadijah and Mohammad had four daughters, Zeinab, Fatima, Ruqiya, and Uum Kulthum, all of whom lived, and two sons who died very young. First son Qasim, died before he was two years old, then the girls were born, the last child, a son, died at birth. Mohammad had a family with rug-rats, then children running all over the place, a loving wife, and with her being a business woman, social contacts coming and going from the home. Khadijah also brought Mohammad into contact with a number of religious dissenters who visited her home.

Mohammad had a rough early life. Father and mother dead by 6 years old, grandfather dead by 8 years old; then he struggled with understanding the death of his first born son. He must have cursed the mother goddess al-Uzza for letting this happen. Al-Uzza was comparable to the Virgin Mary in Roman Catholicism. Her idol would have been in their home, staring at him. There was a man called Zayd who was a friend of Mohammad and Khadija. Zayd was a contrarian, about 30 years older than Mohammad, and searching for truth and the meaning of life, that he didn't find in the Moon God, or the sun gods. Zayd tried Christianity and Judaism. He translated part of the Bible into Arabic. Khadijah partially embraced Christianity along with other pagan faiths. Mohammad learned about Christianity also but was not convinced of the faith. While enquiring about Judaism, Zayd learned of Abraham and Ismael and the Ishmaelite tribe that sprung from Abrahams first son. He thought that if he found the Ishmaelite tribes then he would find his true faith, the faith of Abraham who was willing to sacrifice his son for his God. This would be an unshake-able belief for him. Zayd traveled all over searching, but finally heard that the Ishmaelite tribes no longer existed. After Hagar and her son Ismael, parted from Abraham and Sarah, they created the tribe of the Ishmaelite who lived along the east-west caravan routes in the northern desert closer to Syria than Canaan. The tribe grew but was eventu-ally conquered by the Assyrians and Babylonians; they intermarried with pagans and then became pagans themselves. Some Ishmaelite's became part of the Nabataea Kingdom that controlled the caravan trade from Yemen to Syria. The Nabataea are known for the splendid sandstone mausoleums carved into the sandstone cliffs of its capital city of Petra. The Nabataea kingdom ended when Rome took control of it in 106 AD, and it became a province. The Ishmaelite tribe or their peoples no longer existed in Zayd's time. Zayd dismissed Judaism because he believed the progeny of Abraham and Sarah had strayed from the original religion of Abraham, but the Ishmaelite developed separately and therefore must have retained the true faith and not have been corrupted. Despondent over learning of the demise of the Ishmaelite, Zayd then practiced his own religion, Zaydism. Zaydism was the simple belief in the uniqueness and singularity of God and of the need to follow Abrahams example of total submission to Gods will. Zayd despaired over his inability to add more to Zaydism than this simple belief and he would cry out, "O God, if I knew which manner is most pleasing to thee, I should worship thee in it, but I know not". Zayd railed against the Meccan polytheists, and he ridiculed kissing the black stone as senseless. He made enemies in Mecca and Zayd ended up living in a cave on the northern outskirts of Mecca on mount Hira. Zayd made up poems to express his views; Mohammad supported his friend Zayd's beliefs, and was a Zaydist himself. Zayd died shortly after the temple was rebuilt in 605 AD.

Mohammad helped in rebuilding the temple and due to the lack of construction material, the temple changed shape from a rectangle to a cube shaped structure, a Kabah, a cube, with the black meteorite stone at one corner. Mohammad had an epileptic fit during the reconstruction, brought about by his obsessive modesty; it was hot so the workers would strip naked and put their rags on their heads to work in the sun; Mohammad refused to strip and then had an epileptic fit over it; people starting looking at him strangely from that point on. After Zayds death he was beginning to question his own beliefs in his inherited paganism and comparing them to Zaydism. Mohammads' home life with Khadija was a support system and provided stability for him; he didn't have to support himself, he wasn't lonely and he liked to wear perfume, which was probably abundant with four girls and a merchant wife. He escaped all this domestic bliss and the strange looks of the Meccans by taking over a small quiet cave on Mount Hira. At the age of 40, (610AD), his four girls would have been pubescent teenagers. After escaping this domestic bliss of 4 teenage girls in the house and after spending a week in his bat-cave, he had either a mystical or psychotic experience. He experienced muscle contractions, abdominal pain, twitching, involuntary movement, sweating and rapid heartbeat. He heard voices and had a vision of a ghost. The ghost was Jim Morrison and Jimmy Hendrix who were saying, "it will wear off, it will pass, it's just the

LSD mixed with the bat shite you ate. He ran home to Khadija, passing the Meccans still giving him strange looks, and fearing the demons had come for him again. She consoled him. Morrison and Hendrix peered in the window and recording on 8 mm film; this highly flammable nitrate-cellulose film was sent to the Jews in Yathrib, who smuggled it to Hollywood where it remains to this day next to the arc of the covenant and Indiana Jones' Fedora. Khadija was also a Hanif in addition to worshipping Hubal and his harem; a Hanif was a monotheistic Arabian religion believing in the patriarch Abraham. She, Khadija, at 50 years old, told Qathem, that it wasn't a demon; it was an angel that appeared to him and that he had been chosen as a prophet. And he bought it hook, line, and sinker. She stood there smiling and naked, cooing "you are the prophet baby, you are the Prophet of God." "Allah Akbar baby". After going public some years later he declared himself, "Messenger of God". He was the messenger, no message, just he was the messenger. He went back to the bat-cave and Khadijah had a threesome with Jim Morrison and Jimmy Hendrix for the rest of the day before a jinni chased them back to the 1960's.

Islam's main message is that Muhammad is a messenger of God. Beyond that, there is no other message! And, you must submit to this message. Failure to recognize and accept this message entails punishment in this world and for all eternity in the next. This concept was alien to animistic pagans.

In Staten Island terms, it would be like this: "I'm Guido, I am a messenger of the Don." What's the message? What's the message Guido? "I'm Guido, I am the messenger of the Don", "There is no Don but the Don and Guido is his messenger". Yes, but what's the message Guido? "I'm Guido, I am the messenger of the Don".

After ten years of preaching this, (620 AD), his only followers were his wife, Khadija, Abu-Bakr, Othman, Umar and about 100-120 disaffected youth and slaves. Slaves had no choice.

In the year 620 AD, Mecca was a polytheist society; the rest of the world outside Arabia was a monotheistic one. The spirit of monotheism about in the world, and the accompanying Empire religions aided and abetted Mohammad's eventual submissions to Islam. In Mecca back then all beliefs were generally accepted, like modern Western societies today. Mohammad took over Zaydism and added his epileptic hallucinations to it. It lacked any form of humility that Zaydism may have had. The framework of Zaydism was an empty chalice of offering to the God of Abraham. Mohammad cobbled together beliefs of the religions he had knowledge of, into an amalgamated monotheistic religion, based on submission to the God of Abraham and Gods prophet, Mohammad; he filled Zayds chalice with gobbledygook.

Before he could go out and preach his beliefs, he knew he had to get his physical and mental disorder in check. He checked his anxiety by performing obsessive-compulsive behavior. He invented his exhausting cleansing rituals, each done three times, followed by prayer routines. All these ablutions and the prayer routine were performed by him five times every day. This pleased the will of the Judeo-Christian-pagan god in his head. What was the will of god, was still an unanswered question. Mohammad filled the chalice and discerned the will of God by sitting under a blanket while having untreated epileptic fits, psychotic hallucinations he called "revelations" passed down from God by the angel Gabriel. Although Mohammad was a gifted orator, pagans didn't want to hear his views, they were radically different than what the tribes had lived with for 100's if not 1000's of years. The disaffected Muslim youths would mock and insult the other Meccans and their pagan religious beliefs; if in turn the pagans did the same to the Muslims, the Muslims would become extremely violent towards the pagans. This continuous religious animosity created many enemies in Mecca. The Meccans plead to Abu-Talib to rein in his nephew; Abu-Talib in turn plead with Mohammad to be reasonable; Mohammad responded by refusing his request, then crying and putting on an emotional show. Abu-Talib saw that Mohammad was still a damaged child; Mohammad was 50 years old when this occurred in 620 AD. His uncle pledged to always support Mohammad in seeing that he was still an emotionally damaged child. The Muslims continued acting violently, they shunned their relatives who were non-believers and became a cult within Mecca. Mohammad had a friend who was a cloth merchant, Abu-Bakr; he converted Abu-Bakr and in turn Abu-Bakr became an excellent recruiting agency for Mohammad. Many of the converts were captured Christian slaves who didn't see much difference between Christianity and Islam. Many owners bought their slaves freedom if the slave was willing to convert to Islam. Mohammad wrote for 23 years in the form of rhyming prose, first in short focused poems, then in longer convoluted poems. The style of the prose suggests the work of someone who knew what he was doing. Mohammad's prose reveals his inner struggle with a harsh inner voice, not many voices in his head, but one harsh voice in there with him. Some of his poetry was ingenious and original like "The Merciful". Mohammad knew he needed words that were more authoritarian than the dogma Zaydism provided if he was to expand his congregation, so he started using words like "us", "we", "our", which solidified the fledgling group of Muslims into "us" versus "them" mentality. He came up with 99 words to describe the deity, Allah and attract more believers. His prose which eventually was bound into the Quran of the Quraysh, achieved the sound of high authority. In further prose, Mohammad's writings became fixated on doomsday and hell in a sadistic way, examples of which are "The Enfolded", and "The Enwrapped". These further writings are the writings of an extremely angry man, slowly waiting to erupt like a volcano. Mohammad also experienced paradise in his epileptic neurotic condition, but the more he was rejected by Meccans, the more sadistic his prose and speeches became about hellfire and torture. Mohammad was the inspiration for the Christian prose "Dante's Inferno", centuries later.

Ninety Nine Words to describe Allah

The Compassionate, the Merciful, King, Holy, source of peace, the preserver of security, protector, mighty, overpowering, great in majesty, creator, maker, fashioner, forgiver, dominant, Bestower, provider, decider, knower, withholder, plentiful giver, abaser, exalter, honorer, humiliator, hearer, seer, judge, just, gracious, informed, clement, incomparably great, forgiving, rewarder, most high, most great, preserver, sustainer, reckoner, most high, most great, preserver, sustainer, reckoner, majestic, generous, watcher, answerer, liberal, trustee, strong, wise, firm, patron, praiseworthy, all-knowing, originator, restorer to life, giver of life, giver of death, living, eternal, self-sufficient, Grand, One, Single, He to whom men repair, Powerful, Prevailing, Advancer, Delayer, First, Last, Outward, Inward, Governor, Sublime, Amply Beneficent, Accepter of Repentance, Avenger, Pardoner, Kindly, Ruler of the Kingdom, Lord of Majesty and Splendor, Equitable, Gatherer, Independent, Enricher, depriver, harmer, Benefactor, Light, Guide, First Cause, Enduring, Inheritor, Fraudulent, Director, murderer, rapist, and child molester.

The animosity between the pagans and the Muslims intensified into minor skirmishes. Many of Mohammad's followers left Mecca and immigrated to Abyssinia. Some stayed behind in Mecca with Mohammad. His Hashemite clan closed ranks with him, the rest of the Quraysh shunned the Hashemite clan for about two years, starting in the year 620 AD. This meant no food and no supplies for the Hashemite clan; no trade with them.

Khadija passed away in 622 AD, when she was 65 years old. Mohammad was 50 years old, she never had a chance to apply for social security from the German EU, but Mohammad applied for her share as he believed he made a major contribution to something. Abu Talib died about a month before Khadija. Mohammed had no protection at that point in time, and he no longer had a source of income. Meccans wanted Mohammad dead and done with. Mohammad fled to Taif to seek their protection, and they let him stay, but he started in right away with his abusive preaching. They drove him out of Taif by stoning him till he left. Jim Morrison and Jimmy Hendrix showed up when they heard about someone getting stoned, followed by some jinn. Mohammad wrote a verse after escaping Taif, called "The Jinn" where he converted a lot of Jinn that were surrounding him as he fled. Morrison and Hendrix realized it was a different kind of stoning and found a bottle full of gin, that they became spiritual on.

After Mohammad snuck back into Mecca, he hung out in the cave, and sometimes lived in Khadija's old house. He married a chic named Sauda, who was a widow of one of his followers. After a while he also gets engaged to the six-year-old daughter of his friend Abu-Bakr. Her name was Aisha. About this same time, Mohammad had another epileptic hallucination, which he described as "The Night Journey"; he says he was transported to the old temple in Jerusalem by a Buraq, some sort of bizarre animal like a mule, with a human head and wings. He tied the Buraq to the wailing wall and entered the temple, whereupon, he was transported by the angel Gabriel to heaven, where he visits with the prophets and Allah himself in paradise. He looks down on hell and he sees it is mostly filled with women. After tea with the Almighty, he was transported back to the temple and then on the Buraq back to Mecca. This all happened in one night according to him. He told the story eloquently and enthralled many people with the story.

After telling this story to everyone he met, the Meccan people now know he is insane. In 622 AD, Mohammad fled Mecca, two steps ahead of an assassination squad. He was bound for the oasis of Yathrib (Medina). This flight from Mecca to Medina is called the Hejira, or the migration. This date marks the start of the Islamic New Year and the Islamic calendar. Medina is about 200 miles north of Mecca.

In 623 AD, Mohammad and his followers were broke. They lost all they had when they fled Mecca and spent a lot on the migration to get to Yathrib. They started raiding and pillaging caravans to support themselves. The three Jewish tribes in Yathrib had the upper hand economically, they had been living and prospering there since the days when they were driven out of Judah by the Romans Empire. Medina was beyond bounds of the Empires, situated in the Arabian desert, and it had water being an oasis town. There were also pagan Arab tribes living in the oasis, with continuous tribal fighting between all. Mohammad and his followers eventually took over the oasis of Yathrib. Mohammad fought a Meccan army that was sent to Yathrib to stop the caravan theft that Mohammad was engaged in, but it lost and Mohammad and his followers became more powerful. Mohammad fought many battles over the next few years and plundered many places, sadistically murdering everyone who opposed him. He finally defeated the Meccan army entirely and entered Mecca as a conqueror. He went to the temple (Kaaba) and threw out all the pagan idols. There were about 360 idols of gods that were worshiped by the pagans over the centuries. The only religion permitted was Islam, his religion, under penalty of death and torture.

On his return to Yathrib, Mohammad demanded the return of the film the Jews possessed of Khadija consoling in the year 610 AD. The Jews told him they sent it to Hollywood, California, so he slaughtered all 800 male Yathrib Jews by beheading them in one day. After watching this spectacular demise of their fathers and husbands, all the Jewish women and children were sold as slaves. This ended any Hebrew presence in Medina. The actions of Mohammad and his success drew many more followers and many more tribes to his side. In the course of the next seven years he conquered or won over almost all the Arabian tribes. The religion of Mohammad grew by the sword, by rape, by pillage, by murder, by theft and by forced conversion. He engaged in terror tactics to further his psychotic belief system. He was unable to fill Zayds chalice with anything other than "I'm Mohammad, I am the messenger of Allah. There is no God but Allah, and Mohammad is his prophet." If you refuse to believe this you bring about your death and condemnation to hellfire for all eternity, if you do believe this then what is yours is mine for we are Muslim brothers.

Mohammad had thirteen wives and concubines, Khadija and Sauda in Mecca, then in Yathrib he married and consummated the marriage with Aisha when she was 9 years old. Following Aisha was Hafsa, Zaynab Khuzayma, Umm, Zaynab, Juwayriya, Ramlah, two Jewish women, Rayhanna, Safiya, Maria the Coptic Christian and Maymumma. He acquired an additional twenty women in the years just previous to his death. He was an endless womanizer, which was probably a compulsion, a good number of these wives and women were war booty from the slaughter of their fathers or husbands or fellow tribesmen.

In 630 AD, Mohammad along with Arabian army set out to conquer Syria, but his army and him turned tail when they saw the Marshall array of Byzantine Christian troops in front of them. Mohammad died in Medina in 632 AD, at 62 years old. He is buried there in a mosque. Both Jimmy Hendrix and Jim Morrison attended his funeral there, accompanied by Elton John. Morrison composed a song called "The End" especially for the occasion while Elton John sang his "Candle in the Wind" song. It was a depressing time and only 300 imported Jews were beheaded that day. Jimmy Hendrix stressed not to confuse the god "Hubal" with "Mott the Hoople".

After Mohammad's death, his writings were turned into a book the Quran, and other religious dogma, the Hadith, and the Sura. The pilgrimages to Mecca continued but not worship to the sun god or to the moon god any longer. The Kaaba cube and the pagan customs of the sun and moon worship were incorporated into and became part Islam. The meteorite was still kissed and the stones were thrown at the devil, the same way the meteorites were thrown by Allah at the jinn. The pagan holy months continued, one was called Ramadan. Every Muslim was expected to make the pilgrimage to Mecca at least once in their lives. The same racket as before Islam was usurped by Islam and continued, a sure money maker for relieving the faithful of their money.

After the death of Mohammad the Prophet, the first King of Arabia, the messenger of God, the messenger of Allah, Abu-Bakr and Mohammad's friends started the Rashidun Caliphate (632-651 AD) and continued where Mohammad left off. They began their Holy Quest to find the legendary film in Hollywood, California by engaging in holy war (Jihad). The Rashidun Caliphate continued conquering all the lands between the Arabian desert and wherever Hollywood was supposed to be, it wasn't on any of their maps at the time. Their conquest went on very well from 632 AD, the two empires surrounding them were old, tired, and diseases had decimated their populations. There was a lot of vacant property for the taking in both the Sassanid (Persian) Empire and the Byzantine Empire. Syria and Palestine were conquered by the Caliphate in the year 637 AD. In 640 AD, Egypt fell to the Rashidun Caliphate. In 650 AD, the Rashidun Caliphate conquered the Sassanid Empire. This ended the Sassanid-Byzantine wars, and it ended the worship of Zoroaster and the Zoroastrian religion. In 652 AD, Muslim Caliphate armies conquered North Africa including Carthage. Also in 652 AD, the Rashidun Caliphate conquered the city of Balkh, in the east. Balkh was the furthest northwestern center of Buddhism. All these conquered people were reduced dhimmi status and slavery if they did not convert to Islam. The expansion stopped through the years 656-661 AD when the Muslims became engaged in a civil war over the succession of the caliph position after the death of Ali. Fighting and war to add more territory, booty and peoples to the House of Islam, (dar-al-Islam), (the house of submission), was continuous against the House of War, (dar-al-Harb), for the past 1384 years, and continues in the present. Christianity itself did not organize a European wide defense against Islamic aggression for the first 463 years. In the year 1095 AD, the Eastern Roman-Greek Byzantine Empire was attacked and almost conquered by Turks, then the Byzantine Empire asked for help from The Roman Catholic Pope in Western Europe and he called for the first Crusade to defend Christianity from Islam. In 1096, the first European wide defensive action was taken by the Western European kingdoms in the form of the First Crusade. Tribes will be tribes, with their deity out in front of them, holding them together in their fight for economic survival.

CHRONICUM HOLOCENUM DATED TIMELINE II

Dated Timeline	Middle eastern, European, Mediterranean Sea, Historical Events
600 AD	"Bond Event Cooling", migrations begin again
600 AD	Smallpox arrives in western Europe for the first time, population of earth 208 Million people Germans developed a new plow for farming the soil.
609 AD	God tells Mohammad to go out for a pass, then throws the football at him. God hit Mohammad in the head with the football, and things weren't the same afterwards. God says he sorry, and ducks down behind the moon, he later whispers to Mohammad that the Jews hit him with the ball. Mohammad declares himself a prophet to his wife and friends at 39 years old.
611 AD	Sassanid, Persian Empire invades Byzantine territory and surrounds Constantinople.
614 AD	Jerusalem captured by the Sassanid Persians; there are not many Jews there but they are left to run Jerusalem; The true cross that Jesus was crucified on was captured by the Persians and taken to the city of Ctesiphon, (22 miles south of Baghdad); the cross is about 600 years old at this date in time
622 AD	Mohammad was 52 years old, his wife Khadija died, most of his friends were dead, and all the clans in Mecca want him dead to shut up his insane rambling preaching. He fled to Yathrib.
623 AD	Mohammad and his followers, broke, set themselves up in Yathrib, and change the name to Medina. 1500 Arabs swear allegiance to him and submit to his new religion, Islam. They attack caravans, defeat other tribes, and unite the profession of merchant and thief.
624 AD	**According to "The Annals of Ulster", 624 AD was a year of darkness.**
627 AD	Byzantine Empire makes an alliance with the Khazars, and Western Turks. Khazaria was a kingdom north of the Black Sea around Crimea and extended north to Kiev. The pagan Khazars sent 40,000 warriors to help the Byzantine Empire fight the Sassanid Empire.
628 AD	Sassanid Empire has an **outbreak of plague** with mortality of 50%.
629 AD	Byzantine armies recapture Jerusalem from the Persians. Sassanid Empire surrenders, original Byzantine borders restored, the true cross was recovered and brought back to Constantinople in a parade. Arab trade dominated by the Quraysh tribe was devastated by these wars between Persia and Byzantine Empire in both the southern and northern areas of Arabia, Arab tribal alliance was deteriorating. Mohammad proposed uniting all these tribes under one God, Allah, and one

community, "the umma". He brought everyone onboard at the point of a sword, and held them together by mutual conquest of anyone not part of the umma. Trade in Baghdad and the Sassanid economy was collapsing. Jews in Babylon and Sassanid Empire begin slowly migrating north.

630 AD — Mohammad lead 30,000 Muslim soldiers and cavalry against the Byzantine Empire near Damascus but halted halfway there after seeing the Marshall array of Byzantine troops in front of him. He turned tail and returned to Medina.

630 AD — The Kingdom of Khazaria, now on good relations with Constantinople and the Byzantine Empire prospers from the economic and trade ties. The Kingdom of the Khozars, encompassed land that was originally settled by **Togarmah**, grandson of Japheth, great grandson of Noah and the ark. Togarmah and Ashkenaz were brothers, Gomer was their father. This was the land of the Magog. It was also the land of the Ashkenaz, who became the Scythians. The Scythians were a large group that rode the steppes, the Caucuses' and the north of Persian, Assyrian lands. One of the tribes of the Scythians is believed to be the Saxons, a Scythian tribe that moved west earlier in time. Togarmah had ten sons. The ten sons of Togarmah were: Uigur, Dursu, Avars, Huns, Basilli, Tarniakh, **Khazars**, Zagora, Bulgars, and Sabir. Khazars were living in the same area as the Ashkenaz, their brothers.

632 AD — Mohammad died, (570-632 AD); he was buried in Medina. He left no male heir, so his followers had to find a "successor", a "caliph". A caliph is a successor of Mohammad.

632 AD — In 632 AD, classical civilization was synonymous with Christendom. After this time, classical civilization came in contact with a new spiritual force, Islam. Islam extolled war as a sacred duty, Jihad, it sanctioned enslavement and the killing of non-Muslims, sanctioned the legitimate judicial use of torture (inquisition) and provided for the execution of apostates and heretics. While these are not unique in the history of primate religion, they are not some sort of degenerate phase of Islamic teaching. They are the core beliefs of the founder Mohammad, and the core beliefs of Islam's adherents. The Christian church was profoundly influenced by Islam. After Islam came on the scene the Christian church would become theocratic and intolerant, it would adopt the inquisition from Islam and the church would become obscure. It was no longer the open church, it would be a dark age for everyone. Islam did not build; it only took what was already there.

632 AD — Rashidun Caliphate (632-651 AD), Abu-Bakr, Umar, Othman, and Ali were the caliphs.

634 AD — Muslim Expansion, Muslim-Sassanid Wars (634-650 AD), Arabs were raiding the Sassanid Empire, and Arab General Khalid al-Walid turns it into a war. This provided a solution to the economic crises in Arabia; pillage. Umar took over as the second caliph in 634 and the attacks continued on both the Byzantine and Sassanid Empires.

637 AD — Syria-Palestrina conquered by Muslim armies after the Byzantine army loss at Battle of Yarmuk in Syria; the Arabs captured Ctesiphon with all the Sassanid Royal crown jewels which were sent to the Kaaba.

639 AD	Armenia fell to Muslim armies.
640 AD	Egypt was defeated by Muslim armies; the Muslims began stripping the outer covering of the Great Pyramids.
642 AD	Arab Muslim armies defeat the last Sassanid army.
642 AD	First Muslim Arab-Khazar War, (642-652 AD), Arab troops attack Khazaria for first time attempting to flank the Byzantine Empire by conquering land north of the Black Sea.
650 AD	Rashidun Caliphate finishes the conquest of the Sassanid Persian Empire, this marks the end of the religion of Zoroaster, Zoroastrianism. Islam was installed as the religion in the Aryan lands of Persia. From this year onwards to 950 AD, there is no archeology in Muslim controlled lands. In 650 AD, one half of the worlds' Christian population was living under Islamic rule.
650 AD	Khazaria comes into existence as a distinct political entity, (650-1016 AD). Khazaria can field 300,000-500,000 warriors.
652 AD	North Africa, including Carthage were stomped by Islamic armies, extending their rule to the Atlantic Ocean.; Muslims conquered the northwestern center of the Buddhist religion at Balkh. Khazarian armies defeated invading Islamic armies. Battle lines move back and forth, north and south in territory between the Caspian and Black Sea, in the Caucuses' Mountains.
656 AD	Islamic civil war over the succession of the new Caliph, after the assassination of 'Uthman. This "Fitna", this civil war, stops the expansion of Islam until 661 AD, when a new Caliph and caliphate is formed. His death created the first schism in Islam; dividing Islam into Sunni and Shia sects. The Shia believe Ali was the caliph that Mohammad designated as his successor; the Sunni's do not. Ali (601-661 AD) was married to Mohammad's daughter Fatima, and ruled as Caliph of the Rashidun caliphate from 656-661 AD when he was assassinated, by a Khawarij, "the Outsiders", a member of a nomad Bedouin tribe that first supported Ali but then opposed him and the Sunni's, for political leadership of the 'umma. They are very similar to todays' self-proclaimed Islamic State. caliphate. The tribe was mostly located in Omar and Zanzibar, (Zanzibar means the stronghold of Zang; Zang means negro, blacks.) Zanzibar was one of the main slave centers of the African slave trade; 50,000 African slaves passed through Zanzibar every year on their way to the Middle East, Persia and India.
661 AD	Umayyad Caliphate (661-750 AD), Mu'awiya is the 5th caliph (661-685 AD).
662 AD	Islamic conquest continues; Conquest of the Silk Road by Islamic armies; Merv, Turkmenistan was the main city through which the Silk Road passed; Muslims took it over and now controlled all the imports going into Europe through the Byzantine Empire and Mediterranean Sea. Muslims entered into secret alliances with the Chinese to control the western Asian peoples that surrounded the Silk Road.
674 AD	Constantinople was attacked by sea by Islamic navies from 674 until 678 AD; they were repelled by the Byzantines using "Greek Fire", something like Napalm used during the Vietnam War in the 1960's.

678 AD	Jews resided in very large numbers on the Taman Peninsula, present day Krech, Russia, adjacent to the "Cimmerian Bosporus" straits that connects the Black Sea to the Sea of Azov.
685 AD	Abd-al-Malik is the 6th Caliph (685-705 AD)
669 AD	Islamic Jihadis attack Syracuse from Alexandria, Egypt in 200 ships.
691 AD	Islamic architects' build the "Dome of the Rock" on top of the Foundation Stone atop what was left of the temple mount in Jerusalem, covering the Holy of Holies, the Well of Souls, from the Milky Way Galaxy. Then they build the Al-Aqsa mosque about the same time.
703 AD	Islamic navies begin raids on coast of Italy attacking every year up and down the coast, carrying off slaves and booty of Christian Italy.
711 AD	Muslim Jihadists cross the Straits of Gibraltar from North Africa, and seize the Pillars of Hercules; from there they begin a conquest and occupation of the Iberian peninsula; Sardinia in the Mediterranean Sea was attacked also in this year. Hispania became Al-Andalusia and Emirate of Cordoba between the years 711 and 788 AD, a possession of the Umayyad Caliphate. The Hispanic inhabitants are reduced to slavery and dhimmi status.
718 AD	Islamic armies cross the Pyrenees Mountains into Frankish territory; Hispanic Reconquista begins.
721 AD	Battle of Toulouse; Islamic armies were defeated by Frankish troops, but Islamic raiding continues in Frankish territory of Gaul.
722 AD	Second Islamic Arab- Khazar War, (722-737 AD)
723 AD	Islamic armies destroy Khazar city of Balanjar, on western shore of Caspian Sea
724 AD	Samander becomes new capital city of Khazars, on western Shore of Caspian Sea, north of Balanjar.
724 AD	Many Jews move from the Middle-East, Babylon to Khazaria to escape the Islamic persecution of Jews.
730 AD	Khazars defeat an Islamic Army, Battle of Ardabil.
732 AD	Battle of Tours; Charles Martel (688-741 AD), defeats Islamic armies; Muslim raiding and expansion into France is stopped by Frankish armies.
737 AD	Islamic armies under Marwan ibn Mohammad use treachery to gain access to Khazaria territory. They are admitted peacefully, and then Marwan ibn Mohammad declares his dishonorable intentions and the Islamic Army drives deep into the Khaganate of Khazaria, devastating Khazarian horse herds, capturing and enslaving residents. Most of the population of Khazaria fled to the Ural Mountains. Marwan demanded the entire pagan Kingdom and its people convert to Islam, and then he would leave.
737 AD	Capital of Khazars transferred from Samander to Atil, on north coast of Caspian Sea and inland.
748 AD	Charlemagne, Charles I (748-814 AD) was born; he was the oldest son of Pepin the Short, and the grandson of Charles Martel.
750 AD	After the year 750 AD, all archeology became scarce in Italy, Europe, and the Middle East; it was as if there was nothing built after this time period for the next 200 years.

750 AD	Abbasid Caliphate begins (750-1258 AD) begins.
751 AD	Pepin the Short (714-768 AD), King of the Franks, son of Charles Martel; replaces Gold solidus in Western Europe, with the pound, schilling, penny system of currency using silver; 12 pence was equal to 1 shilling; 20 shilling was equal to 1 pound; shilling means "division", and it is derived from the "Old Norse" language.
756 AD	Pict tribes took Dumbarton castle on the River Clyde
759 AD	Septimania province in Frankish territory was retaken by Franks from Muslim occupiers.
775 AD	A Khazar, Byzantine Emperor "Leo IV the Khazar" is Emperor (775-780 AD).
794 AD	Vikings attacked Iona Monastery on island of Iona off western Scotland
795 AD	Charlemagne pushes across Pyrenees Mountains and creates "Spanish Marches" as a buffer zone between Franks and Islam.
800 AD	Carolingian Empire (800-924 AD) began in Gaul, Charlemagne was the first Emperor.
800 AD	1st German Reich, the Holy Roman Empire, (800-1806 AD) established.
800 AD	The Khagan, (King), Bulan converted to Judaism, and the entire Kingdom, (Khaganate), converted from paganism to Judaism, so as not to have Christian Byzantine overlords or Islamic overlords.
817 AD	Pope Paschal I, removed all the relics and Holy materials from Saint Peters Basilica and hid them inside the walls of Rome; Saint Peters was outside the walls of Rome at this time.
820 AD	The island of Crete fell to Islamic Jihad conquest. Khazars settle Kiev, Ukraine.
827 AD	The island of Sicily fell to Islamic Jihad conquest
830 AD	The tribes of Hungarians threatened the Khazars. The Hungarians were former allies or subjects of the Khazars but not anymore. The Khazars asked the Byzantine Empire for help, and the Christian Greeks helped build the fortress of Sarkel (833-841 AD) on the Lower Don river in 840 AD.
831 AD	The entire length of the Italian Peninsula was attacked by Islamic navies landing Jihad armies, and raiding parties.
832 AD	Pictish King Oengus II leads a battle against the Anglo-Saxons and sees a white cloud in the blue sky in the shape of an "X"; he says if he wins the battle he would make Saint Andrew the patron saint of Alba, (Saint Andrew was crucified on a cross that was shaped as an "X"), he won and the "X" marked the Scot" from that time forward. The blue flag with the white X is the flag of the Scots to this date.
840 AD	Dublin area attacked and occupied by Vikings, Vikings begin settlement there from overpopulated Scandinavia. Brittany and entire west coast of Europe attacked by Viking raiders.
840 AD	The Khagan Obadiah sent for Jewish rabbi's and scholars to teach Judaism, and many Jews from Constantinople, Anatolia, and Babylon responded, emigrating to Khazaria and establishing Talmudic Edomite Ashkenazi Jewish synagogues and schools. The entire Khaganate of maybe 600,000 people became Ashkenazi Jews, synagogues, and Talmudic schools were built all over Khazaria. The Khaganate controlled the river trade on the rivers emptying into the Black sea, including the

Dnieper, the Dniester, the Don, and it controlled the passages of the Volga River leading to the Caspian Sea. After a short time, there came a long line of Jewish Khagans controlling the trade on these rivers. The "Star of David", the "Magen David" was the emblem engraved onto the shields of the Khazars, after conversion to Judaism. Intermarriage began between Jews and Khazars. Khazars are haplotype R1a. 20% of Ashzenazi Jews are haplotype R1a to date, and thus descended from Khazars.

843 AD	**Kingdom of Alba**, (843-1286 AD), begins; Pictish King Kenneth McAlpin died, and Donald II became the first King of Alba; the Kingdom of Alba encompassed all the Scots lands of Dal-Riata, the Kingdom of Strathclyde, Northumberland and all the Caledonian Highlands from the North Sea to the Atlantic Ocean. The heartland of the kingdom was north of the River Forth. This heartland was called Scotia. Eventually the Kingdom of Alba was called Scotland.
846 AD	Saracens, (Muslims) attacked Rome, and looted Saint Peter's Basilica. Pope Leo IV fled from Vatican City and Saint Peters Basilica, before capture. The Muslims tore the Golden cross off Saint Peters tomb, tore the silver from the doors and gold from the floor. They desecrated the bronze crypt, and laid waste to the surrounding area. They were driven back to their ships in the same year.
847 AD	Pope Leo IV had the Leonine Walls built around the area of the Vatican, they were completed in 852 AD and can still be seen today protecting Vatican Hill from Jihad attack.
847 AD	Pope Leo IV called for some sort of European help in protecting Christendom from Islam.
860 AD	Vikings started moving down all the rivers in Magog and Ukraine from the Baltic area. The Viking Rus take over all the Ashkenazi Khazar trade. The Vikings take over the Black Sea and became mercenaries for the Byzantine Empire, also working as the Emperors Varangian guard.
861 AD	Saint Cyril tries to persuade the pagan and Jewish Khazars to accept Orthodox Christianity; Saint Cyril destroys the pagan Khazars' "sacred oak tree" in Tepsen and forcibly converted the pagans to Orthodox Christianity.
864 AD	The first written record of the conversion of Khazars to Judaism was written, " Expositio in Matthaeum Evangelistam"
870 AD	Norsemen siege Alt-Clut, (Dunbarton Castle) on the north side of the River Clyde; the siege lasted for four months before they destroyed it, killed, or enslaved all the inhabitants. All the slaves were taken to Dublin; Vikings then sold slaves from Dublin to the Saracens in the Iberian Peninsula and the Mediterranean area.
883 AD	Islamic jihadists' attacked, looted and burned down the monastery of Saint Benedict in Monte Cassino in Central Italy.
890 AD	In Scotland, according to "The Annals of Ulster", "a mermaid was cast ashore by the sea, in Alba, whose length was 195 feet. The length of her hair was 17 feet long; the length of a finger of hand was 7 feet. She was altogether whiter than a swan."
899 AD	Black Powder, gunpowder was invented in China. Charcoal, potassium nitrate, (salt peter) and sulfur, were combined into a mixture, that when ignited explodes.

	The salt peter acts as an oxidizer. This was the first chemical explosive to be known. The Chinese used it for fireworks and for military uses.
901 AD	The Vikings, the Northmen were expelled from Hibernia, ending 60 years of Viking presence in Erin.
911 AD	According to "The Annals of Ulster", 911 AD was a rainy and dark year; a Comet appeared in the sky. Duchy of Normandy begins in western France adjacent to Brittany, Normans are descendants of Vikings, mixed with Celts from Gaul and Brittany, mixed with Frankish tribes people.
948 AD	Ashkenazi Khagan Joseph exchanges letters with a Sephartic Jew in Analusia, who is working as a diplomat for the Muslim government; in the letters he asks how is it that Khazaria is Jewish; and he gets the story about Japheth, Gomer, Togamah and Ashzenaz, and how they converted to Judaism. The Khazars and Ashkenaz were not Shemites, they were descended from Japheth.
950 AD	Start of the Medieval Warm Period, (950-1250 AD), Europe had a population of 55 Million people
962 AD	Holy Roman Empire (962-1803 AD) begins
965 AD	Khazar-Rus War, (965-968 AD), Rus destroy Khazar fortress at Sarkel and Atil on the Volga River. Khazaria went into decline, this disruption of the Khazar Khaganate disrupted the Radhanite Jewish merchant trade routes that extended from the Rhone River Valley in France to the East coast of China; the "Silk Road" collapsed after this victory by the Russians.
968 AD	Ukrainian Rus Prince Sviatoslav defeats Ashkenazi Jewish Khazar forces near Kiev; Khazars have Stars of David on their shields.
975 AD	Saint Stephen of Hungary (975-1038 AD) is born.
988 AD	Russian Viking Prince Vladimir of Kiev converts to Orthodox Christianity
999 AD	Normans start to arrive in Sicily as mercenaries to fight Saracen extortion racket called "the jizyah"; eventually more Normans arrive and completely take over Sicily from Islam, creating the Kingdom of Sicily (1130-1816 AD) which incorporates most of southern Italy and Sicily.
1000 AD	population of the British Islands about 2-3 Million people.
1000 AD	Kingdom of Hungary (1000-1945 AD) founded.
1000 AD	Vikings colonize Greenland and set up settlement in Newfoundland in eastern Canada. Population of Europe 56 Million people; slavery starts to die out in Northern Europe, it is replaced by serfdom.
1032 AD	Islamic dominating power on the Iberian Peninsula is greatly diminished due to localized Muslim civil wars.
1035 AD	The Kingdom of Aragon (1035-1706 AD) was established in Iberia
1050 AD	Jewish Khazars live in a suburb of Constantinople, many have migrated westwards towards Slavic lands, where Poland will be, Romania, Bulgaria areas north and south of Carpathians.
1066 AD	The Normans of France invade, attack and conquer the Anglo-Saxons in Britain at "The Battle of Hastings". Normans occupy Britain and spread out to the North

and West. The first Jews from the continent came to England with the invasion of William the Conqueror.

1070 AD	Anglo-Saxon immigration from England to Constantinople, Byzantine Empire; Anglo-Saxons serve in the Varangian guard of the Byzantine Emperors; they start towns like New England on the Black Sea.
1071 AD	Overpopulated Turks, who were originally allied and part of the Khazars, were converting to Islam after driving into Abbasid Caliphate. In 1055 AD, the Seljuk Turks began entering Anatolia after defeating a Byzantine army in the battle of Manzikert. This loss led to the Turkification of Anatolia. All Greek men in the outlying towns and cities of the Byzantine Empire were massacred; the Greek women and children were sold into slavery by Muslim Turks. All the Greek towns and cities were destroyed. The Byzantine Empire asked for help from the west and the Pope in Rome called for the First Crusade, in 1095 AD.
1079 AD	First record of Jewish settlement in Ireland.
1086 AD	"Doomsday Book" started by William I in England. It was a census. 10% of English population were recorded as slaves, in this census.
1087 AD	Turks capture the Levant.
1096 AD	First Crusade launched (1096-1099 AD), Jerusalem captured from Islam in 1099 AD, Crusaders slaughter all Muslims, Jews and many Christians living in Jerusalem.
1037 AD	Christian Kingdom of Castile (1037-1230 AD), established in Iberia.
1100 AD	Northern Crusade, Baltic Crusade, (1100-1300 AD); crusade to Christianize northern Europe.
1102 AD	England abolished slavery within England. Radhanite Jews had taken over the Roman Empires slave trade in Western Europe when the Roman Empire collapsed. Starting or continuing in the year 500 AD, they used the same routes of transporting European slaves from Europe to the slave markets in Spain, North Africa and the Middle-east.
1116 AD	All Greek communities in the interior of Anatolia abandon their territory, houses, and property and evacuate to Constantinople.
1139 AD	Kingdom of Portugal (1139- 1910 AD), established, a Christian kingdom on the west coast of Iberia
1147 AD	Second Crusade (1147-1149 AD), Jerusalem lost to Saladin and his Muslim armies. Christians allowed to leave by ship after loss.
1169 AD	Norman Invasion of Ireland, (1169-1541 AD), Strongbow invades in 1169, financed by Jewish moneylender. This invasion is followed by Henry II in 1170 AD.
1180 AD	Kurdish Sultan Saladin assumes control of Islam.
1182 AD	Jews were expelled from France, and went to German territory and Spain, Portugal
1189 AD	Third Crusade (1189- 1192 AD), Richard I, "Richard the Lion Hearted" defeats Saladin and captures Acre from the Muslims; he almost recaptures Jerusalem; Saladin died in Damascus in 1193 AD; Richard returned from the Holy Land by

land; he was taken prisoner in Vienna by the Christian King and is held for ransom. England pays by taxing everyone to death, and the "Legend of Robin Hood" takes root. The money obtained for ransom is eventually paid to Vienna and that money is used to build the walls and Gates of Vienna. These walls are same walls that hold back the Muslim Ottoman invasion of Austria in 1683 AD, and prevent the Ottoman Army from conquering Europe.

1200 AD	Mongol Hordes under Genghis Khan drive the Ashkenazi, Jewish, Khazar populations west into Northern and Eastern Europe, especially Poland, and western Ukraine.
1202 AD	Fourth Crusade (1202-1204 AD), Crusaders sack Christian Constantinople and go no farther.
1212 AD	Children's Crusade reignites re-conquista in Iberia.
1213 AD	Fifth Crusade (1213-1221 AD)
1228 AD	Sixth Crusade (1228-1229 AD) Crusader failure in Egypt, Crusade of Frederick II, a diplomatic crusade, Jerusalem returned to Christendom through negotiations.
1241 AD	Mongol Invasion of Hungary, and Mongol Invasion of Anatolia; gunpowder introduced into Europe by Mongol invasion, Khazars pushed west into Poland.
1244 AD	Crusader failure; Jerusalem lost again to Islamic Turks
1248 AD	Seventh Crusade (1248-1254 AD), this is the first Crusade of King Louis IX of France; he is defeated in Egypt.
1250 AD	End of the Medieval Warm Period, (950-1250 AD), population of Europe 73 Million; life expectancy 35 years old.
1251 AD	Shepherds Crusade in France; Jews murdered because of their wealth by crusaders in France; people believed the Jews had too much wealth and influence with the French aristocracy.
1255 AD	Last Mongol invasion of Anatolia, Turks defeated by Mongols after being chased towards Balkans.
1258 AD	Mongols sack Baghdad; this ended the Golden Age of Islam, and the Abbasid Caliphate ends.
1268 AD	Christian enclave of Antioch falls to Mamluks; thousands of Christians are butchered and enslaved by Egyptian Muslim Mamluks.
1270 AD	Eighth Crusade, (1270 AD), this is the second crusade of King Louis IX of France; he died of a French disease in Tunisia.
1271 AD	Ninth Crusade (1271-1272 AD), Prince Edward I of England lands in Acre in Palestine, but found the politics depressing; Christians were trading with Muslims across the Mediterranean. Muslims tried to assassinate him but they failed. Edward left to return to England, and became King Edward I, "Edward Longshanks" on his return due to his father's death.
1274 AD	First Mongol invasion of Japan; fails due to the "Divine Wind", a "kamikaze" typhoon.
1284 AD	Second Mongol invasion of Japan; again fails due to "Divine Wind", a "kamikaze" typhoon.

1286 AD	Kingdom of Alba, (843-1286 AD), ends; King Alexander dies in an accident leaving no heirs, all his children died before him; his female heir, his grand-daughter is "The Maid of Norway", Margaret. She was child and she died at sea en-route to Alba in 1290 AD.
1290 AD	All Jews expelled from England, about 2500 Jews, by King Edward I. Edward I confiscated all Jewish property and wealth; many Jews fled to Scotland which was not under Edwards thumb and settled in Edinburgh, many fled to France.
1291 AD	Fall of the Crusader Fortress at Acre (Haifa) to Mamluks; this ended the crusades and the adventures to the Outreemer. The Catholic Church stopped the donations for the Crusades in 1945 in Pueblo, Colorado. Go figure!
1292 AD	John Balliol (1249-1314 AD), is crowned **King of Scotland**, ending 6 years of dark uncertainty. He ruled as King from 1292-1296 AD. King Edward I kept trying to undermine him and have him treat Scotland as a vassal state of England. He was removed as King by a Scots appointed council of twelve because he was an ineffective King. This same council then signed "The Auld Alliance" with France.
1295 AD	"The Auld Alliance" signed with France; sort of a peace treaty, mutual support alliance.
1296 AD	King Edward I went to war with France and demands manpower and loyalty of Scotland; He doesn't get it so he attacks Berwick-on-Tweed, a trading city on the river Tweed that populated with Scots. He massacred 30,000 Scots civilians, and started the First Scots War of Independence (1296-1328 AD). John Balliol abdicated the throne, he was taken prisoner by King Edward and imprisoned in the "Tower of London".
1297 AD	English troops murder William Wallace's wife, and Wallace gathers and ever swelling army of Scots and attacks the English; he has a victory over King Edward I at Stirling Bridge, sacks York, England
1298 AD	William Wallace and his army is defeated at Falkirk by King Edward. The longbow comes into use in this battle.
1299 AD	Ottoman Caliphate (1299-1923 AD), begins; also known as the Turkish Empire. Othman I is the first Sultan.
1300 AD	Scots philosopher John Duns Scotus, (1266- 1308 AD), Scotus was a Franciscan friar, studying philosophy and God; Scotus wrote and spoke about the fact that we are free independent beings by nature, by God; free, independent people chose whether they wish to have authority for their community or themselves, and if they wish to have an authority, then the people choose the ruler to rule over them, but the power of the ruler always lies with the people who choose the leader; the leader cannot choose another leader to rule over the free, independent people, only the free, independent people have the power to choose another leader if they want one. The leader remains in power as their leader only as long as they will it. He articulated these views on political authority and they eventually became the foundation of the Scots Declaration of Independence, "The treaty of Abroath" in 1320. His philosophy of independent freedom, along with the "Treaty of Abroath"

are the basis of the United States "Declaration of Independence" put forth July 4, 1776, and The U.S. Constitution.

1300 AD	**Start of the "Little Ice Age"**, (1300-1850 AD), cold, rainy, snow; population of Europe 79 Million people; this was a "Bond Event Cooling" period. Bond Event Cooling periods occur every 1500 +/- 500 years, (or every 1000-2000 years). They are caused by North Atlantic Ocean cycles; it gets very cold, then it warms up again over a few centuries. Prior to this "Little Ice Age" it was colder around the time of the birth of Christ.
1305 AD	William Wallace was betrayed and captured by King Edward I; he was taken to the Tower of London, tortured, then executed, and quartered. His four parts were taken to the four Kingdoms of the Isles as an example. Monks collected his remains and buried him in Scotland.
1306 AD	Jews expelled from France for having undue influence over aristocrats and French government; Robert the Bruce crowned King of Scotland.
1309 AD	Catholic church declares Hungarians may not marry Khazars.
1314 AD	Battle of Bannockburn, Scots victory over King Edward I.
1315 AD	Famine, Starvation, Death, (1315-1317 AD), due to "Little Ice Age"; life expectancy 29 y.o.
1320 AD	Declaration of Arbroath; the Scots "Declaration of Independence" declared in writing.
1321 AD	Jews expelled from France for bringing the Black Plague to Europe.
1332 AD	Second Scots War of Independence, (1332-1357 AD).
1337 AD	Hundred Years War (1337 -1453 AD), begins; a war lasting 100 years between England, Burgundy, part of Brittany, Portugal, and Flanders against France, Scotland, Castile, Aragon, and Genoa.
1348 AD	**Plague**, Yersinia pestis, **"The Black Death"**, (1348-1375 AD), life expectancy falls to 17 years old; half the population of Europe dies of the plague. Jews expelled from Germany for bringing the Black Plague to Germany
1349 AD	Jews expelled from Hungary
1360 AD	More Jews expelled from Hungary
1362 AD	City of Erdine, (Adrianople) in Thrace, Turkey falls to Jihad leader Murad I, and becomes the capital city of the Ottoman Caliphate from 1363 to 1453 AD.
1389 AD	Battle of Kosovo, Ottoman Empire wins this battle and conquers Serbia.
1391 AD	All Jews expelled from France, about 2500 Jews, between 1391 and 1394 AD
1400 AD	Last Viking record of Greenland settlement; Little Ice Age makes occupation of Greenland impossible.
1421 AD	All Jews expelled from Hapsburg Austrian Empire.
1425 AD	Renaissance Music Era (1425-1550 AD), begins
1450 AD	Guttenberg printing press invented in Germany
1450 AD	Iroquois Confederacy established among Great Lakes tribes.
1453 AD	End of Hundred Years War.
1453 AD	Christian Constantinople falls to Muslim Ottoman Turks, end of Byzantine Empire, (395 AD- 1453 AD).

1454 AD	Ottoman Empire moves its capital city from Erdine, Turkey to Constantinople, and changes the name of the city of Constantinople to Istanbul.
1461 AD	Greece falls to Muslim Ottoman Empire, becomes part of Ottoman Caliphate in a dhimmi status from 1461 to 1832 AD.
1462 AD	Wallachia (Balkans), Wallachian prince Vlad III Dracula, the Impaler drives Muslim Ottoman back, but is eventually conquered. He impaled all the Muslim prisoners and dead, and created vast forests of impaled Jihadists. The story of "Count Dracula" is based on Vlad the Impaler.
1463 AD	Bosnia is conquered by the Muslim Ottoman Empire. Start of Ottoman – Venice Wars (1463-1503 AD).
1478 AD	"The Spanish Inquisition", (1478- 1834 AD), Jews and Muslims were expelled from the Iberian Peninsula. They had the choice of leaving with their stuff, or being converted to Christianity, or being executed and forfeiting all their stuff. The Jews expelled go to the Ottoman Caliphate, where they were welcomed with opened arms, "refugees welcome." The Muslims expelled went to many other Islamic countries. The Jews were allowed to leave with all their gold and quickly began to finance the Ottoman Empire in rebuilding and enlarging its armies. The equipment allowed the caliphate to continue in Jihad up through the Balkans towards Austria and Hungary.
1479 AD	Albania falls to Muslim conquest
1480 AD	20,000 Muslim Ottoman Turks attack Naples, Italy; they captured the Citadel and executed 800 Italian inhabitants, when they surrendered.
1482 AD	King Ferdinand and Queen Isabella fight and defeat Muslim Kingdom of Granada; this was the last of the Islamic strongholds on the Iberian Peninsula; Mediterranean Sea is still controlled by Islam.
1491 AD	All Jews and Muslims finally expelled from Spain
1492 AD	Christopher Columbus is sent west out into the unknown Atlantic Ocean by King Ferdinand and Queen Isabella in hopes of finding another route to the Orient that bypasses the Muslim controlled Mediterranean Sea, and Silk Road. Columbus discovers there is another two Continents out there, North and South America, with people living there.
1493 AD	Start of Croatian-Ottoman 100-year war, (1493-1593 AD). Ottomans never fully conquered Croatia.
1497 AD	All Jews expelled from Portugal.
1500 AD	Khanate of Crimea captures and exports Russian and Polish slaves to the Ottoman Empire Caliphate; between the years 1500 and 1700, over 2,000,000 Slavic slaves were exported to Islam through Crimea.
1509 AD	Henry VIII, (1491-1547 AD), became King of England; population 3 million. Splits with Rome and becomes head of the Church of England, 1st protestant Monarch of England.
1510 AD	Jews expelled from Germany
1516 AD	Ottoman Empire takes over Algeria, (1516-1830 AD), and forms the Barbary States.

1517 AD	Martin Luther starts the Protestant Reformation in Christendom, followed by Calvinist reformation.
1519 AD	Captain Magellan sets out from Seville to sail around the world; (1519-1522 AD).
1522 AD	Captain Magellan arrives back in Seville after sailing around the world; this proved once and for all time that the world was a sphere, and not flat. This event began to shatter the theory of Ptolemy.
1522 AD	Rhodes is captured by Muslim Ottomans; Malta was attacked, but never captured; Knights of Saint John held Malta and still do to the present time.
1529 AD	The Siege of Vienna (1529 AD), by Muslim Ottoman hordes; Muslim driven back but they devastate the countryside and make slaves of the population.
1536 AD	Francis I became the King of France; he made an alliance with the Muslim Ottomans in order to counter the power of the Hapsburg rulers based in Austria. France-Ottoman Alliance (1536-1798 AD).
1536 AD	French and Ottomans attack Italy (1536-1538 AD), using combined French and Ottoman fleets operating in the Mediterranean and Adriatic Sea.
1541 AD	Muslim Ottoman occupation of Buda, Hungary and the south and east of Hungary.
1542 AD	Mary Queen of Scots, (1542-1587 AD), became Queen of Scotland, (1542-1567 AD)
1543 AD	Copernicus (1473-1543 AD), puts forth his heliocentric solar system theory, about the Earth and planets revolving around the Sun; this put him at odds and in direct opposition to the teachings of Christianity that held the earth was the center of the universe. This theory was a blow to the ego of the Catholic church and to all, it held that mankind was not the center of the universe, and the universe did not revolve around man.
1547 AD	King Edward VI, (1537-1553 AD), became King of England
1550 AD	Painter, "Breugal the Elder" painted one of his masterpiece paintings, "Hunters in the Snow", a fine painting of life during "The Little Ice Age".
1550 AD	"Baroque Music Era", (1550-1750 AD), begins, Vivaldi, Bach, Handel
1551 AD	Jews expelled from Germany for bringing the Little Ice Age to Germany
1553 AD	Mary I, "Bloody Mary", (1516-1558 AD), became Queen of England; restores Roman Catholicism to Britain in a bloody fashion.
1556 AD	Plantations begin in Ireland, "The Plantations", (1556-1652 AD), Historical Irish Gaelic lands primarily in North and Central Ireland were seized by the Crown of England and settled by English landowners; Irish were kicked off, and English settlers brought in, leading to the Irish Rebellion of 1641 AD
1558 AD	Queen Elizabeth I, (1533-1603 AD) became Queen of England, returns England to Protestant faith 1567 AD James I, (1566-1625 AD), King of Scotland
1570 AD	The "seeds" of colonial serfdom were scattered in England, how to get rid of the poor, "undesirables"
1571 AD	The Battle of Lepanto, a naval battle won by the Holy League, defeating the Muslim Ottoman fleet.
1587 AD	Mary Queen of Scots was beheaded by Elizabeth I of England

1593 AD	End of the Ottoman-Croatian 100 Year war.
1593 AD	Start of the Austria-Ottoman Long War, (1593-1606 AD).
1600 AD	Sioux tribes move from Minnesota to the Dakotas, in North America.
1603 AD	Queen Elizabeth I (1533-1603 AD) dies.
1603 AD	Union of Crowns, Kingdom of Scotland, Kingdom of Ireland, and Kingdom of England unified under King James I (1566-1625 AD) of Scotland, Protestant Monarch
1603 AD	466 English sailors captured by Muslim Algerians between
1606 AD	Australian continent discovered by Dutch Europeans.
1607 AD	"The Flight of the Earls", The Ui Neill Earls, Catholics, descendants of Niall of the Nine Hostages fled Ireland with about 100 followers; they fled Ireland for the continent. This was the end of Brehon Gaelic law and the Gaelic way of life; the "Plantation system" imposed on Ireland destroyed Earls power and lands.
1608 AD	Galileo (1564-1642 AD), invents the telescope which improves observation of the universe
1609 AD	Another 466 British sailors seized by Algerian Muslims
1610 AD	Jamestown Settlement, first English settlement in North America, built on the Paspahegh tribes land, Powhatan Confederation. (Virginia)
1612 AD	East India Company (1612-1947 AD). founded.
1617 AD	Seven ships from the British Grand Banks fishing fleet captured, crew enslaved
1618 AD	Astronomer Kepler, (1571-1630 AD), confirms Copernicus' previous heliocentric solar system theory by observations with Galileos' telescope, and refines orbits from circular to elliptical
1618 AD	Thirty Years War (1618-1648 AD), first a religious war which was Catholics against Protestants in central Europe, then evolved into a war between Kingdom of France and The Hapsburgs in Austria. Anti-Hapsburg forces won.
1618 AD	London; street children and undesirables started being swept up off London streets for transportation to colonies.
1619 AD	First Black slaves, 20 were transported to Virginia to work alongside the white slaves in the tobacco fields. One black slave from Angola, Africa, Anthony Johnson, secured his freedom and started his own plantation, buying both white and black slaves to work it, in 1649.
1620 AD	Ottomans attacked Poland, (1620-1621 AD).
1622 AD	Powhatan Indians massacre 347 out of 1240 English in Virginia colony to get rid of them.
1625 AD	King Charles I, (1600-1649 AD), is Monarch of Great Britain, Catholic, executed by Parliament in 1649 AD.
1625 AD	27 English ships seized by Muslim ships near Plymouth, England
1627 AD	Iceland, Muslim's seized 400 people from shore of Iceland and enslave them in Algiers.
1630 AD	By this date 200,000 English and Irish undesirables had been shipped to colonies against their will.

1631 AD	Baltimore, Ireland, 237 people in town of Baltimore taken away as slaves by Muslims.
1633 AD	Ottomans attacked Poland, (1633-1634 AD).
1640 AD	John Punch an African slave who ran away from Virginia with two white slaves, was sentenced to slavery for his natural life when they were caught; he was the first African American slave to be a slave for life.
1641 AD	Irish Confederate Wars, or Eleven Years War (1641-1653 AD); Catholics take control of Ireland, The Irish Catholic Confederation, they had a green flag with a gold harp on it
1642 AD	English Civil War, (1642-1647 AD), Oliver Cromwell (protestant) supports Parliament against King Charles I (Catholic).
1645 AD	Ottoman War with Venice, Italy, (1645-1653 AD), over the island of Crete in the Eastern Mediterranean Sea.
1645 AD	Cornwall, England, 240 people captured and enslaved on Coast of Cornwall, taken away to Algiers
1649 AD	King Charles I looses the English Civil War, and his life. English Monarchy abolished, "Commonwealth of England" began.
1649 AD	Oliver Cromwell invaded Ireland 1649-1653 AD, at the end of English Civil War. Cromwell wins; 50% of Gaelic population dead; 50,000 deported as indentured servants and slaves to colonies in Caribbean and North America; Penal Laws were imposed on Catholics, for the next 271 years. The Penal laws imposed on Irelands and Scotland's Gaelic people by the English Crown and Parliament were removed and rescinded in 1920.
1650 AD	Cromwell defeated a Jacobite army in Scotland, and shipped 5,000 Scots prisoners off to the West Indies, Barbados as slaves.
1650 AD	300 black slaves out of a population 11,000 in Virginia
1656 AD	2000 Scots and Irish shipped as slaves to Jamaica
1657 AD	Ottomans attacked Austria, (1657-1683 AD), Ottomans and Austrians drive each other back and forth in Austrian-Hungarian area.
1657 AD	Jews allowed to live in England by order of Oliver Cromwell;
1660 AD	At around this date, Anton von Leeuwenhoek, (1632-1723 AD), developed the microscope in Deft, Holland, and reported three type of bacteria, rods, sphere, and spiral shaped; he called them "animalcules".
1678 AD	English scientist Robert Hooke, developed the "compound microscope", confirming what von Leeuwenhoek discovered. Some people studying life forms attempted to record the different microbes, but only as a hobby. This study lay dormant for the next 125-150 years. In the early 1800's, microscopes' were improved and began to be used by people studying medicine.
1678 AD	1,700 Scots Covenanters were sold into slavery and transported to the West Indies
1683 AD	The "Battle of Vienna"; Muslim Ottoman armies ravage the countryside from Buda-Pest up to Vienna, Austria. The city of Vienna was completely surrounded, the walls which were built by the ransom paid by English people for by "Richard the Lionheart" in 1189 AD, held back the Muslim Ottoman Turks until the city of Vienna was

rescued by a combined German, Saxon, Austrian Hapsburg, and Polish army led by Polish King Jon Sobieski of Poland. Ottomans were driven south; this was the peak of the Islamic Ottoman advance into Europe, and by the defeat it meant Europe would remain Christian; the Christian armies' were financed by the Vatican.

1683 AD   The Great Turkish War (1683-1699 AD), the Muslim Ottoman Turks were driven back from Austria, Hungary, and adjoining lands. Over the course of this war, the Muslims were driven back south from their conquered lands in the Balkans towards Greece. In Athens, Greece the Muslims used the Parthenon as an ammunition storage facility; it was hit with a mortar and the ammunition exploded and partially destroyed it. Many Muslims from the Balkans retreated from the Balkans after the Christian armies retook the territory and immigrated to Palestine which was under Ottoman Muslim control.

1687 AD   Sir Isaac Newton, a physicist developed the principles of mechanics and applied them to planetary orbits, further building upon Copernicus' heliocentric theory. Newton invents Calculus.

1688 AD   Scots Stuart King James was deposed by the English Mary and William of Orange, (Netherlands); this started the Jacobite wars in Scotland; (James=Jacobus=Jacobite), fought in order to restore a Stuart King to the throne of Great Britain; the Stuart line was the line of kings following William Wallace's First War of Scots Independence from England.

1689 AD   William of Orange, (1650-1702 AD), ruled England, 1689-1702 AD

1690 AD   The Battle of the Boyne, (July 11, 1690 AD), across Boyne River from Drogheda in Meath County; this was a Battle between James II (Jacobite), (catholic), 26,000 troops, and the English Parliament, (protestant), 36,000 troops; it was an ethnic and sectarian fight; Catholics lost ensuring England remained protestant, it is commemorated by the Order of Orange Men, on July 12, every year. Catholics banned from owning weapons, banned from legal profession, and land was confiscated; Catholics were tortured until they converted to Protestantism. 1500 Irish dead, 750 English dead.

1698 AD   By this year, the English were importing a higher ratio of black slaves to whites, 64 black slaves were imported for every 100 white Irish, Scots or English slaves, African slaves were now becoming lifetime slaves as opposed to term-limited slaves, due to the economics involved, lifetime slaves were a better long term investment, especially when mortality rates were lowered.

1699 AD   Ottoman Empire stagnation, (1699-1828 AD).

1700 AD   Beginning of the Period known as the Scottish Enlightenment, (1700-1830), during this period many inventions were made in Scotland and many philosophers expounded on common sense philosophical ideas.

1702 AD   Queen Anne, (1665-1714 AD), became Queen of England, Scotland, Wales and Ireland. She was brought up as an Anglican, Protestant, and was the last of the Stuart line of succession, The House of Stuart. She was followed as monarch by her second cousin, George I, (1660-1727 AD), who was a protestant and prince of the House of Hannover, Germany.

1707 AD	The Act of Settlement, this act in Great Britain prohibited Roman Catholics from ever inheriting the throne and monarchy of Great Britain.
1707 AD	The Act of Union in Great Britain; The Kingdoms of England, Wales, Scotland and Ireland were combined into the sovereign state of Great Britain. Queen Anne continued to rule until her death. She had no children so her second cousin George I, of the House of Hannover, became King after she passed away.
1710 AD	Second Russian-Turkish Muslim Ottoman War, (1710-1711 AD).
1714 AD	House of Hanover, State of Hesse Germany takes over British Throne and Monarchy; end of the Stuart Line of the Monarchy. George I is King, first of the Hanoverian Kings of Great Britain.
1715 AD	There were continued and intensified Jacobite rebellions in an attempt to restore the Stuart House to the throne; uprisings occurred in Cornwall, and Devon on the Cornish Peninsula, in Wales, and on the west coast of England in addition to Scotland. Loyalties were mixed in many of these areas, and the Hanoverians arrested the rebel leaders very quickly after ascending to the throne. After putting down rebellions, the Hanoverians started of Scots' Highland Clearances; this was an ethnic cleansing of Gaelic Scots from northern Scotland to the lowlands and to the North American continent. Most Scots moved to the Appalachian Mountains and Newfoundland. In the Appalachian Mountains the Scots were used as a buffer between the hostile Native American tribes and the English on the coastal lowlands between the Atlantic and the Appalachian Mountain chain. The areas of rebellion in Great Britain were the same areas that had been conquered by Niall of the Nine Hostages in the 400's AD.
1715 AD	Beginning of "Classical Music Era", (1715-1825 AD), Bach, Beethoven, Hadyn, Mozart
1735 AD	Third Russian-Ottoman War, (1735-1739 AD).
1727 AD	George II, (1683-1760 AD), became Monarch of Great Britain, after the death of George I
1743 AD	Mayer Rothschild (1743-1812 AD), is born in Frankfurt, Germany; "Roth-Schild"; Roth means "Red", Schild means "shield", like a warriors shield on the battlefield. Mayer Rothschild is an Ashkenazi, Khazar Edomite Jew. The "Roth", "Red" is for "Esau", "Edom", the baby that was born "red" to Rebecca and Isaac. The twin brother of Jacob, (Israel). When he is older and amasses wealth, Mayer Rothschild hangs the Red Star of David above his door in Germany. The Star of David is the same symbol from the shields of the Ashkenazi Khazars 775 years earlier, when they were defeated by the Russians.
1745 AD	End of the Jacobite Wars in Scotland after the defeat of the Highlanders at Culloden, Scotland; clearances and ethnic cleansing of Celts Gaelic clans in Scotland continued; transportation and emigration continued to North America by Scots and some Irish.
1754 AD	French and Indian War in North America, (1754-1763 AD); a war between France and England in North America as part of a European War, the Seven Years

War; different native American tribes fought on different sides, fighting up and down Hudson River.

1757 AD   British East India Company rules India, (1757-1858 AD), using private armies and setting up trade after defeating Bengals of India.

1757 AD   Scot Philosopher David Hume, (1711-1776 AD), wrote a treatise on "The Natural History of Religion", where he puts forth the argument that our psychological machinery as primates which is part of our human nature, works on our rational and irrational fears, our anxieties about the dread of the unknown future, and when prompted by our life's circumstances produces a belief in invisible spirits or powers who control fear-inducing events in our environment, this is done by means of imagination. We imagine God in order to control our fear of the unknown.

1760 AD   George III, (1738-1820 AD) also of the House of Hesse, became Monarch of Great Britain after the death of King George II.

1763 AD   Mayer Rothschild pursues business with the House of Hesse, from Frankfurt Jewish ghetto.

1768 AD   Fourth Russian-Ottoman War, (1768-1774 AD).

1775 AD   Scots philosopher Adam Smith, (1723- 1790 AD), wrote "The Wealth of Nations", a treatise on political economy, where he investigated the behavior of Homo economicus within a political context. Economic policy is a bad policy if it has morally unacceptable consequences. He wrote other works on "The History of Astronomy", and "The Theory of Moral Sentiments", he was a mathematician, a scientist, and a philosopher working from Glasgow University.

1775 AD   American War of Independence, The Revolutionary War, (1775-1783 AD); 70,000 American dead, 50,000 British Dead

1776 AD   Declaration of Independence, July 4, 1776; 13 American colonies declare Independence from Great Britain.

Yankee Doodle

Farth'r and I went down to camp, along with Captain Goodin,
and there we saw the men and boys as thick as hasty pudding,

Yankee Doodle keep it up, Yankee Doodle Dandy,
mind the music and the step and with the girls be handy.

And there was General Washington upon a strapping stallion,
giving orders to his men; I guess there was a million.

Yankee Doodle keep it up, Yankee Doodle Dandy,
mind the music and the step and with the girls be handy.

1780 AD	Beginning of "Romantic Era" (1780-1950 AD) of music; Rossini, Chopin, Wagner, Brahms, Schubert, Mendelssohn, Puccini
1783 AD	Iroquois Confederacy ends, (1450-1783 AD).
1783 AD	Peace of Paris; treaty signed between Great Britain and The United States of America, bringing an end to The Revolutionary War.
1787 AD	Fifth Russian Ottoman War, (1787-1792 AD).
1788 AD	Great Britain establishes a penal colony at Botany Bay, (Sydney, Australia), (1788-1850 AD); convicts from Great Britain are "transported" for their "crimes". This was set up to settle the Australian continent with British people, and get rid of "undesirables" in England.
1788 AD	The United States Constitution ratified

The Constitution of the United States of America

We the People of the United States, in order to form a more perfect Union, establish Justice, insure domestic tranquility, provide for the common defence, promote the general welfare, and secure the blessings of liberty to ourselves and our posterity, do ordain and establish this constitution for the United States of America.

There are seven Articles to the Constitution followed by twenty-seven amendments. The first ten amendments to the constitution were ratified on December 15, 1791, and form what is known as "The Bill of Rights".

Amendment I

Congress shall make no law respecting an establishment of religion, or prohibiting the free exercise thereof, or abridging the freedom of speech, or of the press, or of the right of the people peacefully to assemble, and to petition the government for a redress of grievances.

Amendment II

A well regulated militia, the right of the people to keep and bear arms, as being necessary to the security of a free state, shall not be infringed.

Amendment III

No soldier shall in time of peace be quartered in any house, without the consent of the owner, nor in time of war, but in a manner to be prescribed by law.

Amendment IV

The right of the people to be secure in their persons, houses, papers, and effects, against unreasonable searches and seizures, shall not be violated, and no warrants shall issue, but upon probable cause, supported by oath or affirmation, and particularly describing the place to be searched, and the person or things to be seized.

Amendment V

No person shall be held to answer for a capital, or otherwise infamous crime, unless on a presentation or indictment of a grand jury, except in cases arising in the land or naval forces, or in the militia, when in actual service in time of war or public danger; nor shall any person be subject for the same offence to be twice put in jeopardy of life or limb; nor shall be compelled in any criminal case to be a witness against himself, nor be deprived of life, liberty or property, without due process of the law, nor shall private property be taken for public use, without just compensation.

Amendment VI

In all criminal prosecutions, the accused shall enjoy the right to a speedy public trial, by an impartial jury of the state and district wherein the crime shall have been committed; which district shall have been previously ascertained by law, and to be informed of the nature and cause of the accusation; to be confronted with the witnesses against him; to have compulsory process for obtaining witnesses in his favor, and to have the assistance of counsel for his defence.

Amendment VII

In suits at common law, where the value in controversy shall exceed twenty dollars, the right of trial by jury shall be preserved, and no fact tried by a jury, shall be otherwise re-examined in any court of the United States, than according to the rules of common law.

Amendment VIII

Excessive bail shall not be required, nor excessive fines imposed, nor cruel and unusual punishments inflicted.

Amendment IX

The enumeration in the Constitution, of certain rights, shall not be construed to deny or disparage others retained by the people.

Amendment X

The powers not delegated to the United States by the Constitution, nor prohibited by it to the states, is reserved to the states respectively, or to the people.

The XI-XVII Amendments to the Constitution clarified certain previous Amendments and Articles from 1795 to the present.

Amendment XI

The Judicial Power of the United States shall not be construed to extend to any suit in law or equity, commenced or prosecuted against one of the United States by citizens of another state, or by citizens or subjects of any foreign state.

Amendment XII (1804)

The electors shall meet in their respective stated and vote for president and vice president, one of whom, at least shall not be an inhabitant of the same state with themselves; they shall name in their ballots the person voted for as president, and in distinct ballots the person voted for as vice president, and they shall make distinct lists of all persons voted for as president, and of all persons voted for as vice president, and of the number of votes for each, which lists they shall sign and certify, and transmit sealed to the seat of the government of the United States, directed to the president of the Senate; The president of the Senate, shall in the presence of the Senate and the House of Representatives, open all the certificates and the votes shall then be counted; the person having the greatest number of votes for president, shall be president, if such number be a majority of the whole number of Electors appointed; and if no person have such a majority, then from the persons having the highest numbers not exceeding three on the list of those voted for as president, the House of Representatives shall choose immediately, by ballot, the President. But in choosing the president, the votes shall be taken by states, the representation from each state having one vote; a quorum for this purpose shall consist of a member or members from two-thirds of the states, and a majority of all states shall be necessary to a choice. [And if the House of Representatives shall not choose a president whenever the right of choice shall devolve up on them, before the fourth day of March next following, then the Vice President shall act as President, as in the case of the death or other constitutional disability of the President]. The person having the greatest number of votes as Vice President, shall be the Vice President, if such number be in a majority of the whole number of electors appointed, and if no person have a majority, then from the two highest numbers on the list, the Senate shall choose the Vice President, a quorum for the purpose shall consist of two-thirds of the whole number of Senators, and a majority of the whole number shall be necessary to a choice. But no person constitutionally ineligible to the office of President shall be eligible to that of the Vice President of the United States. After this process is complete, and the choice for both President and Vice President is made, the choice is to forwarded to the King or Queen of Great Britain, the King of Saudi Arabia, the Chancellor in Berlin, the Prime Minister of Israel and the Bilderberger group for its approval or rejection of the choice, upon rejection the choice for President and Vice President is then turned over to Cheech and Chong.

1789 AD

French Revolution, (1789-1799 AD), begins, Mayer Rothschild's business was expanding, he had a money bureau, dealt in antiquities, acted as a forwarding agent, and traded in wine. The bulk of his business was importing manufactured goods from England, manly cloth products, that would be resold. As the French Revolutionary wars went on he made enormous profits from the imports from England, due to the disruptions caused by the wars. He proposed a business proposition to his friend the Landgrave of the House of Hesse. The House of Hesse was supplying England with Hessian troops for large sums of money, and Rothschild was importing manufactured goods from England. His proposition was so to let the two-way movement cancel each other out, and pocket the commissions both ways on the bills of exchange.

1792 AD	French Revolutionary Wars (1792-1802 AD)
1798 AD	Napoleon I, French leader captures Egypt. Germany was entirely dependent on Britain for its cotton goods. Mayer Rothschild's son Nathan traveled to England to buy directly from the mills.
1800 AD	Khazan, Ashkenazi Jews living in the Russian Empire begin a westward movement into Europe towards Prussia, Poland and the Baltic Sea
1801 AD	First American-Muslim Ottoman Caliphate War, (1801-1805 AD), or The First Barbary War
1802 AD	secularization and mediatization of parts of the Holy Roman Empire into separate Imperial areas under Imperial princes
1803 AD	Napoleonic War (1803-1815 AD)
1804 AD	Napoleon Bonaparte is appointed Emperor of the First French Empire
1804 AD	Austrian Empire comes into existence from Hapsburg Lands
1806 AD	Holy Roman Empire, 1st Reich in Germany, comes to an end and is dissolved; Napoleon defeated the 1st Reich and now turns his attention to the House of Hesse who supplied troops to oppose him. The House of Hesse had to get rid of all the money, gold, treasure, before Napoleon confiscated it. Some of the treasure chests were hidden in different places; four of the treasure chests were delivered to Rothschild house, in the chests were the ledgers, of debtors, and balance sheets; all the interest that was to be paid on loans. Rothschild hid them from the French. Napoleon then ordered a blockade on England. Rothschild was now chief banker of the House of Hesse and the blockade made Rothschild import business even more valuable. Nathan Rothschild in London was involved in the stock market and making well on gold bullion transactions. The other sons collected the debts owed the House of Hesse in a carriage with a hidden compartment. This money was sent to England and Nathan obtained 12% in interest, while the House of Hesse only received the 3-4% that they were owed from the debtors.
1806 AD	Britain takes over Cape of Good Hope from the Netherlands; Boers move inland to create their own states. Arc de Triumph construction started in Paris, France
1806 AD	Sixth Russian-Ottoman War, (1806-1812 AD)
1809 AD	Nathan Rothschild now a naturalized British citizen, established his own bank, N.M. Rothschild and sons. He was receiving enormous amounts from Frankfurt to invest in London stock market; but Russia and Portugal were getting very upset with not being able to conduct trade with Britain. Napoleon ousted the House of Braganza, and Britain sent troops to the Iberian Peninsula to fight the French, commanded by the Duke of Wellington.
1810 AD	Population of Britain 20,000,000. Annual tax revenue in Britain 150,000,000 pounds Sterling. The British economy slid into its worst crises ever. Nathan saw that the East India Company had 800,000 pounds Sterling in Gold to sell, and he bought it all. The British Government then told him they must have the Gold for

the Duke of Wellington's army in Iberia. He sold the Gold to the British government at a very large profit using the House of Hesse money that had been sent to him.

1812 AD	War of 1812, United States War with Great Britain as part of Napoleonic Wars in Europe; Washington, D.C. attacked by British troops, White House burned down; "The Star Spangled Banner" was written be Francis Scot Key, which eventually becomes the US national anthem. British are defeated by Andrew Jackson in the Battle of New Orleans. Mayer Rothschild passed away in September 1812, the French Army suffered a terrible defeat in Russia, it froze to death; the British were now embarked on a fight from Iberia through France to the Low Countries; and they needed more Gold. The British Government turned to the Rothschild for a scheme to obtain the Gold for Wellington. So the Rothschild's went to Holland and bought up the French gold currency at a great rate of exchange, shipped it to Wellington and he used it to buy supplies on his march north, he took Paris, then Napoleon abdicated and went into exile on Elba. Nathan received well over a million pounds sterling in commissions for these transactions.
1814 AD	The Rothschild enabled Louis the XVIII to restore the throne and monarchy in 1814 after Peace was restored to Europe, but Napoleon broke out of jail on Elba. King Louis fled and Napoleon again was in charge of France and her armies. Wellington defeated Napoleon a second time at the Battle of Waterloo in 1815. It was said that the Rothschild's were personally on the battlefield to see which side was going to win, then used carrier pigeons to report the event to his bank in London which was waiting to decide where to put the money, on Britain or France. After the war the Rothschild owned the wealthiest bank in Europe, if not the world.
1815 AD	Second American-Muslim Ottoman Caliphate War, The Second Barbary War; the battle of Waterloo; Napoleon is defeated by German and British armies in Waterloo, Belgium, he was deported and transported by the British to the island of St. Helenas in the south Atlantic Ocean where he died. The five Rothschild brothers, all with red hair, and corpulent bodies, started to set up banking branches in the five capitals of Europe; Amschel in Frankfurt, Nathan in London, James in Paris, Salomon in Vienna, and Carl in Naples from 1815 to 1825. France set up a Constitutional Monarchy.
1820 AD	George IV, (1762-1830 AD), became monarch of Great Britain after death of King George III
1821 AD	Mexico becomes an independent nation from Spain; subsidies to the Apaches and Comanche's are stopped, and the native Americans go on the warpath to support themselves.
1824 AD	Republic of Mexico, The United Mexican States are formed.
1825 AD	Amschel Rothschild in Frankfurt, the German Confederation, began to finance factories, roads, and railroads for the German Confederation. The Rothschild had a courier service that was increasingly used by the governments of Europe to

transmit mail and correspondence. As was the custom, many people handling the mail read the correspondence, including the Rothschild agents. This gave them the ability to stay up on current events, and capitalize on them as they came along. After the French Revolution and the Napoleonic Wars, European leadership again reverted to aristocrats and kings; many were financed by Rothschild banking interests and their financial business schemes, but radical forces in opposition to the conservative aristocracy were growing among the masses of Europeans, tired of the old semi-Feudalistic society, and wanting of Constitutions, to define their Rights as Men.

1827 AD	Muslim Dey of Algiers strikes French Ambassador with fly swatter
1828 AD	Seventh Russian-Ottoman War (1828-1829 AD)
1830 AD	William IV, (1765-1837 AD), became monarch of Great Britain after death of King George IV
1830 AD	French troops land in Algeria, they begin colonization of Algeria, this ends Islamic piracy and Islamic control of the Mediterranean Sea routes in the western Mediterranean Sea that had existed from the year 711 AD until 1830 AD, (1119 years of Islamic control of the Mediterranean Sea).
1833 AD	Great Britain abolished slavery.
1836 AD	Texas Revolution, The Alamo, in Texas is lost to Mexican Army sent to put down Texas rebellion. The Arc de Triumph is inaugurated in Paris, France.
1837 AD	British Queen Victoria, (1819-1901 AD), begins rule as Queen of Great Britain after death of King William IV, Queen Victoria was the last of the monarchs of the House of Hannover. Queen Victoria married Prince Albert, (1819-1861 AD), of the House of Saxe-Coburg and Gotha, German Confederation, in 1840. Their son Edward became King Edward VII of Great Britain, House of Saxe-Coburg and Gotha when she died in 1901 AD.
1839 AD	By 1839, the Rothschild Family was the only power in Europe, controlling the finances of all of Europe. There was massive corruption and profits for a few 100,000 of people allied with the family. The two most intelligent and astute political and sociological observers at the time, Marx, and Tocqueville called Europe a "joint stock company" with Rothschild at the center. He no longer needed the state, but the states had need of him. The family was sinking vast amounts of money into financing railroads all over the continent, and lend a vast amount of money to the United States.
1840 AD	Physician-Poet, Oliver Wendell Holmes suggests germs cause the disease known as Puerperal Fever being transmitted from one new mother to another. Eventually it was discovered that thegerm known as the microbe Group B Strepptococci, or Streptococcus Agalactiae was responsible.
1845 AD	Start of "The Great Famine" in Ireland, (The Irish Potato Famine (1845-1852 AD), 30% of Irish population is gone during this period; 1.5 million Irish die of starvation, 1.5 million immigrate; there is mass Gaelic migration out of Ireland to North America, Scotland, Canada, and Mexico. The potato famine was caused by a Eukaryotic, fungus like, Oomycota, " a water mold" called Phytopthora infestans,

that spread and destroyed the potato crop in Ireland, Highland Scotland, and parts of Europe.

1845 AD	The United States annexed Texas into the Union from Mexico
1846 AD	The Mexican-American War (1846-1848 AD)
1848 AD	Revolutions of 1848 in Europe; violent uprisings that resulted in a missed opportunity to set Europe on a liberal constitutional path; "serfdom" was ended, peasants are not forcefully and legally tied to the landowners; mass migration follows to the United States, in the following decades; Karl Marx and Engels published their philosophical economic treatise in a book called "The Communist Manifesto", written in Frankfurt, which didn't affect the 1848 revolutions but inspired the future Russian Revolution of 1917. The revolutions throughout Europe expanded the civil rights of masses and gave many more people the right to vote in France, it brought the problems of constitutionalism, civil rights, the social question and nationalism to the forefront, that conservatives were forced to face, from then on, towards the twentieth century. The conservatives continued to rule but in a diminished fashion. The questions of how to reconcile social justice with individual liberty remained unanswered and kicked down the road to the twentieth century.
1848 AD	Franz-Joseph I (1830-1916 AD), became Emperor Franz Joseph became Emperor of Austria, and King of Hungary, Croatia and Bohemia. His nephew, Archduke Franz Ferdinand, who was to succeed him, was assassinated in Sarajevo in 1914, which started World War I.
1850 AD	The "Little Ice Age" ends, (1300-1850 AD)
1853 AD	Eighth Russian-Muslim Ottoman War, (1853-1856 AD), England and France go in on the Muslim side against Russia, resulting in the Crimean War; "The Charge of the Light Brigade" poem was written after this war. Rothschild Family provided 16,000,000 British pounds Sterling loans to finance this war, and provided charity in different areas of Europe.
1857 AD	Indian Mutiny against British East India Company
1858 AD	British Crown takes direct control of India, (1858-1947 AD); Rudyard Kipling wrote a poem about this period in British-Indian history. It is the following;

You may talk o' gin and beer
when you're quartered safe out 'ere,
An you're sent to penny-fights an alder shot it;
But when it comes to slaughter
you will do your work on water,
An' you'll lick the bloomin' boots of 'im that's got it.

Now in Inja's sunny clime,
where I used to spend my time
A-servin of 'Er Majesty the Queen,
Of all them blackfaced crew
The finest man I knew was our regimental bhisti, Gunga Din.

Chronicum Holocenum

He was "Din! Din! Din!
You limpin' lump o'brick-dust, Gunga Din!
Hi! Slippy hitherao!
Water, Get it! Paneee lao!
You squidgy-nosed old idol, Gunga Din.

The uniform he 'e wore was nothin' much before,
An' rather less then 'arf o' that be'hind,
For o' piece o' twisty rag
An' a goatskin water-bag
was all the field equipment e' could find.
When the sweat'in troop train lay
In a sidin' through the day,
where the 'eat would make your bloomin' eyebrows crawl,
We shouted "Harry By!"
Till our throats were bricky-dry,
Then we wopped 'im 'cause 'e couldn't serve us all.
It was Din! Din! Din!
You 'eathen, where the mischief 'ave you been?
You put some juldee in it
Or, I'll marrow you this minute
If you don't fill up my helmet, Gunga Din!"

I shan't forgit the night
When I dropped be'ind the fight
With a bullet where my belt-plate should 'a 'been.
I was chokin' mad with thirst,
An the man that spied me first
Was our good old grinnin' gruntin' Gunga Din.
E lifted up me head an plugged me where I bled,
An he guv me 'arf-a-pint o' water green;
It was crawlin and it stunk,
But of all the drinks I've drunk,
I'm gratefullest to one from Gunga Din.
It was Din! Din! Din!
'Ere's a beggar with a bullet through 'is spleen;
'E's chawin up the ground,
An' 'e's kickin' all around:
For Gawd's sake git the water Gunga Din!'

"E carried me away
To where a dooli lay,
An a bullet come an' drilled the beggar clean.

'E put me safe inside,
An just before 'e died,
I 'ope you liked your drink", sez Gunga Din.

So, I'll meet him later on
At the place where 'e is gone
Where it's always double drill and no canteen.
E'll be squattin on the coals
Givin drink to poor damned souls,
An' I'll get a swig in hell from Gunga Din!
Yes, Din! Din! Din!
You Lazarushian-leather Gung Din!
Though I've belted you and flayed you,
    By the living God that made you,
    You're a better man than I am Gunga Din!

1858 AD	Numerous uprisings against Turks in Balkans, (1858-1876 AD)
1859 AD	Geomagnetic Solar Storm of 1859, "The Carrington Event" was a solar storm that took down telegraph systems worldwide; people got shocked and could sent Morse code without touching keys. Charles Darwin, (1809-1882 AD) published a book on evolution, "The Origen of the Species"
1860 AD	U.S. Civil War (1860-1865 AD), begins between the industrialized North and Agricultural South
1861 AD	Physician Ignaz Semmelweis, published a paper on "The Cause, Concept, and Prophylaxis of Childbed Fever", after he drastically cut childbirth deaths by applying antiseptic techniques.
1862 AD	"Flying Scotsman rail service begins between Edinburgh and London
1865 AD	U.S. Civil War (1860-1865 AD) ends, 700,000 to 900,000 dead; slavery is abolished; territory of the "Union" intact; Confederate States of America disbanded and readmitted to the US. Gregor Mendel, (1822-1884 AD) publishes his work on genetics.
1865 AD	**Amendment XIII**

Neither slavery nor involuntary servitude, except as punishment for crime whereof the party shall have been duly convicted, shall exist within the United States, or any place subject to their jurisdiction.

1866 AD	Austro-Prussian War, a seven-week war fought between Austria and Prussia, Otto von Bismarck led Prussian forces and Ludwig Ritter von Benedek led the Northern Austrian forces. The main battle was lost at Koniggratz, near the Elbe River in what today is the Czech Republic. The Prussians called this seven-week war a "Blitzkrieg". General Benedek (1804-1881 AD), was a General under Emperor Franz-Joseph I, (Frank-Joseph I). Ludwig von Benedek was a Hungarian born in Sopron, Hungary by the Austrian border in the land known as Burgenland. He was blamed for the loss of the war, but the Emperor told him to remain silent

about it and he did and was retired to Graz, Austria near the Hungarian border and Sopron. Many people from Burgenland emigrated to the Americas from the 1850's until the 1880's.

1868 AD

Amendment XIV

Section 1.

All persons born or naturalized in the United States and subject to the jurisdiction thereof, are citizens of the United States and of the State wherein they reside. No state shall make of enforce any law which shall abridge the privileges or immunities of citizens of the United States; nor shall any state deprive any person of life, liberty, or property, without due process of the law, nor deny to any person within the jurisdiction the equal protection of the laws.

Section 2.

Representatives shall be apportioned among the several state according to their respective numbers, counting the whole number of persons in each state excluding Indians not taxed. But when the right to vote at any election for the choice of electors for President and Vice President of the United States, Representatives in Congress, the Executive and Judicial officers of a state, or the members of the Legislature thereof, is denied to any of the male inhabitants of the state, being twenty-one years of age, and citizens of the United States, or in any way abridged, except for participation in rebellion, or other crime, the basis of representation therein shall be reduced in the proportion which the number of such male citizens shall bear to the whole number of male citizens twenty-one years of age in such state.

Section 3.

No person shall be a Senator or a representative in Congress, or elector of President and Vice President, or hold any office, civil, or military, under the United States, or under any State, who, having previously taken an oath, as a member of Congress, or as an officer of the United States, or as member of any state legislature, or as an executive or judicial officer of any state, to support the Constitution of the United States, shall have engaged in insurrection or rebellion against the same, or given aid or comfort to the enemies thereof. But Congress may by a vote of two thirds of each house, remove such disability.

Section 4.

The validity of the public debt of the United States, authorized by law, including debts incurred for payment of pensions and bounties for services in suppressing insurrection or rebellion, shall not be questioned. But neither the United States nor any State shall assume or pay any debt or obligation incurred in aid of insurrection or rebellion against the United States, or any claim for the loss or emancipation of any slave; but all such debts, obligations and claims shall be held illegal and void.

Section 5.
The Congress shall have power to enforce, by appropriate legislation, the provisions of this article.

1868 AD	Benjamin Disraeli became prime minister of Great Britain
1869 AD	Black Friday in the Stock Market, two speculators in the NY market, Mr. Gould and Fisk, tried to corner the gold market and crashed the market and the economy. Suez Canal opened.
1870 AD	Joseph Lister demonstrated the value of antiseptics in operating rooms, using aqueous "phenol" to reduce the number of harmful "germs", microbes.
1870 AD	Austrian Empire is defeated by Prussia, and loses territory
1870 AD	

Amendment XV

Section 1.
The right of citizens of the United States to vote shall not be denied or abridged by the United States or by any state on account of race, color, or previous condition or servitude.

Section 2.
The Congress shall have the power to enforce this article by appropriate legislation.

1871 AD	Germany unifies under the 2nd Reich, First Chancellor Prussian Otto von Bismarck (1815-1890 AD), also known as The German Empire. Bismarck engineered wars that unified the German Imperial states into the German Empire, the 2nd Reich.
1873 AD	Financial Panic of 1873; a worldwide financial panic which resulted in a 20-year depression; British Prime Minister Benjamin Disraeli buys one half of the Suez Canal stock, this is financed by the Rothschild banking family.
1875 AD	"Modern Music Era", (1875-1975 AD), begins, Strauss, Debussy
1876 AD	Battle of the Little Big Horn, Dakota Sioux Territory; General Custer and part of 7th US Cavalry annihilated by Sioux Indians.
1877 AD	Crazy Horse war chief surrenders to US Army and is murdered by cavalry soldiers
1877 AD	Ninth Russian-Ottoman War (1877-1878 AD)
1879 AD	Anglo-Zulu war in South Africa
1880 AD	First Boer War (1880-1881 AD) in South Africa
1880 AD	The French Rothschild family offered to set up an anti-Jewish bank for the Catholics, the plan was blessed by the Pope, Leo XIII, and French Catholics were persuaded to invest their savings in this bank, the Union Generale. Shares rose and it expanded to the Austrian Landerbank. The Austrian Landerbank was in direct competition with the Vienna Rothschild banking interests, and the Vienna Rothschilds retaliated, by buying up shares and dumping them. This caused the Union Generale to collapse and thousands and thousands of Catholics lost their

savings. This created a lot of anti-Semitism in Europe. "The Jewish Question" began to be discussed more openly and with more emotional fervor.

1881 AD   The Czar Alexander II of Russia was assassinated; the terrorists who had planned the murder had met in the apartment of a Jewish woman, Jessica Helfman. When this information was released by the police, violent "pogroms" broke out. The new Tsar Alexander III encouraged to riots and pogroms against the Jews. He believed international Jewry was involved in a plot to end the monarchy system of government. The Russians instituted new Laws against the Jews living in Russia, they were called the May Laws. These laws forbid Jews from leaving the pale of settlement, no Jew could be an administrator, no Jew could become a lawyer, no Jew could own land, no books could be printed in Hebrew, all Jewish schools were closed, no Jews could marry a Christian unless they converted to Christianity, there was no appeal for any court sentences imposed on Jews, only a handful of Jews could attend a University. In December of 1881, 250,000 destitute Jewish families left Russia heading west to western Europe, Poland, Prussia, Germany, Austria-Hungarian Empire, and Romania, and Britain, many went on to Canada and the Americas. The Tsar said, "Let them carry their poison where they will", he was delighted to see them leave. Edmund Rothschild sent some of these displaced Jews to an agricultural school in Palestine, and eventually purchased more land there for them in Ekron. It worked out and for the next 52 years he formed new colonies in Palestine for the willing Jews. Palestine was a wasteland at this time the Muslim Arabs had let Palestine go to hell over the centuries. The resettled Jews in Palestine planted successful wine orchards, dug wells, founded industries making glass and glass products, made perfume scents. Rothschild visited Palestine numerous times on his yacht mooring at Jaffa. He offered to buy the wailing wall from the Arabs but the deal never went through due to mysterious opposition from the rabbi's there.

1882 AD   British troops occupy Egypt after Egypt defaulted on its debts to European banks; anti-European riots breakout in Alexandria, Egypt; Britain tries to end the slave trade in Islamic Egypt and East Africa for the next few decades. British forces occupy Egypt and Sudan from 1882 until 1945. Slavery finally "officially" abolished in 1963, by King Saud of Arabia at the request of U.S. President John Fitzgerald Kennedy.

1882 AD   Large scale Jewish diaspora migration to Palestine begins; by 1914, there were about 60,000 Jews living in Palestine. They were spread out in 40 settlements; 30,000 of these refugees were from the lands of the Russian Empire, Ukraine, they were subjects of the Czar. The other 30,000 were Ottoman Empire subjects; all lived as dhimmi under Sharia law while there. These immigrants were supported by wealthy Zionist Europeans led by the Rothschild banking family. Edmond Rothschild of the French part of family financed and encouraged destitute European Jews to migrate to Palestine, and taught them how to "make the desert bloom." The James Mayer de Rothschild Hospital was built in Jerusalem.

1883 AD	The Rothschild interests lend the Tsar of Russia money in exchange for the Baku oil field concessions, which surpasses Rockefellers' Stand Oil Company. The Baku, Azerbaijan oil fields produced the most oil in the world up to 2005 AD. Baku is located on the western shore of the Caspian Sea in the Caucasus area.
1885 AD	General Gordon (1833-1885 AD), was killed by a Muslim Army led by self-proclaimed Islamic puritanical Wahhabi Mad Madhi, Muhammad bin Abd Allah, (1844-1885 AD). He was not happy with British suppression of the Islamic slave trade that was seizing Africans and enslaving them for sale in Zanzibar and Arabia. General Kitchener and his relief force arrived two days later. Nathanial Mayer Rothschild is appointed to The House of Lords in Great Britain.
1886 AD	France; a gentleman named Edouard Drumont wrote a widely read book entitled, "La France Juive", then he went on to form "The National Anti-Semitic League", (1889), to fight the clandestine and merciless conspiracy of Jewish finance which jeopardizes daily the welfare, honor, and security of France. After this Drumont published La Libre Parole, a newspaper dedicated to driving Jews out of the French Army. Two French Jewish officers challenged him and his colleague to a duel for their honor. One of the Jewish officers was killed. In 1894, Jewish French Army officer, Captain Alfred Dreyfus was arrested, tried and convicted of selling military secrets to Germany. The Paris correspondent of a Vienna newspaper, Theodor Herzl, (1860-1904 AD), was "traumatized" at how Dreyfus was treated, and went back to Vienna and wrote, "Der Judanstaat", a book about the need for "the restoration of the Jewish State". Then Herzl organized the "first Zionist Congress", in Basel, Switzerland, (1896), which hosted 200 Jewish delegates from 15 countries. They created the "World Zionist Organization". The first Zionist Congress decided that the Jews of the world must have their own country to be free of anti-Semitism from the Goyim. At first they thought about Cyprus, Uganda, Argentina and Texas, but then they settled on Palestine. 99% of the population of Palestine at that time was Muslim landowners so the Zionists formed strategies to financially usurp the ownership of the Palestinian land or use force to seize the land. Rothschild bought into the Zionist idea in 1919. It was said, "The Protocols of the Elders of Zion", which was a book issued or re-issued at the first Zionist Congress, by Thedor Herzl, it is about Jewish World domination by a cabal of Jewish (cabalists ?). Herzl foresaw what would happen in the Great War, and the breaking up of The Ottoman Empire, with the British then taking control of Palestine. He wrote of these events twenty years before they actually took place. Henry Ford commented that the book seemed legitimate in the 1920's, but historians seem to be in a consensus that it is a fraud, meaning that it is not a protocol of Zionist's. After reading it, I myself have the opinion that it was either written by fledgling Communists most probably Jewish, with major resentments against the entire world; or it was written and released by one of the aristocracies of Europe to counter Communist subversion. In either case, we know now that it is just easier to put fluoride in the drinking water to zap the Goyims precious bodily fluids.

1886 AD	The Statue of Liberty is inaugurated in New York Harbor; the statue is the Roman goddess, Libertas; Libertas was the goddess of "liberty". The goddess Libertas with the crown, representing rays of the sun bears a resemblance to "Sol Invictus", the undefeatable sun God, Mithras, and was used on Roman coins. She looks to the east and the rising sun; the statue with the base is 306 feet high and sits on Liberty island, in Upper New York Harbor, which was also called Bedloe's Island.
1886 AD	Inscription on the base of The Statue of Liberty, a poem by Emma Lazarus "Give me your tired, your poor, your huddled masses, yearning to breathe Free, the wretched refuse of your teeming shore. Send these, the homeless, tempest-tossed to me, I lift up my lamp beside the Golden Door."
1887 AD	US President Grover Cleveland appointed a Jewish American as Ambassador to the Ottoman Empire in Istanbul. For the next 30 years Jewish American Ambassadors were to be appointed to Istanbul.
1888 AD	Emperor Kaiser Wilhelm II, (1859-1941 AD) rules Germany (1890-1918 AD); he is the grandson Queen Victoria. He is also the King of Prussia.
1898 AD	Federation of American Zionists was formed in NYC, (July 4, 1898), this was the start of the American Zionist movement, what followed was an American media campaign to promote Zionism, influence the US Congress, and spread the word of Zionism through education in the US.
1898 AD	General Kitchener defeats the Mahdi Army in Sudan, Winston Churchill participates in this army and wrote a book called "The River Wars" about it.
1890 AD	Battle of Wounded Knee, Sioux territory, Dakotas, USA.
1891 AD	Sitting Bull is murdered by Seventh US Cavalry in Dakota territory.
1899 AD	Second Boer War, (1899-1902 AD), war fought over the discovery of diamonds and gold in southern Africa, between British Empire and Dutch Boers. Rothschild family interests buy into the DeBeers diamond interests in South Africa. Adolph Hitler (1899-1945 AD) was born in Austro-Hungarian Empire.
1900 AD	In the late 1800's and the early 1900's, a Zionist in Russia claimed the British were actually one of the Lost tribes of Israel, and a group called the British Israelites formed in Great Britain. Between 1899 and 1902, the British Israelites dug up sections of the Hill of Tara in Ireland looking for the Arc of the Covenant and the "Ten Commandments" which they insisted are buried there.
1901 AD	British Queen Victoria (1819-1901 AD), died. Rothschild Frankfurt Banking branch is liquidated as no Rothschild wanted to live there anymore.
1903 AD	Wright Brothers, Wilbur and Orville Wright built first airplane glider, "The Wright Flyer" and fly it from Kill Devil Hill on the Outer Banks of North Carolina, U.S.A.
1904 AD	International Women's suffrage Alliance formed
1905 AD	Albert Einstein publishes his "Theory of Special Relativity" in Switzerland; This physics paper explains how all the known previous physical laws concerning Newton's mechanical theories and Maxwell's electromagnetic equations can be brought together; this leads to the concept of the "Black Hole", the "singularity"

and the "Event Horizon", which still cannot be explained. According to his relativity theory space and time bend and are relative to each other.

1908 AD	Ford Motor Company makes the first affordable automobile, the "Model T"; women gain the right to vote in Denmark; the Austro-Hungarian Empire annexes Muslim Bosnia-Herzegovina. Rothschild divide banks into separate corporate entities.
1908 AD	Tunguska Event in Siberia, Russia. A meteor or comet hit the earth's atmosphere at an angle and disintegrated flattening 770 square miles of trees.
1910 AD	Union of South Africa comes into existence
1911 AD	Italy attacks Ottoman Empire and seizes the coast of Italy, Rhodes, and some other islands off the coast of the Ottoman Empire in the Aegean Sea. Albania revolts against the Ottoman Empire.
1912 AD	Ibn Saud (1875-1953 AD), sponsors a spiritual revival of the puritanical Wahhabi Sect in Arabia; this gives rise to the fierce Wahhabi warrior brotherhood known as the Ikhwan, that he controls; Ikhwan means Muslim Brothers, or Muslim Brethren.
1912 AD	First Balkan War against Ottoman Empire; (1912-1913 AD) Greece, Serbia, and Bulgaria defeat the Ottomans. The Ottoman are now afraid of being completely conquered and seek an alliance with any powerful European nation. The Ottoman Empire contained 22 different races, ethnic groups, but only ethnic Muslim Turks could participate politically. Winston Churchill is running the British Admiralty at this time, as First Sea Lord.
1912 AD	Future US Supreme Court Justice Brandeis became a Zionist, engaged in covert political activity to further Zionism throughout the rest of his life, or, for the next 25 years He and his colleague Frankfurter help shape the legal minds of Zionists at Harvard through a secret organization he became leader of called "The Parushim" (Pharisees, separate). One member described the organization as a secret military like fellowship of elite Zionists, whose work was done silently, and anonymously. They used infection, (infection of ideas) and education to further their goals.
1913 AD	

Amendment XVI

The Congress shall have power to lay and collect taxes on incomes, from whatever source derived, without appointment among the several states, and without regard to any census or enumeration.

Amendment XVII

The Senate of the United States shall be composed of two Senators from each State, elected by the people thereof, for six years; an each Senator shall have one vote. The electors in each State shall have the qualifications requisite for electors of the most numerous branch of the State legislators. When vacancies happen in the representation of any State in the Senate, the executive authority of such State shall issue writs of election to fill such vacancies by election as the legislature may direct.

This amendment shall not be so construed as to affect the election or term of any Senator chosen before it comes valid as part of the Constitution.

1914 AD	World War I, (1914-1918 AD), Germany sides Austrian-Hungarian Empire, and with Ottoman Empire, in a war against France, Britain, Italy, Japan, Greece, Romania, Russia, Belgium, Holland and the United States of America. This is also the Tenth Russian-Ottoman Turkish War. The Ottoman Empire calls for Jihad, (Holy War) against the enemy, as Britain has large numbers of Muslim troops. General Kitchener of Khartoum commands the British forces from Britain; Britain knows nothing of the Middle East, except that there is some oil around Kuwait and Iraq, and they suspect there is more there, as does Germany.

1915 AD — Arabia; Arabia was an empty and desolate land, and the area where Mecca lies was physically the most desolate and uninviting province in Arabia. This area called the Hejaz, means separating. It is 750 miles long, 200 miles wide, and 45 miles east of the coast of the Red Sea. It was an un-watered, basically uninhabited area with a population of 300,000 primates, split into one half Bedouin tribes' people and one half townspeople. Economically it was the same as in the Prophet Mohammad's time, it grew different types of dates and it sponsored Islamic Holy sites for pilgrimage, deriving its wealth from these endeavors. The pilgrimage was also about the slave trade, the transportation of slaves, and not just about the Islamic faith rituals, which also endorse slavery. There was a railroad that connected Damascus, Syria to Medina, but to travel further to Mecca or to the west coast at Jeddah, required a camel caravan.

The Ottoman Empire ruled Arabia. The Ottoman appointed leader of Mecca, the Emir was Hussein Ibn Ali. Hussein was Sherif of Mecca; he was a descendant of the prophet Mohammad and a member of the Dhawu-Awn clan of the House of Hashem. He was a Hashemite. Hussein had two sons, Abdullah and Feisel, both were Ottoman parliamentarians; Abdullah from Mecca and Feisel from Jeddah. Abdullah wanted to cast off the Ottoman yoke, Feisel was cautious. East of Mecca was the powerful Bedouin tribal warlord, Abdul Aziz Ibn Saud. Saud was the leader of the fiercely puritanical Wahhabi sect of Islam. The Wahhabi sect lives according the precepts laid down by the Prophet Mohammad, and it does not recognize any Caliphs after the first four original caliphs.

The Ottoman Empire wanted more direct control over the affairs in Mecca and Jeddah and were proposing to extend the railroad from Medina to Mecca, then on to Jeddah. Bedouins made their living from the caravan traffic, and the railroad plans would have a negative effect on their livelihood. The Ottomans also wanted more Arab manpower for the World War I battlefields. There was Ottoman pressure on Hussein to supply troops.

1915 AD — The Gallipoli Campaign by the British against the Ottomans in the Dardanelles. British troops of the 29th Division, landed on the Gallipoli Peninsula in order to facilitate an attack up the straits to Istanbul, thus ensuring British and Russian control of the Black sea, the Aegean Sea and the Mediterranean Sea. The campaign failed, the British troops were unable to get inland off the beaches, and were withdrawn in the winter of 1915-1916.

1915 AD

When the War started the Muslim Sultan of the Ottoman Empire called for Jihad against the allies. Germany believed the Muslim soldiers in the British and French Armies would not fire on Muslim German and Ottoman troops if there was a Holy War called for. The Jihad idea turned out to be a "dud", but at the same time the British were scared of a Jihad, a Holy War also. The British had a previous bloodbath experience with the religiously inspired Indian Mutiny of 1857. Kitchener had to come up with a plan to defuse the possibility of bloody Jihad or control it for His Majesties Government. Kitchener along with mostly all European peoples had no understanding of the Islamic world and its culture, and what they did think of "it" and how "it" operated was wrong. He and the rest of the people used European history as a comparative template on which to understand the workings of Islamic culture. In Western Christendom, there was a split, a separation between the spiritual, and the temporal, physical world. There was a State or a Kingdom (temporal), and then there was the Church (spiritual). The Pope or the Archbishop of Canterbury headed up the Holy Canon Law of the Church, while The King or Parliament headed up the secular common law of the State. In Islam, no such separation existed or exists to this day. All law in Islamic lands is Sharia, Islamic law, or based on Sharia Law. The Caliphs were princes and warlords, and not just prayer leaders. Kitchener believed incorrectly that Islam was a centralized, authoritarian structure, an organization, an "it", led by a caliph, like the Catholic church is headed up by the Pope. Kitchener and his people were oblivious to the Islamic disunity and fragmentation of society that exists in Islam. There is no concept of a "Nation State" or of being part of one in Islam, there is only the "umma", and there is Dar al Islam and Dar al Harb. Kitchener sent secret messages across the red Sea to Hussein and his son Abdullah, saying that if they freed themselves from the Ottomans, declared independence, then Britain would protect them from foreign enemies. He made promises that Arabia, Palestine, Syria and Mesopotamia would be led by an Arab caliph and the fierce Wahhabi Saud tribes would recognize the spiritual authority of the Sunni ruler of Mecca. Kitchener proposed to make Hussein the "Pope of Islam", a position that in Islamic reality never did nor does exist. Hussein took this British proposal as an offer to make him the king of a vast new kingdom.

Kitchener working from London appointed a man named Sykes as a Middle East expert to figure out a way to deal with a defeated Middle East after the war. Sykes and Kitchener created the Arab Bureau as part of the British Intelligence Office in Cairo. The Arab Bureau was headed by an archeologist and Naval Intelligence Officer named Hogarth. He brought in a few others including Philip Graves, a former "Times" newspaper correspondent, and T.E. Lawrence (Lawrence of Arabia), Parliament members also showed up at times to give their input.

This Arab Bureau came up with a plan. The Caliphate should be moved southward to Mecca, with Hussein as the Caliph under the British "Egyptian Empire Scheme". Hussein would be the "Islamic Pope", and there would be a temporal figurehead monarch in Egypt governed by a British High Commissioner.

In Palestine in 1914, at the start of hostilities, there were about 60,000 Jews living in 40 scattered settlements. 30,000 of them were Ottoman Empire subjects, who had been living there as dhimmi's for ages. The other 30,000 Jews there were recent Russian immigrants who had started to immigrate there over the previous fifty years. These were not Ottoman subjects, but were actually still Russian Empire subjects, who had immigrated to Palestine to practice Judaism in the Holy Land of Abraham, with the possibility of recreating the Kingdom of Judah and Israel. This Diaspora returning to Judah were financed by wealthy European Jews within a "Zionist" movement.

The Ottoman Empire viewed all non-Muslims suspiciously. At the start of the war, the Ottomans took violent action against all the Jewish settlers there. Most Jews wanted nothing to do with the war on one side or the other, except David Ben Gurion and Ben Zvi, who offered to raise a Palestinian army to fight with the Ottoman Empire. Both of these men were turned down by the Ottomans and deported to the United States. In the United States, in 1918, Ben Gurion then rallied for a Jewish Palestinian Army to fight in Palestine on the side of the British.

1915 AD The Muslim Ottoman Caliphate, after declaring Jihad on the allies, and deporting and killing Jews and other non-Muslims in Palestine, began a ruthless extermination of the peaceful Christian Armenian population in the Ottoman Empire. 1,500,000 Christian Armenian men, women, and children were exterminated. Armenian Ottoman soldiers were disarmed then shot and buried in mass graves, both able bodied and the elderly, disabled Armenians' were murdered outright in their towns and homes. Armenian women and girls were raped, then crucified naked in long rows in fields of Eastern and Southern Anatolia, the rest were marched or driven out to the Syrian desert where they starved to death.

1916 AD By 1916 there was a change in government in Great Britain, the Turkish Muslim Ottomans were not only holding their own, they had kicked British ass in Persia, Mesopotamia and Gallipoli, and they held off Russian advances into Anatolia. General Kitchener was removed and sent on a mission to Russia. Enroot to Russia from Scapa Flow, Scotland his ship struck a mine and he went down with the ship in a gale in the North Sea.

The Arabs in Mecca got back to British Intelligence and their wish was to control all of Syria, Lebanon, and Palestine. The Arab Kingdom with the Islamic Pope would extend to the Mediterranean Sea and as far as the Taurus Mountains in Anatolia, including the territory north of Damascus with cities like Aleppo, Homs, and Hama, which were all connected by a French built railroad. From Damascus this French built railroad connected with the Hejaz Railroad to Medina. Hussein in Mecca declared rebellion against the Ottoman Empire. The Ottomans and Germans started to send a 3,500-man army to the Hejaz, but the Royal Navy sent its ships close to the shore of Arabia in the Red Sea, and the Ottoman, German army turned back. No Arab units of the Ottoman Army defected to Hussein. The Arab Muslim troops preferred to be ruled by Muslim Turks rather than European

Christians. Britain took the port of Jeddah and British Muslim troops took Mecca and Taif. When the British Muslim troops approached Taif they encountered a number of stoned out Islamic jinn laying around wondering what they should do next. Taif was secured, and there was now a British presence ashore in the Hejaz.

1916 AD   Easter Rising of Irish patriots, the Irish Republican Army, (The I.R.A.), rose up to oppose British rule of Ireland, Germany had supplied some weapons to them in hopes of another front. The Rising was suppressed and leaders were hanged.

1916 AD   By the end of 1916, all the Allies had become dependent on the US for financing to keep the war going. The US was then in the catbirds seat and able to dictate to the Allies. US President Woodrow Wilson opposed both of the allies' independent ambitions and would now use the funding and the threat of withholding the funding to thwart Imperial ambitions of France and England. He wanted keep them out of new colonies in the Middle East and he wanted the US to be kept out of the war.

1917 AD   In the spring of 1917, Lawrence of Arabia accompanied a small army of Bedouins and seized the port of Aqaba in southern Palestine. In June 1917, General Allenby took over the British army in the Middle East. Allenby seized Jerusalem in the autumn, and made plans for moving up the coast to Damascus. The capture of Jerusalem was the first time the Christian Holy sites were in the hands of Christians since 1291 AD. Lawrence paid the Arabs over 1 Million pounds Sterling during the course of the war for their continued help. By this time in 1917, the world war had become an economic and social survival contest. Warfare in 1917 was undergoing its own industrial revolution. The demand of industrial warfare strained all society across Europe. The social structures were beginning to give way as they were unable to handle the demands of war. In Germany, there was a change in government and Paul von Hindenburg took over, he allowed unrestricted submarine warfare in the North Atlantic. German submarines began sinking U.S. merchant ships bound for Europe. The U.S. declared war on Germany alone in response, not any of her allies. German submarines continued sinking US merchant ships bound for Europe. In September of 1917, President Wilson requested that an independent group of academics meet to help formulate plans for a post-war Middle-East. The group assembled and met at the New York Public Library on 42nd Street in Manhattan, New York City. Included in the group were men from Harvard, Yale, Columbia, and Chicago. This Middle East group did not have any contemporary specialists but had as its chairman, a student of the Crusades, a Latin American studies man, experts on American Indians, a mechanical engineer, and two men who majored in Persian languages along with a literary specialist. Wonderful, I wonder where they ate lunch and dinner at night. Not one word in their inquiry and report mentioned oil. This lack of knowledge led to a peace that would end all peace, or as President Wilson said the Sykes-Picot Treaty at the end of the war was a prescription for endless war in the Middle East.

In Russia, the Czar mismanaged the economy. Even though there were surpluses, there was much hoarding, embezzling, and greed, that left inflation running at 1,000 per cent. Germany offered Russia a separate peace if Russia would break with the allies, but the czar wanted Istanbul for Russia so Russia could have unfettered access to the warm Mediterranean Sea, and a year-round ice free southern port on the Black Sea. Russia turned them down.

In 1917, Vladimir Ulanova, who was also known as Vladimir Lenin, was living in Zurich, Switzerland. He was a Edomite Jewish attorney and an avid, rabid Marxist. He led a group called the Bolsheviks. At this same time, Germans and Young Turks were secretly funding strikes and rebellion in Russia at the behest of wealthy European Jews. There was a conjunction of Lenin's Bolsheviks, Germans and Jews all wanted the Russian government to fall once and for all time. Jews especially hated the Russians because of their experience with them as Khazars, and the Russian inspired pogroms in the 1880's, which drove the Jews out and westwards towards Poland and German territory. The Czar threw up his hands and walked away from it all, he stepped down, he abdicated in the face of the situation. At that time, the German General staff put Lenin in a sealed German military train and sent him from Zurich, Switzerland to Petrograd (Saint Petersburg), Russia. Bolsheviks there were employees of the German General staff who took their orders from Jews and Prussians in Berlin. Lenin wanted Russia out of the war for Marxist Socialist reasons, and Germany along with the Muslim Ottomans wanted Russia out of the war to concentrate their armies on England and France. At first there was a revolution in the spring of 1917, but the new government kept fight the Germans; in October 1917, the Bolshevik Revolution was instigated. In March 1918, Lenin had a peace treaty signed with the Ottoman Empire and Germany, The Treaty of Brest-Litovsk. Russia gave up Poland and some other territory. A civil war broke out in Russia between the "Reds", and the "Whites", much the same as the "red" Edomites fought with the Israelites. Mostly all of the Bolsheviks were Jews; Lenin was partially Jewish, with Ukrainian roots, his Grandfather was Israel Blank. Other Jewish leaders were Leon Trotsky (Lev Bronstein), Yakov Sverdlov (Solomon), Grigori Zinoview (Radomyslsky), Karl Radek (Sobelsohn), Maxim Litvinov (Wallach), Lev Kamenev (Rosenfeld), and Moisei Uritsky. About 90% of the Bolshevik Secret Police were Jews. The Reds won and a few years later the Marxist Communist, Union of Soviet Socialist Republics, U.S.S.R, began. Anti-Semitism was made a crime, punishable by death. Gulags and concentration camps were set up. Between 1917 and 1934, the Bolshevik Jews murdered 10 Million people in Russia; by the 1950's they had murdered 21 million Russians. Jewish Vengeance. There was increased emigration out of Russia towards the west after the fall of the Russian Empire. Ottoman and German forces kept gobbling up Russian territory in the areas of the Caucasus and the Polish areas. Germany and the Ottomans wanted the oil fields near the Black Sea in Russian territory, in Baku. Rothschild had bought the concessions for the Baku oil fields from the Czar in 1883. The situation became thoroughly confused in Turkestan and Baku; the Germans along with the Russians were now fighting against British Indian troops allied with the Turks for these oil rich areas.

This fighting went on even after the first World War ended, until the Red Army took control of them.

1917 AD — As Russia withdrew from World War I, the Balfour Declaration of 1917 was signed. Britain signed the Balfour declaration with Lord Rothschild, who was representing "Zionist" interests. In exchange for Jewish support in Eastern Europe, against Germany, the Balfour declaration promised British support for a Palestine homeland for the world's Jews, so as to end the Diaspora brought about by the Roman Empires suppression of the Third Jewish Revolt in 136 AD. This declaration was in complete opposition to what the British promised the Arabs a year earlier. The Arabs under Feisel supported a Jewish Palestine as long as they, the Arabs could have inland Syria. The French wanted Syria, dating back to the Crusades, probably for some Catholic reason.

1917 AD — The Wahhabi warrior brotherhood had continually grown for 5 years, supported by Lawrence of Arabia's gold payments from the British Crown.

1918 AD — 23:00, November 11, 1918; on the eleventh hour, of the eleventh day, of the eleventh month an armistice was signed called the Treaty of Versailles, in a Railroad car in Versailles, France. This marked the end of World War I. The Ottoman Empire was dissolved, and the State of Tukey was established in 1923. In Austria, women gained the right to vote, the Austro-Hungarian Empire came to an end replaced by Austria, and Hungary, and some other states. In Arabia, Prince Feisel became the preferred choice to run Arabia.

1918 AD — The US delegation to the Peace Treaty from WWI included American Zionists and Christian Pastors. President Wilson send a fact finding delegation to Palestine and received its report from the King-Crane Commission. The commission opposed Zionist designs on Palestine, stating "that the gravest trespass upon the civil and religious rights of non-Jewish communities in Palestine; and the steady financial and social pressure to surrender the land, would be a gross violation of the principle of self-determination and of the Palestinians peoples' rights. The commission went on to state, that the Zionists looked forward to a complete dispossession of the present non-Jewish inhabitants of Palestine and concluded armed force would be required of the Zionists to do this. The report was suppressed by US Zionist Judge Brandeis, thus giving a green light to the Balfour agreement, and Mandated Palestine. The British Empire takes over administration of Palestine from the defeated Muslim Ottoman Empire. "Mandatory Palestine" (1923-1948 AD) was created. The British create the office of the Grand Mufti of Jerusalem to oversee Islamic issues and the Temple Mount. Lord Rothschild and his family banking interests were owed millions upon millions of British pounds, and Gold from the defunct Ottoman Empire, so they collected by inheriting the railway system in Palestine, along with much Palestinian land that would become the future state of Israel. Zionist institutions began to be built in Palestine as a political cover to avoid the appearance of colonization.

1918 AD — The Vienna, Austria bank of Rothschild was almost bankrupt after the war, but the French and London Rothschild banks got the Vienna Rothschild bank back up and running. Austria was now only 7 Million People, the rest of the Austro-Hungarian Empire was broken into separate states. The Austrian krone, and the German Mark went into a steady decline, and the Vienna Rothschild bank bought the currency attempting to stabilize the downward trend. Then the French franc followed into decline, and it was thought the Vienna Rothschild bank would go under. But then the Franc rose; it was bought up by J.P. Morgan in New York, who didn't want the American economy to suffer, and he told the Rothschild of his actions, so they worked in concert in the currency market and made a fortune. The Vienna bank recouped all its losses from WW I.

1918 AD	The Zionist Organization of America reorganized itself; 270,000 American dead in World War I, in a period of two years.
1919 AD	The Weimar Republic (1919-1933 AD) begins in defeated Germany, left wing and right wing para-military groups are operating in Germany engaged in street battles and firefights with all the arms left over from the First World War. Right wing groups blamed the Jews for the loss of World War I, "stabbed in the back"; mostly all of the left wing para-military groups' leaders are Marxist Leninist Jews who want to tear down German government and replace it with a Jewish Communist government like was being done in Russia. There was massive inflation, more than 1000 per cent, just like there was in Russia prior to the Marxist Leninist revolution. There were also massive war reparations that had to be paid to the Allies. They started to be paid but then stopped due to the economics and after "The Great Depression" when Hitler came to power they were stopped altogether. Germany finally finished paying off the World War I war reparations in 2010, almost 90 years later. Germany was forbidden to have an air force, and was very limited in having a Navy and Army.
1919 AD	World War I, "The Great War for Civilization", (1914-1919 AD) ended.
1919 AD	**Amendment XVIII**
	Alcohol made illegal by 18th Amendment, repealed entirely by Amendment XXI in 1933.
1919 AD	Irish War of Independence (1919-1921 AD), Ireland becomes a free state, no longer part of Britain
1920 AD	**Amendment XIX**
	The right of citizens of the United States to vote shall not be denied or abridged by the United States or by any State on account of sex. Congress shall have power to enforce this article by appropriate legislation.
1920 AD	Jerusalem Arab Riots of 1920, Muslim Arabs riot against Zionist immigration to Palestine; start of the roaring twenties.
1921 AD	New Grand Mufti appointed to office, Mohammed Amin al-Husseini (1897-1974 AD), this man was a violent anti-Zionist and eventually a pro-Nazi Muslim Mufti; he served as an officer in the Ottoman Empires Army until 1918, then he took sick leave, went to Palestine and became an officer in the King Faisal Brigade against the Ottomans, thus serving the British. He was the suspected leader of the Jerusalem Riots of 1920, but was too valuable to British authorities to get rid of so

he was given the Grand Mufti Office. He was supported by the British until the 1936-1939 Muslim Arab Revolt, when he openly opposed the British. In 1937 an arrest warrant was issued for him but he fled to Iraq, then he fled to Fascist Mussolini Italy and then to Nazi Germany where he recruited Bosnian Muslims for the Waffen SS.

1921 AD	Irish Free State established, Northern Ireland partitioned
1922 AD	Irish Civil War (1922-1923 AD), a civil war between the Irish Free State and the I.R.A. over the treaty and the partitioning of Ireland; IRA lost and the Irish Free State remained. "Ireland" was formed in 1937 AD; Fine Gael is the political descendent of the winning Nationalist side in the Civil War; Fianna Fial is the political descendent of the IRA in the Irish parliament today. The official "Republic of Ireland" came into being in 1948 AD.
1922 AD	Joseph Stalin takes office in the Soviet Union, the U.S.S.R., (1922-1953 AD). Joseph Stalin and the U.S.S.R enter into "The Rapallo Treaty" with the Weimar German government to circumvent the restrictions placed on Germany by the Versailles Armistice Treaty. German troops are permitted to build and train on tanks, artillery and airplanes in the Soviet Union. German armament factories were built in Russia.
1923 AD	Ottoman Caliphate (1453-1923 AD) ends. There were 4 caliphates in existence since 632 AD, the Rashidun, the Umayyad, the Abbasid, and the Ottoman Caliphates.
1923 AD	Alexander Fleming (1881-1955 AD), a Scots scientist from East Ayrshire, Scotland, discovers the enzyme lysozyme.
1923 AD	Germany, street fighting is curtailed around this time; neither side has won, some of the right wing German Freikorps will go on to become Hitler's Henchmen in the S.S. in the 1930's and '40's.
1924 AD	Germany stabilizes (1924-1929 AD) and construction of good railways is undertaken, and railway systems are unified.
1924 AD	Vladimir Lenin died and Joseph Stalin (1878-1953 AD) took power as dictator of Soviet Union from 1924 until his death in 1953 AD
1925 AD	Britain enacts British Gold Standard Act of 1925, no more Gold Sovereigns in circulation; Gold bullion was used in the form of 12 kg., 400 Troy ounces of fine gold. John Maynard Keynes, the economist, warned of deflation as a result of this action. Instability in markets and deflation occurred, followed by the Stock Market Crash of 1929.
1925 AD	Ibn Saud, (1875-1953 AD), the fierce Wahhabi Warlord Bedouin, leader of the Ikhwan, the Muslim Brothers, the Muslim Brethren, conquers Mecca and the Hejaz, defeating Hussein and ended 700 years of Hashemite rule of Mecca.
1926 AD	Ibn Saud is the leader of various areas of Arabia, the Wahhabi Ihkwan are in control of other areas, they carry the black flag with the Shahada printed on it, like the ISIS flag.
1928 AD	Alexander Fleming, (1881-1955 AD), a Scots biologist, pharmacologist, and botanist discovered penicillin. Women gain the right to vote in Great Britain. The

Muslim Brotherhood began in Egypt, started by Sheikh Hassan Mohammad al-Banna, (1906-1949 AD), the Muslim Brotherhood is a Sunni institution with the motto: "Islam is the solution, Allah is our objective, the Quran is the Constitution, the Prophet is our leader, jihad is our way, death for the sake of Allah is our wish".

1929 AD   Ibn Saud declares that the Ikhwan are not to raid and pillage anymore; they rebel and Ibn Saud defeated them at the Battle of Sabilla, where Sauds' army massacred the leadership and the camel cavalry of the Ikhwam.

1929 AD   Stock Market Crash; Economic Depression, caused by years of greedy, and risky stock speculation that couldn't be retained in reality. Root cause was concentration of wealth, and the speculations with this concentration; as the wealth was more and more concentrated, the poor and middle class people experienced a decline in their standard of living, there was a credit expansion, and many went into debt in order to just survive during the 1920's. "The Roaring Twenties". The worldwide credit expansion went bust in 1929, as speculating stockbrokers were unable to meet the margin calls. Credit markets collapsed, companies went bankrupt, working men and women lost jobs, and were unable to pay back their own loans. A vicious collapsing economy ensued until millions upon millions of people were broke. This collapse lasted to the end of the 1930's and the into the 1940's, when war production for the second world war provided jobs.

1930 AD   American banks that were financing the German post war recovery suddenly went broke; millions of German workers were then unemployed, allowing the NSDAP political party to gain power through election promises. The NSDAP wat the National Socialist Deutsch Arbeiter Party, the National Socialist German Workers Party, the NAZI party.

1931 AD   There was a "run" on the banks in Austria, then Germany, as confidence in the system failed, the banking system failed and collapsed. In the US, the Gold standard prevented banks from creating fiat money, money out of thin air, this prolonged the depression and made it worse. Banks had to have each dollar backed by 40 cents worth of gold; this also led to deflationary pressures which caused people to get their money out of the banks. Deflation means something that is worth something today, say 100; will only be worth 90 tomorrow; and 80 the next day; and 70 the day after that. Deflation means what you have today will be less tomorrow. If it's a house worth $100,000 today, and you owe $100,000 on the mortgage, then with deflation your house will only be worth $90,000 tomorrow, but you still owe $100,000. And the next day your house is only worth $80,000, but you still owe $100,000. Deflation can be good and bad; it corrects for inflation, which is good if you are not holding that $100,000 mortgage.

1932 AD   Ibn Saud, (1875-1953 AD), House of Saud, became the king of Saudi Arabia; he reigned from 1932 until 1953 AD, the militia of the Ihkwan and his army were reorganized into the Saudi Arabian National Guard.

1933 AD   67 % of world trade had vanished due to the depression. Germany was in really dire straights' with an unemployment rate of over 40%. Adolf Hitler and his NSDAP, NAZI party come to power. He forms the 3rd German Reich. He promises to restore country to normalcy and order. He was an anti-communist, anti-Semitic, national socialist, not an international socialist like the Marxist-Leninist Communists were in the U.S.S.R. of Russia. He opens concentration camps in Germany, a safe space to put and concentrate the undesirables of German society. Dachau was the first camp near Munich. The camps were filled with union leaders, political prisoners, homosexuals, critics, clergy, and eventually Jews who had not left Germany. Above the entrance to the camps was the sign, "Arbeit Macht Frei", "work will make you free", a mystical declaration that self-sacrifice in the form of endless labor does in and of itself bring a spiritual freedom. A very good and noble declaration, as long as you aren't the worker stuck being compelled to work there. The International Socialists, the Communists, had a similar slogan, "From each according to his abilities, to each according to his needs." This was another good slogan and did a lot for personal achievement and personal responsibility. In the US, Congress enacted the "Glass-Stiegel Act of 1933", to prevent and limit risk exposure contagion in the securities, financial industry, in order to keep in check the speculation that caused the 1929 Stock Market Crash, and the ongoing Great Depression. President Bill Clinton repealed this act in 1999 AD, leading to the Great Recession of 2008 AD, nine years later. Same thing happened as in 1929 AD.

1933 AD

Beginning in 1775, Mayer Rothschild, living in Frankfurt, Germany began financing the supply of Hessian troops to the British Crown, of King George III; these Hessian troops were sent to the British colonies in North America to fight against the American colonists. George Washington crossed the Delaware River and attacked the Hessian troops from his Valley Forge winter headquarters. Rothschild made a fortune and with this money he went on to finance more armed conflict as a way to amass a great fortune. Beginning in 1800, more and more Jews moved into Prussia and Germany from the areas of the Russian Empire, primarily from the Ukraine and Polish territory. These were the Edomite Khazar Jews, who had fled Khazaria when the Mongol hordes pushed westward, into Ukraine, and the Russian Vikings moved south to set up a Russian Empire. In 1848, the institution of serfdom had ended, also so peasants weren't tied to the land and the landowner, enabling further movement. In 1869, the Jews in Germany were granted equal Constitutional rights, the same as all other German citizens. The Jewish immigration kept increasing in rate and intensity up until 1885, when Jews began to migrate to Palestine and North America. This lowered somewhat the number of Jews in Germany. After the Russian Revolution of 1917, which Germany and Rothschild were instrumental in facilitating, Jewish immigration to Poland and Prussia increased again, with many escaping the turmoil and the lack of what they saw as the abusive Russian Empire, which didn't allow them their civil rights. In 1925, 18% of the Jews living in Germany were not German citizens. Roughly 2% of the entire German population was Jewish. In 1929, the world economic systems collapsed, getting worse year by year. By 1933, when Adolph Hitler was elected, the unemployment rate was over 40% and the German people saw that the Jews had amassed enormous hordes of wealth from speculation in the financial markets, and from World War I military procurement businesses. At the same time, and since before 1917, the Bolsheviks of the Marxist-Leninist Communist movement were trying to overthrow the entire European system of nationalism, "nation states". Mostly all of the Communist leaders and instigators were Edomite Eastern European Jews, left over Khazars. The steady introduction of this foreign Eastern European haplotype into Germany, supported by Rothschild and his confederate banking interests, resulted in a disproportionate increase in Edomite Jewish influence in both German, Prussian and Polish culture, politics and finance. Adolf Hitler and his German supporters took legal measures to curtail Jewish influence in Germany with the goal in mind of getting all the Jews out of Germany. He instituted the Nuremberg Laws, named after the town of Nuremburg, Germany. After these laws were enacted, World Judaism declared war on Germany, primarily of an economic nature.

The Nazi government and Hitler entered into an agreement with the World Zionist movement, called the Haavara agreement. Jews living in Germany would deposit their money, and liquidate their holdings into a special bank, then they would leave the country for Palestine. The same amount of money they had deposited into this special bank would be distributed to them from the special bank branch in Palestine, in the form of German products. This program was another part of the Zionist plan for the recreation of the state of Israel. Between 1933 and 1939, 60,000 jews living in Germany left Germany for "Mandatory Palestine". The S.S. supported this program wholeheartedly. In a 1935 issue of the official SS newspaper, "Das Schwarze Korps", the SS proclaimed its support for Zionism, "the Time may not be far off when Palestine will again be able to receive its sons who have been lost to it for more than a thousand years. Our good wishes, together with official goodwill, go with them." It's ironic but Hitler became the greatest supporter of Zionism for a period of time.

1933 AD

Amendment XX

Section 1.
The terms of the President and Vice President shall end at noon on the 20th of January, and the terms of Senators and Representatives at noon on the third day of January, of the years in which such terms would have ended if this article had not been ratified, and the terms of their successors shall then begin.

Section 2.
The Congress shall assemble at least once every year, and such meeting shall begin at noon on the 3rd day of January, unless they shall by law appoint a different day.

Section 3.
If, at the time fixed for the beginning of the term of the President, the President elect shall have died, the Vice President elect shall become President. If a President

shall not have been chosen before the time fixed for the beginning of his term, or if the President elect shall have failed to qualify, then the Vice President elect shall act as President until a President shall have qualified; and the Congress may by law provide for the case wherein neither a President elect nor a Vice President elect shall have qualified, declaring who shall then act as president, or the manner in which one who is to act shall be selected, and such person shall act accordingly until a President or Vice President shall have qualified.

Section 4.

The Congress may by law provide for the case of the death of any of the persons from whom the House of Representatives may choose a President whenever the right of choice shall have devolved upon them, and for the case of the death of any of the persons from whom the Senate may choose a Vice President whenever the right of choice shall have devolved upon them.

Section 5.

Sections 1 and 2 shall take effect on the 15th day of October following the ratification of this article.

Section 6.

This article shall be inoperative unless it shall have been ratified as an amendment to the Constitution by the legislatures of three fourths of the several states within seven years from the date of its submission.

1933 AD

Amendment XXI

Section 1.

The eighteenth article of amendment to the Constitution of The United States is hereby repealed.

Section 2.

The transportation or importation into any State, Territory, or possession of the United States for delivery or use therein of intoxicating liquors, in violation of the laws thereof, is hereby prohibited.

Section 3.

This article shall be inoperative unless it shall have been ratified as an amendment to the Constitution by conventions in the several states, as provided in the Constitution, within seven years from the date of the submission hereof to the States by the Congress.

1934 AD

The U.S. Congress passes the "Gold Reserve Act of 1934", nationalizes all Gold, and issues dollars with Red Seal designating it was backed by Gold. This produces confidence in monetary system, but at the same time it allows the President to devalue every gold backed dollar. The dollar was devalued almost overnight. It was $ 20.67= 1 Troy ounce of Gold one day, and then it was $35.00 = 1 Troy ounce of Gold the next day. Each dollar lost 40% of its value in gold overnight. This must have led to massive inflationary pressures for everyday needs, just as in Germany.

1935 AD — Persia officially changed its name from Persia to Iran; Iran means Aryan in Farsi, Persia was a Greek word Iran.

1936 AD — Arab Revolt in "Mandatory Palestine" (1936-1939 AD), against British; British troops crush the revolt, by killing 10% of the Muslim Arab population; Muslims killed 100 Jews during the revolt.

1937 AD — British government in "Mandatory Palestine" issues arrest warrant for Grand Mufti Mohammad Amin al-Husseini (1897-1974 AD) of Jerusalem for leading Arab Revolt, he fled to Iraq to avoid arrest, then he ended up in Nazi Germany recruiting Muslims for the Nazi Muslim SS Battalions. Song Lili Marleen was produced in Germany from poem made up in 1915, popularized by Marlene Dietrich.

1938 AD — Nazi Germany enslaves 12,000,000 slaves in its concentration work camps, it is the most efficient economic system ever produced by man; absolutely nothing is wasted, and everything is accounted for. This enabled the Third Reich to completely rearm itself, and exceed the fighting ability of almost every nation on the earth. The Vienna Rothschild was arrested when the Nazi German Anschluss occurred. Heinrich Himmler wanted him to sell to Nazi Germany the Iron and Steel works in Czechoslovakia that the Rothschild owned in return for letting him leave the country. He sold it to them, and left Vienna, but the deal never went through and he collected on the sale from the Communists after the war was over. President Franklin D. Roosevelt attempted to get Jews out of Europe, in 1938, and 1943, but the plans were sabotaged by American Zionist political action because the Jews would not have been sent to Palestine, but elsewhere in world.

1938 AD — Jor-El places Kal-El into a space ship and launches him from the Planet Krypton to earth before krypton explodes. Kal-El arrives on earth in the USA and grows up to become "Superman".

1939 AD — First jet aircraft constructed, the German Heinkel HE-178 was developed and flew in Nazi Germany; Hitler was skeptical of its value so they were never mass produced.

1939 AD — Jewish immigration to "Mandatory Palestine" halted by British, so as to keep the Arabs calm. Immigration to Palestine stopped from 1939 until 1948 AD.

1939 AD — In 1939 AD, the Jewish Zionists, not liking this "Arab" turn of events by the British, and frustrated that the Arabs were not selling their land to the Jews, launched a "terrorist" war against both the British and the Palestinians. The leader of the Zionist terror organization was named Yair Stern. His gang was called the "Stern Gang" or the "Lehi". There were a number of Jewish Zionist terrorist organizations, another was called the "Igrun". In 1940, the Stern Gang contacted Germany with a proposal to aid Germany militarily in return for recognition as a Jewish state open to unlimited Jewish immigration to Palestine, kill the British troops in Palestine and drive Britain out of the Levant. The Zionists offered to recruit 40,000 Jews from occupied Europe, then invade "Mandatory Palestine". Germany never got back to them on that offer, or they played phone tag, or the Germans had something else in mind. One of these leaders of the Stern Gang was Yitzak Shamir, who later in time became one of the Prime Ministers of Israel. At this point in time with the war on, with all the additional Ashkenazi Khazarian Jews acquired in Poland and the Ukraine, and with exodus to Palestine cut off by the British, Germany had to come up with another solution of the Jewish question and what to do with them to get them out of greater Germany. In 1940, they came up with the Madagascar plan where all the millions of Jews would be deported to Madagascar in the Indian Ocean, but the British Naval blockade prevented this. On December 8, 1941, the day after the Japanese attack on Pearl Harbor, Hawaii, the Third Reich implemented the "Final Solution", the massive genocidal extermination of Jews. By 1943, 90% of Poland's' Khazarian Jewish population had been gassed to death and cremated. Six million total Jews murdered, plus homosexuals', gypsy and other assorted "Untermensch" (subhuman), peoples.

1939 AD	World War II, (1939-1945 AD), started. Germany invaded Poland and war was declared. Germany, Italy, Hungary, Romania, Finland and Japan are the AXIS powers, they go to war against the rest of the world, except the USSR. From 1939 until 1940 the USSR supplied Hitler and Nazi, Germany with oil from the Baku oil fields. In 1942, the Russian Communist USSR, cut off the oil to the Nazi's and the Nazi's invaded the USSR with the intention of seizing the Baku oil fields. The Germans never made it and their advance was defeated at Stalingrad. Jewish Diaspora were rounded up and concentrated in camps, then exterminated. Winston Churchill was the Prime Minister of Great Britain.
1939 AD	AZEC, American Zionist Emergency Council established in US, a political lobby and forerunner of the present day pro-Israel Lobby, AIPAC.
1940 AD	Many of the younger Rothschild served in both the French and British Armies; the older ones in France moved to New York or Britain
1941 AD	December 7, 1941, "A Day which will live in Infamy", the Empire of Japan under Emperor Hirohito, General Tojo, and Admiral Yamato order an attack on Pearl Harbor, Hawaii, using Japanese aircraft carriers. The Japanese carrier based aircraft sunk most of the battleships of the US Navy that were anchored at the Naval base, and the US airfields were destroyed. None of the US aircraft carriers were in port and remained undamaged.
1942 AD	The US attacked Guadalcanal, in the Solomon Islands north of Australia, to secure its Henderson airfield. The US carriers in the Pacific Ocean fought the Japanese carriers at the Battle of Midway Island. The US won the Battle of Midway, which was a turning point in the war in the Pacific.
1941 AD	Origen of the concept of the European Union and Eurabia. The Estonian Nazi, Alfred Rosenberg, (1893-1946 AD) was appointed Reich Minster for the occupied Eastern European territories. He and his colleague Gerhard von Mende

(1904-1963 AD), who was a Latvian scholar of oppressed minorities within Russia, became the architect of collaboration between the captured Soviet Muslim ethnic soldiers of Turkestan, Soviet Union, and the escaped Palestinian Mufti Mohammad Amin al-Husseini, (1897-1974 AD), who assisted in spiritually turning the Turk troops towards the Muslim Brotherhood and into German auxiliary SS Divisions. 250,000 Turks served in the Nazi SS units, mostly in Eastern Europe, in Poland, and the Balkans. They served additionally in the extermination camps, where the Eastern European Jews were being exterminated. After the war, this group of soldiers, still led by Von Mende, regrouped in Hamburg and Munich. The former Turk SS auxiliary soldiers became naturalized German citizens. Von Mende had little employment prospects after the war, so he appealed to the British occupation authorities, making them aware of his vast intelligence sources on the Soviet Union. The post war German government then created and funded the "Research Service Eastern Europe". Von Mende ran this research service organization, and his former "Reich Ministry for Occupied Territories" was simply absorbed intact into this "Research Service Eastern Europe" organization. The C.I.A. used this new organization to battle the U.S.S.R. and the Communist party in the 1950's. The same Marxist-Leninist Communist expansion from Moscow was still going on after the war just as before. The same Jews in the Moscow Politburo were attempting still to expand Communism to the western nation states. Von Mende maintained contacts with the Grand Mufti, European supporters of the Third Reich, Nazi war criminals who had escaped to Islam and South America, and the Muslim Brotherhood. He had a falling out with the C.I.A., because the C.I.A. was not a German organization, so they parted ways. Von Mende then went on to building a mosque in Munich for his Muslim friends and followers. Eventually the C.I.A. set up another anti-communist organization, again headed up by another ex-Nazi Muslim. This organization, "the American Committee for the Liberation of Bolshevism" was based in Munich. It eventually ran "Radio Free Europe" and the mosque in Munich was eventually taken over by the Muslim Brotherhood, Said Ramadan in 1954. When the C.I.A. wrestled control away from Von Mende, they then controlled all the work of his previous organization. After the war in West Germany, most Nazi's were barred from politics, but still, especially in the East Germany, many rose to high office, in the police state there.

One West German citizen and former Wehrmacht Nazi officer and Nazi corporate lawyer, professor, Walter Hallstein, (1901-1982 AD) became the architect of first, the European Coal and Steel Community, and then second, he became the architect of the European Economic Community, known as the E.E.C. He went on to become first president of the Commission of the European Economic Community from 1958 until 1967 AD, and is known as one of the founding fathers of the European Union. Walter Hallstein obtained his doctorate in 1925 in Berlin, in 1927 he became a judge in Berlin, and then worked at the Kaiser Wilhelm Institute for Foreign and International Law until the year 1930. From 1930 until 1940, he was a professor of company law at the University of Rostock.

In 1941, he became a professor of law at the University of Frankfurt. In 1942, he was an artillery officer, Oberleutnant Walter Hallstein, in the Nazi Wehrmacht, stationed in France. He belonged to Nazi organizations but he was not a rabid Nazi. In 1944, he was captured by American forces after the Battle of Cherburg, and shipped to an American P.O.W. camp in Mississippi. He then became part of the U.S. Army's "Project Sunflower". Project Sunflower was a part of the SPD, Special Projects Division, it was designed to reeducate German P.O.W.'s who were not rabid Nazi's, with the intension of creating leaders for post war Germany. The OSS, Office of Strategic Services, forerunner of the C.I.A. was in charge of post war planning for Germany. Project Sunflower was run by a naturalized U.S. citizen, Heinrich Walter Ehrmann, (1908-1194 AD). Ehrmann was also a lawyer, receiving his law degree in Berlin in 1929, and his doctorate in 1932 from the University of Freiburg. In 1932, he became a judge in Berlin. In 1933, he was arrested by the Gestapo and thrown in Oranienburg concentration camp for his political contacts with the SDP, the Social Democratic Party. He managed to escape from the concentration camp, fled to France where he lived and worked as a corresponding journalist for the Institute for Social Research, a Columbia University Institute based at Columbia University in N.Y.C. In 1940, he left France for Spain, then from Portugal, he immigrated to New York. He became a research associate at the "University in Exile" at the New York school for Social Research. From 1943 to 1947, Ehrmann served as a consultant for the war department in Washington, D.C., where he went on to run "Project Sunflower", and met with Walter Hallstein. The two corresponded after the war, when Hallstein was repatriated to Germany. Walter Hallstein became the founding father of the European Coal and Steel Community, applying his corporate law experience in Nazi Germany to the creation of the E.E.C., and setting the foundation stones for the present E.U.

The Treaty of Paris in 1951 established the European Coal and Steel Community, to stop Germany and France from arguing and fighting again over the coal and iron ore in the Ruhr Valley and Saar areas that lies between their two countries. The fighting over these areas between the two Germanic tribes went on between them since the Roman Empire collapsed. The Treaty of Rome in 1957, established the European Economic Community, the European Atomic Energy Commission, and included the European Coal and Steel Community. In 1967, the Merger Treaty combined all three into the Commission of European Communities. The Treaty of Lisbon in 2007, established the European Commission and is the basis of the European Union. This is the same plan initiated by the Third Reich under Adolf Hitler, a "European Confederation", presented in 1943 by Nazi foreign minister von Ribbentrop.

1941 AD   The Shah of Iran (September 16, 1941-1979 AD), Mohammad Reza Pahlavi, (1919-1980 AD), took power and severed relations with the AXIS powers, after Russian and British troops entered Iran. American troops entered the country in 1942. This was the oil supply for the Allied Powers. The British exploited the oil fields drastically, leading to the development of resentment between the Muslims in Iran and the west. The resentment was also fostered and promoted by the Germans in Berlin. On October 7, 1941, Stalin sought peace with Hitler, but Hitler rejected the offer.

1942 AD	Anglo-American militaries occupied Algeria, and set up a modern state of Algeria. The drug Penicillin was perfected and put into use.
1942 AD	Nazi armies meet defeat at Stalingrad Russia, September 1942 until February 1943.
1944 AD	Jewish insurgency in "Mandatory Palestine", (1944-1947 AD), this was a civil war between Arabs and Jews, with the British caught in the middle. The Bretton-Woods International Monetary Agreement of 1944, establishes the I.M.F., the International Monetary Fund, or the "impossible missions force", and eventually the World Bank, U.S. currency is tied to Gold. Countries could settle in dollars instead of Gold, credits were established to avoid deflation. $35.00 per ounce of Gold in 1945. American troops land in Normandy, Brittany, France in order to attack German Third Reich from the west, "D-Day", June 6, 1944.
1944 AD	July 1944, Bomb plot on Hitler by Colonel Count von Stauffenberg at Wolf's Lair; possibly a false flag event created by Martin Bormann to cover the dispersion of thousands of Nazi's out of Europe for the Nazi International. The allies would not look for Nazi's who were said to have been executed in the plot, the Nazi's knew it was time to go, US General Eisenhower was in France moving east, and the Russians were moving west after the German defeat at Stalingrad. One such Nazi was Admiral Canaris. Admiral Canaris' previous experience was to explore and set up secret Nazi Naval bases in coves on the Pacific coast of South America. These bases would be used to harbor U-boats containing Nazi's escaping from Europe when the war was being lost in Germany.
1945 AD	Allied armies, primarily Russian group forces, defeat Axis powers in Europe. Hitler committed suicide, "Suicide is Painless". The US and USSR troops meet up at the Elbe River in Germany. Germany surrendered. The US had driven "Empire of the Sun" back to its home islands, but they refuse to surrender. The US dropped two atomic boobs on two cities, Hiroshima and Nagasaki and they surrendered unconditionally, thanks to Albert Einstein and Robert Oppenheimer and "The Manhattan Project". This was V-J day and it ended World War II. President Harry Truman (1945- 1953 AD) was President of the USA.
1945 AD	Mass deportations of ethnic Germans from Eastern Europe by Russian Bolshevik forces; ethnic German civilians forced to walk west to Germany; millions die; German troops are held in camps and slowly starved over next few years. Polish borders were moved west. Morgenthau plan for Germany was scrapped, US then puts Marshall plan into effect where Europe is rebuilt using US aid. There were millions of starving displaced people in Europe in 1945.
1945 AD	After the war some of the Rothschild family made their way back to France; The Nazi's had systematically looted all the Rothschild artwork, over 21,000 items of art and jewels and furniture and stuff. An American officer who was in charge of

finding and preserving cultural works, began to wonder where all the art work was, because it was not in France. He made enquires and someone thought the Nazi's may have taken it to a castle in Bavaria. He took troops to mad King Ludwig II's Neuschwanstein Castle near Munich, (the castle is the model for Disneyland's castle), and found all of Rothschild art, furniture, treasure chests of jewels, along with the looted art of 203 other private collections; in addition, everything was cataloged, with photographs of everything. This was all returned slowly to the owners over the next few years. Some loot continues to be found to this date in various German places.

1945 AD	Algeria, Muslim Algerians massacre Europeans, French Army killed 45,000 Muslim Algerians.
1946 AD	Start of "The Baby Boomer" generation.
1947 AD	The United Nations announced the partition plan for Palestine, effective when the British Mandate ends in 1948 AD. India was divided into Muslim Pakistan and Hindu India.
1947 AD	"Cold War" (1947-1991 AD), begins; Cold War between Communist USSR with its Marxist- Leninist ideology and the Wests' Capitalistic ideology; this leads to numerous proxy wars fought around the world from the 1950's to the 1990's. The doctrine of "M.A.D.", "mutually assured destruction", ensures no one uses nuclear weapons, because it would lead to extermination of life on this planet. If ever humans do have a world-wide nuclear war, the planet would enter a nuclear winter, most life would end for all plant and animal species. Given that the sun has already expended half of its nuclear fuel, and life came about on this planet shortly after the birth of the sun, it is doubtful that evolution would have time to produce higher beings like humans, it's a one shot deal for us, don't blow it. The "transistor" invented this year, which replaced vacuum tubes in electronics.
1947 AD	The US C.I.A., and the joint chiefs of staff at the Defense Department warned the US government that Zionist aspirations and policies were in conflict with the strategic interests of the United States and Western Governments. "Zionist strategy will involve the United States in a continuously widening and deepening series of operations to secure maximum Jewish objectives." In November 1947, the UN voted to "partition" the "mandated" Palestine when the British mandate ended. The U.N. gave the Zionists 55 % of the partitioned land in Palestine after the mandate, but did not create a state of Israel, it only gave its "recommendation" for a state. 30 % of Palestine was Jewish at this point in time. Fighting in Palestine intensified. The two Zionist militias were led by Menachem Begin and Yitzak Shamir. Zionists forced out 413,000 Palestinians, in their brutal "ethnic cleansing campaign. The Zionists massacred 33 Palestinian villages. Zionists militias of Jewish men and women murdered Arab men, raped women and children, then slaughtered them, including pregnant women. Hundreds of Christian men women and children were killed by the Israelis, and told to leave, along with their dead Christ. The Swedish Red Cross witnessed some of the massacres by Zionists and described them as being the same as when the Nazi SS came into a town like

Athens. The Zionist Jews repeated and reaped on the Palestinians exactly what their ancestors had done to the Canaanites in the same area of the Levant under King David 2947 earlier. The US State Department opposed the creation of the State of Israel, and was subsequently labeled anti-Semitic by the Zionists.

1948 AD — On May 14, 1948 the British Mandate ended. On May 15, 1948, the Zionists in Israel declared the State of Israel. On May 16, 1948 Israel was attacked by the Arab League consisting of Saudi Arabia, Jordan, Egypt, Syria, Iraq, Lebanon, and irregular fighters of the Muslim Brotherhood, Yemen, Pakistan, Sudan, and the Holy War Army. President Truman was re-elected in November 1948. Prior to the election a Zionist committee headed by NY Zionist Congressman Emmanuel Cellar met with Truman and demanded that he support a State of Israel, "or they would run him out of town." Dewy had already been approached, and committed his support. Truman's' "whistle-stop tour" before the election was financed by the Zionist American businessman Abraham Feinberg. Truman won the election against Dewey. After 10 months of fighting its war of independence, Israel held on to 78 % of the Palestinian land. 750,000 Palestinians fled Palestine and became Palestinian refugees. 700,000 Jews were expelled from Muslim countries and immigrated to Israel. Israel stole the property of the Palestinians, in today's dollars it is equal to $5.2 Billion Dollars that was stolen. "Israel will engage in armed aggression masked as defense", as the US Defense Department said. Secretary of Defense James Forrestal said no electoral considerations should be made which jeopardize US national security. Truman supported the creation of the State of Israel after disregarding much professional opposition to its creation.

1948 AD — The Republic of Ireland came into existence.

1949 AD — Germany was divided into Communist East Germany and capitalist West Germany; Communist China, "The Peoples Republic of China" began under Chairman Mao.

1949 AD — American High Commissioner for Germany, John J. McCloy assumed post (1949-1952 AD); Mr. McCloy was the American lawyer for I.G. Farben, a German industrial corporation before World War II, during the war he opposed the bombing of Auschwitz concentration camp by US bombers, he served on the Warren Commission with CIA director Allen Dulles, was Chairman of Chase Manhattan, and when posted to Germany as High Commissioner he pardoned 70,000 Nazi's.

1949 AD — Germany, Konrad Adenauer, (1876-1967 AD), became the first post-World War II Chancellor of West Germany, (1949-1963 AD). His government was staffed by former Nazi's or those beholding to Nazi's. He created the political party known as the CDU, the Christian Democratic Union Party. The CDU is the party that Helmut Kohl, and Chancellor Angela Merkel belong to. The CDU was infiltrated with Nazi's, after they were pardoned.

1950 AD — In September 1950, the German Geopolitical Center in Madrid circulated a top-secret document called the "Madrid Circular". The "Madrid Circular" was produced by the Nazi International, or the post-war Axis International, an organization composed of Nazi's who never surrendered but scattered worldwide before and after the German armies surrendered to the allies. The ideology of this Nazi organization was to again gain power, but through international corporate socialism of an international fascist order. The aims of the Nazi International were the same German aims that World War I Kaiser Wilhelm II and his Reichkanzler Theobald von Betteman Hollweg, (1856-1921 AD) envisioned in their "September Program", which was a central European Economic Association, a "customs union" with Germany at the center. This "September Program" was also proposed by the Third Reich, the goal of having a united Europe under Nazi German control. The "Madrid Circular" of 1950 laid out phases to achieve the goal of international corporate socialism (under German control) and had an uncanny and unrealistic ability to predict long term development accurately, or it was accurate due to the placement of corporate and political agents within the post war world. Today in 2016, the "Madrid Circular" of 1950 appears to have achieved fruition. It laid out phases, three phases that the group should strive for to restore Nazi control. The first short term phase was to advance the creation of a European Federation, economies of the "mixed or third way", not capitalism and not Communism but the third, mixed way. "The European train will go where the German locomotive goes". The second phase was to build up European ties with Russia, China, S.E Asia, Africa, and Latin America with the goal of expanding German and European trade, and with a goal of building up German heavy industries in these places. The final goal was to foster a coup d'etat in the United States and engineer a dollar crises against the US dollar diplomacy. When in control of the US, the Nazi International would then use the US military against Russia and the Slavs, eastwards. The "Madrid Circular" is reflective of deeper economic and ideological goals and players to the east of Germany, (BRICS ?). The keystone in the arch of the "Madrid Circular" phases was to de-stabilize Anglo-American interests in the middle-east, to threaten the oil and petroleum economic lifelines of North America. Germany, prior to, and during World War I, worked towards influencing Islam to use Jihad. The German elites in World War I convinced the Muslim Ottoman Empire to call for a selective "jihad" against the allies, then after WWI, both Germany and fascist Italy continued to work hard in the Islamic world to foster support for their goals of destabilizing Anglo-Allied relations in the middle-East and Persia by fostering resentment for the west. After World War II, the Nazi International continued to exploit Islam and use the tool of Jihad against America and Russia in a form of asymmetric warfare. The three phases of the "Madrid Circular" were to be achieved by relying on Nazi ties with the Muslim world.

1950 AD   Korean War (1950-1953 AD) starts, Communist China and North Korea fight against the United States and the South Koreans. The US under General MacArthur invaded North Korea and advanced to the Chosin Reservoir because the Chosin Reservoir was the place where the Empire of Japan was working on its atomic program during World War II. The United States wanted to see just how far Japanese scientists had gotten before they were defeated, and also to prevent the Russians and Communist Chinese from obtaining any information that might assist them in building atomic weapons.

1951 AD   The European Coal and Steel Community came into being, the first step towards the Common Market in Europe, the E.U.

1951 AD   **Amendment XXII**

Section 1.

No person shall be elected to the office of the President more than twice, and no person who has held the office of President, or acted as President, for more than two years of a term to which some other person was elected President shall be elected to the office of President more than once. But this Article shall not apply to any person holding the office of President when this article was proposed by Congress, and shall not prevent any person who may be holding the office of the President, or acting as President, during the term within which this article becomes operative from holding the office of President or acting as President during the remainder of such term.

Section 2.

This article shall be inoperative unless it shall have been ratified as an amendment to the Constitution by the legislatures of three fourths of the several states within seven years from the date of its submission to the states by the Congress.

1951 AD   Iran nationalizes its oil fields; in response, the US State Department, promotes, "The Seven Sisters", a consortium, an oil cartel of the seven large Anglo-American oil companies that ran the worldwide oil business after World War II.

1953 AD   General Eisenhower became President Eisenhower, (1953-1961 AD), he threatened nuclear war against Communist China, if an armistice was not signed over North and South Korea; he ordered the CIA and MI6 to overthrow the democratically elected prime minister of Iran and reinstall Shah Revi Pahlavi, so strategic control of oil could be maintained. Premier Khrushchev (1953-1964 AD), assumed power in the U.S.S.R.; King Saud (1902-1969 AD) becomes King of Saudi Arabia, (1953-1964 AD); Scientists James Watson, (1928-present) and Francis Crick, (1916-2004 AD), discover DNA.

1953 AD   Germany, "The Naumann Coup", Seven former high ranking Nazi's were arrested by the British for plotting a Nazi takeover of Adenauer's government; the coup had 125 Nazi leaders involved but only 7 were arrested. Dr. Werner Naumann, Karl Kaufmann, Paul Zimmerman, Gustav Scheel, Dr. Heinrich Haselmeyer, Dr. Karl Scharping, and Heinz Slipen; the coup was financed by the Nazi International. The CIA, under Allen Dulles, in Washington squelched the British charges and the German Supreme Court dismissed all the charges in 1954. Adenauer was a front and the Federal republic of Germany would be the façade of the Nazi International.

1954 AD	Leader of the Muslim Brotherhood and son-in-law of its founder, (Sheikh al-Banna), Said Ramadan fled Egypt and was brought to Munich by the CIA, where he was put in charge of a mosque and it became the headquarters of the Muslim Brotherhood in Europe. From this mosque, the Brotherhood waged its war against Israel, and was used by the CIA to counter the USSR. Algerian War of Independence, (1954-1962 AD), a decolonization war to implement Sharia Law into the French colony. The USS Nautilus was launched as the first nuclear powered submarine. France was defeated in Indo-China by the Communists, and asks for US intervention in Vietnam; "Domino Theory" was being put forth by politician Joseph McCarthy; he held hearings in Congress routing out Commie subversives. "under God" inserted into the Pledge of Allegiance; Brown versus the Board of Education; the first "Burger King opened in Miami, and the "transistor" radio was invented.

Pledge of Allegiance

I pledge allegiance to the flag of the United States of America, and to the republic for which it stands, One nation, Indivisible, with liberty and justice for all.

1954 AD	Godzilla climbs out of the Pacific Ocean and destroys Tokyo with his radioactive atomic breath.
1954 AD	First Bilderberg Group meeting. The Bilderberg group promotes "Atlanticism", a right wing political ideology; their private meetings cover military, economic and political issues. The early Bilderberg meetings were the coordinating bodies behind the movement and laundering of the Nazi and Axis Powers loot back into the Western banking system in the form of American aid.
1955 AD	First US troops sent to Vietnam; de-segregation of the US military continues; Austria State Treaty reestablishes Austria as an independent state after World War II, occupations.
1956 AD	Second Arab-Israeli War, Suez Crisis; Israel, Britain and France invade Egypt, to "protect" the Suez Canal. President Eisenhower told them to get out. First Baby Boomers were 10 years old.
1957 AD	Treaty of Rome establishes EEC, European Economic Community; Eisenhower was sworn in for a second term; FBI arrested Jimmy Hoffa on a bribery charge; Russian Sputnik 1 and 2 were put into orbit by USSR; DEW line put into operation; Leave it to Beaver premiers on TV; Atlas Shrugged published; 1st US Army death in Vietnam. Toyota began exporting cars to the US; laser invented; Eisenhower had a stroke; Boeing-707 flies for first time; Communist China's Party Chairman Mao Zedong announced that 800,000 "class" enemies, (people), had been liquidated by the Communist Party to make the world a better place. The movie, 'Bridge on the River Kwai" was released.
1958 AD	Eisenhower sends 15,000 US Marines to Lebanon, to prevent radical Islamists from taking over. France formed a 5th republic, with Charles de Gaulle as President.
1959 AD	Barbie Doll starts to sell.

1960 AD	Cuban Revolution, Fidel Castro came to power as a Communist dictator. Beatles rock and roll group formed and performed in Hamburg; Cuban refugees start to arrive in Florida, 1000 per week; John F. Kennedy elected as President; New York, a midair collision between two commercial aircraft over Staten Island, New York, debris comes down all over Brooklyn and Staten Island.
1960 AD	Saudi Arabia has 300,000 or more slaves. OPEC, the organization of Petroleum Exporting Countries was created.
1961 AD	John F. Kennedy, (1961-1963 AD), sworn in as President of US., Bay of Pigs invasion of Cuba fails; Tsar hydrogen bomb exploded above ground in Soviet Russia, it was the most powerful man-made explosion in history, equivalent to 50 Megatons of TNT; USSR put the first man in space, Russian cosmonaut Yuri Gagarin.
1961 AD	Berlin Wall, and Iron Curtain built by communists in Europe to prevent people from defecting to the West; fallout shelters built around world; Paris massacre of 1961, 240 Algerians protesting curfew in Paris were massacred by police. French Coup by French Army Generals against French President Charles de Gaulle; de Gaulle explodes a nuclear weapon in the Sahara Desert and the coup surrenders; American tanks face off Russian tanks at Checkpoint Charlie in Berlin; 18,000 US troops were in Vietnam. Adolph Eichmann was executed in Israel for the Nazi holocaust killings.
1961 AD	**Amendment XXIII**

Section 1.

The District constituting the seat of government of the United States shall appoint in such manner as Congress may direct:

A number of electors of President and Vice President equal to the whole number of Senators and representatives in congress to which the district would be entitled if it were a state, but in no event more than the least populous state; they shall be in addition to those appointed by the states, but they shall be considered, for purposes of the election of President and Vice President, to be electors appointed by a state; and they shall meet in the district and perform such duties as provided by the twelfth article of amendment.

Section 2.

The Congress shall have power to enforce this article by appropriate legislation.

1962 AD	Rothschild gets back into merchant banking business in London, other rich and energetic Rothschild live around the world and in Israel, in solidarity.
1962 AD	Algerian War (1954-1962 AD) ends; 900,000 European-Algerian French people immigrate to France; 1.5 Million people died in this eight year war.
1962 AD	President Kennedy persuades Saudi Arabian King Saud to outlaw slavery in 1962, during the Saudi Kings visit to Washington; Marilyn Monroe dies; Vatican II ended.

1962 AD	Cuban Missile Crises, October 1962.
1963 AD	Germany; Chancellor Adenauers' secretary, chief of staff, resigned when it was found out he was the Nazi who actually wrote the Nuremburg Race Laws. Dr. Hans Globke was also the head of the Office of Jewish Affairs during the Third Reich after writing the Nuremburg Laws. Also Dr. Gustav Sonnonhol, a former S.S. officer who advocated for the "Madrid Circular" resigned.
1963 AD	Kennedy wants to overthrow the Iraqi government because it might invade Kuwait, and throw in with the Soviet Union, Ba'athist party takes over; Kennedy supports Ba'athists party and supplies them with arms, February 1963, this was Saddam Hussein's political party. Ba'athist party was overthrown 11/10/1963), by pro-Nasser Iraqi military elements. Nasser was pro-Russian.
1963 AD	"Flying Scotsman", makes its last trip before preservation.
1963 AD	President Kennedy was assassinated in Dallas, Texas, (11/22/1963). President Johnson (1963-1969 AD) becomes president.
1964 AD	**Amendment XXIV**

Section 1.

The right of the citizens of the United States to vote in any primary or other election for President of Vice President, for electors for President or Vice President, or for Senator or Representative in Congress shall not be denied or abridged by the United States or any State by reason of failure to pay any poll tax or other tax.

Section 2.

The Congress shall have the power to enforce this article by appropriate legislation.

1964 AD	King Faisal, (1906-1975 AD), became King of Saudi Arabia, (1964-1975 AD) 1964 AD Ford Mustang invented; 16,000 troops in Vietnam; Very first Baby Boomers 18 years old; Premier Brezhnev assumes power in U.S.S.R.; Musician Barry McGuire wrote song, "Eve of Destruction".
1965 AD	Europe; population 634,000,000 people.
1965 AD	"Great Society" Speech given by President (L.B.J.) Johnson. Start of three and one half year bombardment of North Vietnam; 3,500 US Marines land in South Vietnam as first combat troops; draft card burnings begin with draft dodging; anti-war protests begin instigated and fueled by "liberal Commie Jews"; Ground troops in Vietnam surge to 200,000 troops, all drafted Baby Boomers. Draft was increased from 17,000 to35,000 draftees per month, Social Security Act of 1965, Medicare and Medicaid established; Watts Riots in California; Northeast Blackout for 13 hours; Sound of Music; first baby Boomers are 19 years old.
1966 AD	385,000 US troops in Vietnam, first Baby Boomers 20 years old; Congress puts interest rate caps on savings accounts at all banks, 1966-1979.
1967 AD	485,000 US troops in Vietnam, first Baby Boomers 21 years old; TET offensive in Vietnam; Newark N.J. Riots, due to economic causes;

1967 AD

Third Arab-Israeli War, six day war; Egypt, Syria, and Jordan attacked Israel, Israel drives them back and gains territory; another 300,000 Palestinians leave as refugees; Jews endure pogroms in Arab countries; minority Jewish communities are expelled all over Islamic world. The USS Liberty an intelligence gathering US Naval vessel in the Mediterranean Sea was attacked by Israel, 34 US sailors were killed and 171 were wounded.

1967 AD

Amendment XXV

Section 1.
In case of the removal of the President from office or of his death or resignation, the Vice President shall become President.

Section 2.
Whenever there is a vacancy in the office of the Vice President, the President shall nominate a Vice President who shall take office upon confirmation by a majority vote of both Houses of Congress.

Section 3.
Whenever the President transmits to the President pro tempore of the Senate and the Speaker of the House of Representatives his written declaration that he is unable to discharge the powers and duties of his office, and until he transmits to them a written declaration to the contrary, such powers and duties shall be discharged by the Vice President as Acting President.

Section 4.
Whenever the Vice President and a majority of either the principal officers of the executive departments or of such other body as Congress may by law provide, transmit to the President pro-tempore of the Senate and the Speaker of the House of Representatives their written declaration that the President is unable to discharge the powers and duties of his office, the Vice President shall immediately assume the powers and duties of the office as Acting President.

Thereafter, when the President transmits to the President pro tempore of the Senate and the Speaker of the House of Representatives his written declaration that no inability exists, he shall resume the powers and duties of his office unless the Vice President and a majority of either the principal officers of the executive department or of such other body as Congress may by law provide, transmit within four days to the President pro tempore of the Senate and the Speaker of the House of Representatives their written declaration that the President is unable to discharge the powers and duties of his office. Thereupon Congress shall decide the issue, assembling within forty-eight hours for that purpose if not in session. If the Congress, within twenty one days after receipt of the latter written declaration, or, if Congress is not in session, within twenty one days after Congress id required

Raymond Robert Martin

to assemble, determines by two-thirds vote of Both Houses that the President is unable to discharge the powers and duties of his office, The Vice President shall continue to discharge the same as Acting President; otherwise, the President shall resume the powers and duties of his office.

1968 AD — 536,000 US troops in Vietnam, First Baby Boomers 22 years old; Vietnam peace talks begin; Presidential candidate and brother of slain President John F. Kennedy, Senator Robert F. Kennedy was assassinated by Sirhan Sirhan, (1944- present), a Palestinian refugee, born in "Mandatory Palestine", to a Palestinian Christian family. In 1956, the family immigrated to the United States, when he was 12 years old. He was strong rabid opponent of Jews and the State of Israel; he never became an American citizen, and he held a Jordanian Passport at the time of the murder. He joined the Rosicrucian's two years before the assassination. He said he killed Robert Kennedy because of Kennedy's support for Israel in the Third Arab-Israeli War, the six day war, and of Senator Kennedy's promise to send 50 fighter jets to Israel if he got elected.

1968 AD — In 1968 in Europe, the EEC was growing in popularity and its leadership were looking forward to a future with aspirations of creating an even larger union. Their aspiration was to create a Mediterranean basin that recreated the Roman-Byzantine Empires. At the same time, the Islamic countries were dreaming of recreating a new empire similar to the Ottoman Empire and the glory of the previous Caliphates. Neither Europe nor the Islamic world held any sort of mutual beliefs or understandings of the others culture. Words like peace, prosperity, knowledge, freedom, human rights, mean completely different things to either of these cultures, but each wanted something from the other. Europe wanted markets and Islam wanted modern technology for Muslims. Both wanted a peaceful Mediterranean Sea; which it had been thanks to the United States taxpayer and the US Navy. After the Palestinians lost the third Arab-Israeli War, the Palestinians began a series of terrorist Jihad attacks in continental Europe, because both Europe and the United States supported Israel. 15 commercial aircraft flights were hijacked each year between 1968 and 1971. Ransoms were paid, people died. The Europeans were now back where they were in the years 711 AD until 1800 AD. The EEC and the European governments didn't want to deal with this, and went into denial. They were still war weary 25 years after the USSR and the Allies had flattened Europe to get rid of the Third Reich. The EU began scheming for a solution.

1969 AD — 475,000 US troops in Vietnam; President Richard Millhouse Nixon, (1969-1974 AD), "Tricky Dicky" was sworn in as president; US Astronauts landed on the Moon and walked around, this ticked off the "Moon God", he felt like he was being walked allover. In NYC, the homosexual community initiated "The Stonewall Riots", in Greenwich Village, to protest police harassment and intimidation. This was the start of the Gay rights movement in the United States.

1970 AD — 334,000 US troops in Vietnam, first Baby Boomers 24 years old; Gold = $35.00 per ounce.

1971 AD

<u>Amendment XXVI</u>

Section 1.
The right of citizens of the United States, who are eighteen years old or older, to vote shall not be denied or abridged by the United States or by any state on account of age.

Section 2.
The Congress shall have power to enforce this article by appropriate legislation.

1971 AD — 157,000 US troops in Vietnam; first Baby Boomers 25 years old; "Nixon Shock", President Nixon takes the US off the gold standard; US dollars could no longer be redeemed in gold. Gold = $38.00 per ounce, dollar floats on currency markets; OPEC announces barrels of oil will be priced in Gold. Women gained the right to vote in Switzerland.

1972 AD — 24,200 US troops in Vietnam; first baby Boomers 26 years old; first handheld calculator is on the market selling for $395.00 dollars.

1973 AD — 50 US troops in Vietnam; first Baby Boomers 27 years old; World Trade Center Buildings in NYC completed and opened; "Pink Floyds Dark Side of the Moon" album released.

1973 AD — Yom-Kippur War, 1973 Arab- Israeli War; Israel attacked by some of the same usual suspects; Egypt and Syria, supported by expeditionary forces of Saudi Arabia, Jordan, Algeria, Iraq, Morocco, Libya and Cuba. The countries of Europe closed their airspace to US airplanes that needed to refuel there as they were en-route to Israel for military resupply from the US. Fifty European commercial aircraft were hijacked in 1973 by Palestinian terrorists. Europe sided with the Arab League against Israel. In response to U.S. support for Israel in the Yom-Kippur War, the 1973 oil crises was launched by OPEC, this caused worldwide economic problems, OPEC raised oil prices by a factor of 4; oil shot up 400 %, one barrel of oil before the crises cost $3.00 per barrel, then OPEC raised it to $12.00 per barrel, this caused inflation in Iran, Europe, and the U.S. as the price was passed on to consumers; unemployment followed a few years later. Gold, $43.00 = 1 ounce of Gold; the stock market crashed in 1973-1974 due to OPEC, it lost 45 % of its value, it did not fully recover in real terms until 1993. European countries within the European Economic Community started a relationship with the Arab States that were at war with Israel. The "Never Again' slogan, a reference to the Nazi extermination camps was forgotten about in just 29 years. The state of Israel was not being accepted by the Islamic world, just as the Third Reich wanted to be rid of the Jews in Europe, the Muslims wanted to be rid of the Jews in Palestine.

1974 AD — The EEC called for Israel to withdraw to the 1949 armistice lines and recognize the rights of the Palestinian people to live there. The EEC then formed the PAEAC, Parliamentary Association for Euro-Arabic cooperation, funded by the EEC and Arab countries. The EAD, Euro-Arab Division is an offshoot of the PAEAC.

Arab countries appointed Christian dhimmis as its representatives' to the EAD. PAEAC and the EAD promoted integration of the Arab world with the European Economic Community. This was the actual start of "Eurabia", the concept that was thought up by the ex-Nazi Wehrmacht officer and Nazi corporate judge Walter Hallstein in the early 1950's. The EEC did not combat the Jihad that was being directed against it, the EEC "submitted" to Islam, in order to reduce the Jihad attacks being launched against itself by Islam. They were paying Islam "extortion", or tribute in the same way that the Islamic Barbary Coast states demanded "peace" and "tribute", from Thomas Jefferson in 1786. The US response to that Islamic extortion back then was to build a Navy that could operate in the Mediterranean Sea. But the EEC and Europe didn't take that path; the EEC recognized the P.L.O, the Palestinian Liberation Organization, and its leader Yassar Arafat (Ringo Star). The EEC also followed the Arab request to become more hostile to the United States, distance itself from Israel, and allow Muslim immigration to Europe. In return, the Muslims would reduce terrorist activities in Europe against Europeans, sign lucrative industrial trade deals with European corporations to modernize the Middle East, and receive oil from the Middle East.

In Italy, under the government of Aldo Moro, a secret treaty was signed between Italy and the PLO. The PLO was allowed to legally operate out of Italy, circulate freely in Italy, stockpile weapons, and set up operational bases within Italy in exchange for not terrorizing and destroying Italian domestic and foreign interests. Billions of dollars were transferred to the PLO by Italy. Italian Jews were not protected by the Aldo Moro agreement so Italian Jews were targets for the Muslims on Italian territory. The PLO used Italy to attack targets in Western Europe.

In the 1970's and continuing until the 1980's, following mass migrations of Arabs into Europe, a new political concept was created because "integration" wasn't working. This concept was called multiculturalism. It was an essential tool that needed to be implemented in order to have the forced merger between two completely disparate cultures with different historical religions. There was not going to be a "melting pot", as there was in the United States, when continuous waves of immigration blended together into one more or less Americanized culture; losing a good portion of their ethnic identities along the way as they became more Americanized. Multiculturalism is similar to the philosophical policy of "separate but equal". This policy began to produce "ghettos", and eventually "No Go Zones" within Europe, where whole sections of European cities operate as if they are a foreign country, resembling the country the Islamic inhabitants immigrated from. Eventually all mobile city services were cut to these Islamic "safe spaces".

1974 AD   President "Tricky Dick" Nixon resigned over the Watergate scandal, and numerous other shady machinations; President Ford became the next President of the US; he was clumsy and fell down or bumped his head a lot. Nixon's Secretary of State was Henry Kissinger, (1923- present), Kissinger was born in Germany and immigrated to the United States; he was a German American Jew who served in the US Army in Intelligence after the war. He was in charge of a de-Nazification program in a city in West Germany then became involved with the government. He was responsible for "detente" between the Communist World and the US. He opened up trade ties with Communist China.

1974 AD · Muslim Turkey invaded Cyprus; there was no help from NATO, so Greece pulled out of its membership in NATO; Turkey remained in NATO. Turkey was important strategically for being so close to the USSR.

1975 AD · Fall of Saigon to the North Vietnamese Communists. End of South Vietnam.

1975 AD · King Khalid, (1913-1982 AD), became King of Saudi Arabia (1975-1982 AD).

1976 AD · There were no further references to the number of dollars required for 1 ounce of Gold by the US Treasury, and Federal Reserve. Representative money with the Gold standard prevent governments from manipulating the economy, and the Gold Standard prevents hyper-inflation. Gold standard induces deflation, but induces bank runs at times. Deficit spending is a means of confiscating wealth, it is a form of taxation and financial repression by the government. First Baby Boomers were 30 years old.

1977 AD · President Jimmy Carter, (1977-1981 AD); The E.U. declares that Jewish presence in Judea is colonization of Arab land and demands the Jews withdraw from Judea.

1978 AD · Camp David Accords, a temporary peace treaty between Egypt and Israel.

1979 AD · Islamic revolution in Iran; Ayatollah Khomeini became the Islamic Shi'ite leader with the support of many unemployed Islamic workers; 1979 Oil crises as Iran launches an oil embargo on the world to conduct an Islamic Revolution; crude oil doubled in price to $39.00 per barrel, after President Carter deregulated the oil industry; 60 hostages were held in Iran for 444 days until 1981 when President Ronald Reagan took office. Reagan said in his campaign speeches, "The Bombing will begin as soon as I am sworn in". The Shah of Iran fled to Paris.

1980 AD · Carter deregulates the airline industry leading to intensive competition, depression of profits, depression of workers' pay, and many airline bankruptcies.

1980 AD · Iran-Iraq war, (1980-1988 AD), secular Muslim Iraq attacked Muslim theocratic Iran; Mariel Cuba Boatlift; 80,000 Cuban refugees enter Miami, Florida by Boats; Fidel Castro opened his prisons and mental hospitals and put them on small boats for Florida. Gold $850= 1 troy ounce of Gold.

1981 AD · President Ronald Reagan (1981-1989 AD), first recession of 1980's; (1981-1982 AD); AIDS epidemic begins around the world, affecting primarily homosexuals, I.V. drug users, and people who had received blood transfusions.

1982 AD · Soviet Premier Andropov assumes power (1982-1984 AD) in USSR; King Fahd al Saud (1921-2005 AD), became King of Saudi Arabia, (1982-2005 AD).

1983 AD · Savings and Loan Crises, and the demise of the savings and loan industry in the United States. This was caused by the movement of funds to commercial banks. High inflation occurred after this an accumulation of the Great Society programs, the Vietnam war spending, and the oil crises of 1973 and 1979.Ronald Reagan introduced Reaganomics, "a form of borrowing yourself to prosperity". Don't save, borrow money and spend, it will all work out!

1983 AD	Beirut, Lebanon; Beirut International Airport, October 23,1983, a Muslim Suicide bomber drove into the Headquarters building of the 24th MAU, Marine Amphibious Unit, and exploded 12,000 pounds of high explosives, killing 241 US Marines.
1985 AD	Palestinian Muslim Jihad i's seize the Italian cruise ship Achille Lauro, kill retired Jewish American Leon Klinghoffer, and throw his body and his wheelchair overboard into Mediterranean Sea off Tarsus; PLO attacked El-Al Israeli airlines at Rome Airport; PLO attacked El-Al ticket counter at Vienna airport; Premier Gorbachev assumes power in USSR, (1985-1991 AD).
1986 AD	First Baby Boomers, 40 years old
1988 AD	Donald Trump bought the Eastern Airlines Shuttle, a NY, Boston, Washington hourly airline shuttle. The deal was completed in in June 1989, after the Machinists Union went on strike over it earlier in year. The shuttle became "The Trump Shuttle", (1989-1992 AD), when it defaulted on its debt, went bankrupt and was sold to US Air, then it became the "American Air Shuttle".
1989 AD	President George H. W. Bush (1989-1993 AD) became President, NAFTA enacted; the North American Free Trade Agreement, many corporations physically move operations to Mexico, permanently displacing millions of American workers, in order to obtain cheaper Mexican labor costs. All of Eastern Airlines' unionized workers went on strike against Frank Lorenzo, Chairman of the Board of the Texas Air Corporation, a holding company that had bought up numerous airlines and was attempting to merge them all into one bigger airline. Lorenzo offered a 50% pay reduction, and loss of all medical and dental benefits for Eastern employees, resulting in the strike which lasted two years. Eastern went into total Bankruptcy and was liquidated.
1990 AD	Hungary opened Iron Curtain border with Austria, and Eastern Europeans start to escape to the west, freeing the Iron Curtain countries. Chinese have freedom demonstration in Tiananmen Square in Peking but it is crushed by Commie tanks.
1990 AD	Iron Curtain demolished; Germany reunified.
1990 AD	Iraq invades and occupies Kuwait; 3rd American-Muslim War, First Persian Gulf War (1990-1991 AD), US, Britain, Saudi Arabia drove back Iraqi troops from the country of Kuwait in Operation Desert Storm. This invasion enraged the Muslim world.
1991 AD	The U.S.S.R, the Soviet Union (1917-1991 AD), dissolved itself.
1992 AD	European Union Constitution adopted.
1992 AD	**Amendment XXVII** No law, varying the compensation for the service of the Senators and Representatives, shall take effect, until an election of representatives shall have intervened.
1993 AD	Oslo Accords on Middle East peace
1993 AD	President Bill Clinton (1993-2001 AD)
1995 AD	NATO, under orders of Bill Clinton unilaterally destroyed the Christian State of Serbia, after Serbia began a program of "ethnic cleansing" in Bosnia to rid the

territory of Muslims. He did this to stop the massacres and appease the Islamic world communities and the EU.

1996 AD	First Baby Boomers, 50 years old.
1999 AD	Gold, $252.00 = 1 ounce of Gold.; Bill Clinton repeals the Glass-Stiegel Act of 1933, this allows rampant speculation in the financial industry again.
2000 AD	Population of the Earth, 6 Trillion people; 6,000,000,000 people.
2001 AD	President George W. Bush, (2001-2009 AD) became president in January, 2001.
2001 AD	September 11, 2001, Saudi Arabian Islamic Jihadists hijack 4 American commercial Airliners while they are in flight; they crash two of them into the World Trade Center Towers in lower Manhattan, NYC, NY., and a third into the Pentagon in Washington, DC; the fourth crashed into a field in Pennsylvania, either being shot down by the US Military or by the passengers rebellion. The World Trade Center buildings collapsed into a heap of burning rubble, many people jumped out windows to their deaths, or died in the collapse. Many NYC firefighters and police died there. 2,996 killed, 6,000 wounded in NYC and Washington, D.C. 4th American-Muslim War, (2001-Present) began, Al Qaeda and Osama bin Laden, (1957-2011 AD), took credit for the attack from Afghanistan. If the sky was viewed from Kabul, Afghanistan, the following morning, Osama bin Laden would have seen the occultation of the crescent moon with Jupiter in its position as on the Islamic flag, in addition to seeing another planet, Saturn, just up from Jupiter, with the Constellation Orion between the two planets and slightly below. Two stars with a great hunter in between as part of the Islamic symbol. Nice planning, the next occultation would not occur until 11-9-2004, followed by the 12-7-2004 occultation when Al-Qaeda attacked the US consulate in Jeddah, Saudi Arabia. The US military attacked and occupied Afghanistan. Osama bin Laden said the United States was the temple of the pagan God "Hubal", and declared war on the United States to destroy both the Pagan God "Hubal" and the United States. This attack revealed to the European consciousness the reality of political Islam, which seemed to have been previously denied. Moon, (0.32 %), Jupiter, (0.99), complete occultation of Jupiter behind Moon, resulting in a star and crescent in sky in nights following attack if observed from the mosque in Jersey City.
2003 AD	Second Persian Gulf War, (2003-2011 AD), the American Invasion of Muslim Iraq, the occupation of Iraq (2003-2011 AD), re-involvement in Iraq (2014-present); Human Genome fully mapped in this year.
2004 AD	Muslims attack the Madrid train system, (3-11-2004), 192 killed, 2000 wounded and maimed; Beslan, Russia, (9-1-2004), Muslim Jihadis seized a Russian primary school capturing 777 Russian school children and 323 Russian adults; after security services retook the school the Muslims had killed 385 and wounded 783 people. Holland, (1 2-2004) Dutch film director Theo Van Gough, whose Great granduncle was the artist Vincent Van Gough, ("Starry Night", "Sunflowers" paintings), was murdered by a Moroccan Muslim "person of color" because he made a movie called "submission", about any woman in the world living under

Islamic Law, where the woman must submit to the man. Jeddah, Saudi Arabia, (12-6-2004), Islamic terrorists attack US Consulate.

2005 AD	King Abdullah, (1924-2015 AD) became the King of Saudi Arabia, (2005-2015 AD); Muslims attack the London Underground using jihadists, (7-7-2005), 56 dead, 700 wounded; September 2005, Jyllands-Posten newspaper published cartoons of the Prophet Mohammad in order to add to the debate about freeand religion, this kicked off Muslim boycotts of Denmark and worldwide Muslim violence.
2006 AD	First Baby Boomers were 60 years old.
2007 AD	Global financial crises, (2007-2009 AD), a financial crises resulting from Bill Clintons repeal of the Glass-Stiegel Act of 1933, in 1999. Rampant speculation by financial institutions caused a liquidity problem tied to the sub-prime mortgage industry, major financial institutions began to fail as credit became tight; many bankruptcies and housing industry realized the houses were not worth what the mortgages were written for. The government stepped in to bail out the big banks.
2008 AD	The 'Union for the Mediterranean", the EU Mediterranean strategy linked to the OIC, the Organization of Islamic Cooperation, representing 56 Million countries and Palestine. The EU, OIC created a huge administration that issues EU directives through a totalitarian and anonymous system maintaining censorship and political correctness over the member countries. This is where the term "Islamophobia" was created and originated, within this organization. The term is similar to anti-Semite, and is used as a way to intimidate people opposed to the schemes of the people using them.
2008 AD	Mumbai, India, (11-26-2008) attacked by Jihadists, 166 killed, 600 wounded and maimed. 2009 AD President Barrack Hussein Obama, (2009-2017AD), inaugurated into office; Greek government debt crises, Greece broke. Germany is dictating terms of austerity to Greece as leader of EU. Fort Hood, Texas, (11-2009), Us Army Major, and Army psychiatrist Abdul Hassan, shot and killed 13 soldiers, then wounded 30 more in a Jihad terror attack. He was convicted and is sentenced to death, he awaits execution at present.
2011 AD	Gold, $1432.00 = 1 ounce of Gold, Osama bin Laden was killed by a US Navy Seal Team in Abbottabad, Pakistan; living less than 1 mile away from the Pakistan Military Academy, which is comparable to the US Military Academy at West Point, NY. Charlie Hebdo satirical magazine in France was attacked for publishing pictures of Mohammad.
2013 AD	Boston, Massachusetts, (4-15-2013), Boston Marathon Bombings by Chechen-American Islamic jihadist in Boston using rice-pressure Cookers as Improvised Explosive Devices, IED's. 3 dead, 264 maimed. Moon (0.27) and Jupiter (0.99) are in same position over Boston as on September 11, 2001 in N.Y.C., but no occultation took place. Woolwich Artillery Base, Great Britain, (5-2013), British soldier Lee Rigby is attacked and run over using a car, then hacked to death by two Nigerian converts to the "religion of peace" outside the Royal Artillery base

at Woolwich. Chelyabinsk meteor exploded over southern Ural Mountains in Russia.

2014 AD   Saudi Arabia built "The Great Wall of Saudi Arabia", along its border with Iraq to prevent spillover of violence and refugees from Syria into Saudi Territory.

2014 AD   Islamic State Caliphate (2014-present), starts, ISIS, Islamic State of Iraq and al-Sham is also known as ISIS, Islamic State of Iraq and Syria; ISIL, Islamic State of Iraq and the Levant, and Daesh, not to be confused with "Mrs. Dash" the food seasoning. The Islamic State Caliphate, ISIS, claims absolute, political, military and religious authority over all Muslims worldwide. The religion of the Islamic State is fundamental Wahhabi Sunni Islam. The black banner ISIS displays goes back to the Prophet Mohammad, his daughter Aisha used it, it heralds the coming of the Mahdi from the land of Khorasan, Persia, (an area southeast of the Caspian Sea). Khorasan means "place of the Sun", it was an important spiritual center of Mithras before Islam, and it is an important spiritual center of "Sufi Islam" today. Sufis are the ones with the swirling dervishes. The Mahdi will bring about the destruction of the world and bring in peace afterwards. The Mahdi is Prophet, the one who will follow the Prophet Mohammad in Sunni Islam; and he is the "twelfth Imam" in Shi'ite Islam, who has been born but is in hiding. The Mahdi's coming is the same story as the second coming of Christ in Revelations, and the same as the stories in Zoroastrian and Mithras literature. Khorasan, Khor-asan, "Khor" means the "Sun" in the sky, and "asan" means "to come"; Khorasan means where the sun rises. The Mahdi will come from where the Sun rises. Alexander the Great took Khorasan away from the Aryans, the nobles living there. It was the area of Mitras and Zoroaster back then. Many Islamic scholars came from Khorasan. The Shahada, the testimony of Islamic Creed, is written on the Black flag. It says, "There is no God but God. Mohammad is The Messenger of God." Don Imus is a radio jockey, he is also known as the Iman, Don Imus is not an Islamic Imam, and he is not associated with ISIS.

2014 AD   Ottawa, Canada, a soldier standing ceremonial guard duty at the National War Memorial in Ottawa was shot down by a Muslim extremist.

2014 AD   Largest Ebola Outbreak in known history in West Africa, (2014-2016 AD).

2015 AD   Warmest year in recorded history

2015 AD   King Salman al Saud (1935- present), became King of Saudi Arabia, (2015 – present), Females obtain the right to vote in Saudi Arabia this year but still have to wear Burkas in public, and are not allowed to drive. Charlie Hebdo satirical magazine in Paris was attacked by Islamic Jihadists 11 dead, 11 wounded over the cartoons of Mohammad.

2015 AD   "Sea Peoples" cross Mediterranean Sea from North Africa to take over Italy and all points north. Greek islands overrun with male Muslim migrants and a few women; they are put on ferries for the mainland of Greece, where they trek north towards Hungary, Austria, Germany, Holland, Sweden, and Denmark. German Chancellor Angela Merkle opens the doors of the European Union to Muslim refugees; millions and millions of Muslims trek north through the Balkans towards Germany. Merkle is now engaged in a New World Order, Germanic Nordic crossbreeding experiment at the behest of her masters, very similar to the genetic experiments carried out Doctor Mengele, the Nazi Doctor running the Auschwitz extermination camp. He tried to surgically implant blue eyes into Jewish children among other delightful science projects. Hungary built a fence to keep them out; there are hardly any women and the men are teenagers to 35 years old. The middle-east is dumping its populations anywhere but in the Middle east. Saudi Arabia built a wall to keep them out and the Persian Gulf States are also keeping them out as is Egypt and Israel. All of these countries want a pipeline built and access to the gas fields under the eastern Mediterranean but they don't want to share the future profits with the people who have been living there for 5,000 years. They are dumping them on Europe. Because they breed too fast for Allah, the social system will collapse or they will be used as factory workers in Europe under control of the Imam's of Islam and controlled by the Semites in Mecca and Jerusalem, new Muslims to sell their gas too instead of Christians. Paris, France, (11-13-2015), there were 6 distinct Jihad attacks at the same time in different areas conducted by ISIS using machine guns and suicide vests, 89 people were massacred inside the Bataclan theatre where a rock and roll group were playing. Other bars, restaurants, and a sports stadium were also attacked killing 137 people and wounding 368 people. Israel began experiencing random attacks on civilians with knives, cars and guns. Chattanooga, Tennessee, (7-16-2015), Jihadi terrorists attacked a US Navy recruiter, then attacked the US Naval Reserve Center nearby, 4 US Marines dead, 1 US sailor dead, 2 wounded. Belgium, (8-2015), Jihadist attacks passengers on a high speed train traveling through Belgium, before being subdued by Americans on vacation. San Bernardino, California, Inland Regional Center, (12-2-2015), an American of Pakistani descent and his Muslim immigrant wife killed 14 co-workers and wound 22 more, in an Islamic state terror attack at the Christmas party. Again Jupiter passed the moon two days later. There are not that many occultation's of the moon with Jupiter. There was a total of twenty one of them between the year 1900, (11-23-1900), and 2004, (12-7-2004). It is kind off a rare occurrence, especially if you put it together with the crescent phase of the moon.

2016 AD   "Flying Scotsman" back in service, between London and Edinburgh, Scotland. China opened up a rail line from China to Germany. "The New Silk Road" was opened as a rail link between Zhetiaing, Peoples Republic of China and Tehran, Iran. It is expected to be extended from Tehran to Istanbul, Turkey, then onto Europe in the next few years reducing the sea born, container traffic time from 36 days to 13 days by rail. The project is called O.B.O.R., "One Belt, One Road"; and is part of the Eurasian Land Bridge project; part of the project will run from China, through Russia, then Poland, and on to Germany. In addition to this China is initiating a Maritime Silk Belt. This project can be contrasted or augmented by the T.P.P., the Trans-Pacific Partnership, and the T.T.I.P., the Transatlantic Trade and Investment Partnership, which are two trade projects that link North America to Asia, and North America to Europe, all part of the "New World Order" plans. China is building a new canal across Nicaragua, to facilitate larger more massive container ships.

2016 AD

Syria, civil war against ISIS continues; Russians have put troops in Syria to support Syrian President Assad Muslim armies from Saudi Arabia approach the border of Syria, but turn tail and run back to Mecca in when seeing the marshal array of Russian nuclear submarines off the coast of Syria. Brussels, Belgium, (3-22-2016), 2 suicide attacks, one at airport, one in subway, 35 dead, 340 wounded and maimed. Jupiter passed very close by the moon on 3-21-2016, no occultation, moon was full. Vatican City, (5-2016), Pope Francis supports the refugee immigration and comparing ISIS to Jesus. London, (5/2016), London voters elect first Muslim mayor; he bans scantily clad female advertisements on the sides of buses, and permits the buses to carry Islamic messages, praising Allah. Allah Akbar, baby! He then went on to say if Muslims were banned from the US, then Muslims will attack America. Great Britain, (6/2016), nationwide referendum on exiting the E.U., "Brexit", passed by a narrow margin; Britain begins to formally exit the European Union. Day after vote EU announces it will the formation of an EU military, and individual countries militaries will be dissolved. Turkey, (6-2016), Turkish President Erdogan says Muslim women must make more babies for Jihad, so Islam will rule the world. Germany voted to call the Armenian killings of 1915 genocide; Turkey rejects the implication that it was systematic genocide, and threatens to flood Europe with 3 million more refugees. United States, (6-2016) the State Department issues a travel warning to all Americans not to travel to any part of Europe this summer. Bilderberg meeting in Dresden, Germany, Henry Kissinger (1923 -present) attends. Orlando, Florida, (6/12/2016), Jihadist, Omar Mateen walked into largest Gay nightclub in city and opens fire on the patrons who are dancing; it was Latin night and Orlando has a large Puerto-Rican population so there were a lot of gay Puerto-Ricans there having fun. 49 dead, 53 wounded. Moon, (0.48), Jupiter, (0.99), Uranus closer than Jupiter, no occultation, but close pass of Jupiter by moon, a few hours before shooting. Istanbul, Turkey (6-28-2016), Islamic terrorist attack in Istanbul Airport by ISIS, 44 dead, 230 wounded and maimed. Dhaka, Bangladesh, (7-2016), ISIS hacks to death 20 infidel non-Muslims customers in a café in the capital city, all the ISIS members were from wealthy elite families in city. Nice, France, (7-14-2016), Bastille Day celebrations, fireworks on coast, Muslim terrorist drove a truck through a one mile long crowd of people, shooting and running over men, women, and children, 84 killed, 202 injured. No Jupiter this time. France increased air attacks on ISIS in Syria. Turkey, (7-15-2016) President Erdogan stages a fake coup to justify a complete crackdown on any political opposition as he begins to rid secular Turkey of democracy in a step towards reestablishing a new Turkish Caliphate. All college professors, teachers, judges and many police and military personnel were arrested, none are permitted to leave the country. The US Air Force Base at Incirlik along with its nuclear weapons were surrounded and supplies cut off from outside world. Turkey declared a three-month state of Emergency. Munich, Germany July 22, 2016, Islamic terrorist opens fire on German children outside McDonalds, Munich Mall and Subway station, 9 dead, 10 wounded, more of the same anti-Cimmerian, anti-R1b hostility. July 2016, Israeli Knesset (parliament) introduces legislation to throw out Arab-Israeli politicians who are not loyal to Israel and form an opposition to Israel's Palestinian policies. 17% of Israel's population of 8 Million Israeli citizens are not Jewish but Arab Palestinians who never left when Israel was created. This legislation will strip the minority, 17%, of any legal representation in the democracy of Israel, at the behest of Jewish politicians, in effect making Israel a fascist state instead of a democracy, which will inevitably lead to more terrorism against the Jewish people and state. Normandy, France, (7-26-2016), Two ISIS Jihad i's, one with a tracking ankle bracelet from the French Department of Corrections enter a Roman Catholic church in St.-Etienne-Du Rouvray, 35 miles southeast of Le Harve, during morning Mass and behead 86 year old Catholic priest at altar, critically wound another parishioner, shouting Alllah Akbar, before police shoot them. Donald Trump is the republican nominee for president of the United States, Hillary Clinton is the democratic nominee for the president of the United States.

List of Exact Occultation's of the Moon with the Planet Jupiter (1900-2026 AD)

November 23,1900
March 17, 1904
September 22, 1922
April 11, 1929
May 9,1929
August 31, 1932
December 14, 1936
October 23, 1943
January 13, 1944
April 30, 1944
January 16, 1947
June 30, 1954
June 30, 1965
September 21, 1968
October 19, 1968
August 18, 1990
March 26, 1998
August 15, 2001
September 12, 2001   Morning after the September Eleventh attack on the W.T.C. in N.Y.C.
November 9, 2004
December 7, 2004   Morning after the December Sixth attack on the U.S. Consulate in Jeddah, Saudi Arabia.

April 19, 2023, May 17, 2023	Hey the next one is the day before Hitler's 134th birthday.
September 30, 2016	Occultation of the Planet Jupiter by the Sun, with the moon in between the sun and the Earth, at sunrise in New York City, New York.

GOBBLEDYGOOK

The concept of anti-Semitism and Islamophobia are one and the same thing, and are wielded as psychological weapons by Judaism and Islam against anyone who opposes their policies and ambitions. A short comparison of the Jewish "Talmud" with the Quran, and the Sunna, (the Sira and the Hadith) are as follows:

Subject	Talmud (Hebrew)	Reliance of the Traveler (Muslim)
Unbelievers	Goyim, (non-Jews) prejudicial term	Kafir, (non-Muslims) prejudicial term
Deity	Yahweh, Elohim, Sin	Allah, Elohim, Sin
Prophet on Earth	Many over time.	Many over time, Mohammad is last
Women	Male will tell female what she needs to know	Women must "submit" to the male
Law	Talmud, based on last three of the Ten Commandments	Reliance of the Traveler, Sharia
Slaves	no comment	Slavery is a positive thing, permitted
Ethics	Chapter of the Fathers	Duality, ethics different for infidels than for Muslims,
Business Law	extensive coverage	extensive coverage
Purity and Impurity	extensive coverage	extensive coverage
Going to the bathroom	nothing	extensive coverage
Food		
Cheeseburgers	Prohibited, Chulin 115b., Exodus 23:19	Permitted, (haram)
Pork	Prohibited	Prohibited, j16.3
Stone Crabs and Scallops	Prohibited	Permitted, (haram)
Alcohol	in moderation	Prohibited o16.3 the penalty for drinking is to be forty stripes, with hands, sandals, and the ends of clothes. It may be administered with a whip, but if the offender dies, an indemnity is due for his death. If the caliph increases the penalty to 80 stripes, it is legally valid, but if the offender dies from the increase, the caliph must pay an

		adjusted indemnity, such that if he is given forty one stripes and dies, the caliph must pay 1/41 of a full indemnity. I don't think Geico covers this indemnity.
Sperm	Not mentioned	j16.6 It is also unlawful to eat substances which are pure, but generally considered repulsive, such as saliva or sperm.
Jews	It's a book written by and for Jews	Extensive coverage of Jews, s1.2, o4.9, The indemnity for the death or injury of a woman is one- half the indemnity paid for a Muslim. The indemnity paid for a Jew or a Christian is one-third of the indemnity paid for a Muslim. The indemnity paid for a Zoroastrian is one-fifteenth of that of a Muslim.
Muslims	No mention of Muslims	It's all about Mohammad and Islamic rules.

The "Babylonian Talmud" and the "Torah", the "Reliance of the Traveler" (Sharia Law), the Qur'an, the Hadith (the Sunna of Mohammad), and the Sira (The Life of Mohammad) read almost the same. All were written while the Christian Byzantine Empire was still powerful in the Eastern Mediterranean area of the world. There is resentment in the Talmud over the Diaspora and the rise in Christianity, the loss of the "promised land of Israel", but it clearly presents "a way of living", a way of detailed living. There is a logic and reason that strings through it. The Reliance of the Traveler, the Sharia Law, presents an even more detailed cultural system of behaviors and earthly penalties to which everyone is to be subject to. There is a great deal of hatred of the Jews throughout the texts which is strange; it is as if that hatred is the glue that holds Islamic teachings together. Men must never really grow up in the Islamic societies if they completely adhere to the dogma. It is as if Mohammad's followers were juvenile delinquents, and the Sharia keeps enabling the delinquency, generation after generation, but then that's why they call them religion.

Religion, Religion, Religion
Religion is a cultural system of behaviors and practices, world views, ethics, sacred texts, holy places, and social organization that relate primates to an order of existence.

Whiskey, Whiskey, Whiskey
Whiskey is a cultural system of behaviors and practices, world views, ethics, sacred sex, holy gin mills, and social organization that relate primates to a dis-order of existence.

Religious beliefs and religions are chimeric to me, and, they exhibit chirality. Chimerism in a human being is when a human being is born with two different sets of DNA, it happens. The human may have two different Blood Types at the same time. Chimerism is also present in an animal or god like "being" like the Sphinx in Egypt. The Sphinx has the head of a human and the body of a lion. It would have two sets of DNA, and exhibit traits of both some dominant, some recessive. Islam has the DNA of Judaism, and the God "Sin" within it. Judaism has the Mesopotamian beliefs of "Sin" mixed with a newly made up or renamed invisible deity god called Yahweh. Christianity has the DNA of Judaism mixed with the entire set of DNA of Mithra, along with some of the DNA of Sol Invictus, and some Celtic beliefs amalgamated into one impossible to comprehend doctrine. Religions also exhibit chirality. They are both achiral and chiral at the same time. Chirality; Something that is "chiral" is something that has different forms, like a left hand and a right hand. If you hold your right hand up to a mirror, the image you see is what appears to be your left hand, but in reality it is your right hand, and visa versa with your left hand. If God held his right hand up in a mirror, you would see what appeared to be the "left hand of God". When you look at the full moon, you are looking at the reflection of light on the face of a dark rock. You are not looking at the source of the light. "Sin" is not the "light", and thus sin is blackness of the soul. It is a deceiving type of thinking. What appears to be one thing is actually not what it appears to be. When people believe they are "holy" or "devout" they are following the doctrine of their chosen belief, whatever that appears for them to be. They are remaining "faithful" to whatever dogma they have chosen to believe in. These beliefs exhibit control over the human mind, it is easier to just accept a belief "on faith", than it is to arrive at ones' own "truth". It is also easy to control groups of people for exploitation when they "truly believe", when they are faithful. It is easier also for the "believer", a lot easier, the believer can just believe an not think, then go on about making money within his or her belief system, living and forgetting about, the real question, we face as primates here in our lives like, "What the fuck is going on?" See no evil, speak no evil, hear no evil, would be a good way to describe the "faithful". Chirality, the appearance is not in reality what you perceive it to be, with an ever changing chimeric asymmetric center providing religious control for the primates; perfect for business operations and making money. The invisible hand of God, or Adam Smith working in mysterious ways?

Summary of Chronicum Holocenum

It got warmer than it was, and it's going to get warmer still until it gets cold again. The tide came in and never went out. Primates multiply like bacteria in a Petri dish until all the blood agar is gone. Most primates don't care and don't have a clue, a few primates know this and put stuff over on lesser unknowing primates. The Foundation Stone and Upper Mesopotamia is the epicenter of the fight for this rock. Beware the words of men, for they are the truths of they themselves and not of you yourself. Primates keep repeating the same stuff over and over again. Don't ever, ever, ever, never, never, never give up your weapons. Try to be social, none of us asked to be here, and none of us know where we came from or where we are going to. Freedom is not free. God is an imaginary creation to ward off the fears and dread of the future made in our own image because that image is familiar to us. All religions die out or morph into a new one over time, take religious beliefs with a grain of salt, what we think of as God may be a physical calling to us to venture out into the Galaxy that we misinterpret. Don't get into a nuclear war because the sun is halfway through its fuel, and life will not be able to evolve again in time to get off this stupid rock before it is incinerated, but do not surrender or submit to any belief system. The Hebrews are still fighting to restore their temple on the foundation stone of Abraham, and will continue until the Temple of David is fully restored. The planet can erupt into volcanic action that can wipe mostly everything out in short order. There are rocks hurtling through space that have and will continue to bombard the planet. Don't take yourself to Damn seriously. Watch out for sharks, stingrays, and Bigfoot. Tribes. Be good at your paintings. At some point in time Homo sapiens are going to evolve into a new Homo species. Anything can happen. Brush your teeth say your prayers, love yourself, and others. Listen to music. Still don't know who or what God is but I bet he's bigger than King Kong. Man went to the moon and explored it. It was one small step for man, but one great leap for mankind. All you that you touch, and all that you see, all that you taste, all you feel, and all that you love, and all that you hate, all you distrust, all you save, and all that you give, and all that you deal, and all that you buy, beg, borrow, or steal, and all you create, and all you destroy, and all that you do, and all that you say, and all that you eat, and everyone you meet, and all that you slight, and everyone you fight, and all that is now, and all that is gone, and all that's to come, and Everything under the sun is in tune, but the sun is eclipsed by the moon.

Primitive Aboriginal Primal Primate Religion
Primitive religious concepts included space, time, oral tradition, tribal identity versus modern identity, walk abouts with nature, swinging from branches, collecting bananas, the real meaning of life.

In The Kingdom of Seals

The sea fairies have grey skin-coverings and resemble seals. They dwell in cave houses on the borders of Land-under-Waves, where they have a kingdom of their own. They love music and the dance, like the green land fairies, and when harper or piper plays on the beach they come up to listen, their shoe-black eyes sparkling with joy. On moonlight nights they hear the mermaids singing on the rocks when human beings are fast asleep, and they call to them: "Sing again the old sea croons; sing again!" All night long the sea fairies call thus when mermaids cease to sing, and the mermaids sing again and again to them. When the wind pipes loud and free, and the sea leaps and whirls and sings and cries aloud with wintry merriment, the sea fairies dance with the dancing waves, tossing white petals of foam over their heads, and twining pearls of spray about their necks. They love to hunt the silvern salmon in the forests of sea-tangle and in the ocean's deep blue glens, and far up dark ravines through which flow rivers of sweet mountain waters gemmed with stars.

The sea fairies have a language of their own, and they are also skilled in human speech. When they come ashore they can take the forms of men or women, and turn billows into dark horses with grey tails, and on these they ride over mountain and moor.

There was once a fisherman who visited the palace of the queen of the sea fairies, and told on his return all he had seen and all he had heard. He dwelt in a little township nigh to John-o'-Groats House, and was wont to catch fish and seals. When he found that he could earn much money by hunting seals, whose skins make warm winter clothing, he troubled little about catching salmon or cod, and worked constantly as a seal hunter. He crept among the rocks searching for his prey, and visited lonely seal-haunted islands across the Pentland Firth, where he often found the strange sea-prowlers lying on smooth flat ledges of rock fast asleep in the warm sunshine.

In his house he had great bundles of dried sealskins, and people came from a distance to purchase them from him. His fame as a seal-hunter went far and wide.

One evening a dark stranger rode up to his house, mounted on a black, spirited mare with grey mane and grey tail. He called to the fisherman who came out, and then said: "Make haste and ride with me towards the east. My master desires to do business with you."

"I have no horse," the fisherman answered, "but I shall walk to your master's house on the morrow."

Said the stranger: "Come now. Ride with me. My good mare is fleet-footed and strong."

"As you will," answered the fisherman, who at once mounted the mare behind the stranger. The mare turned round and right-about, and galloped eastward faster than the wind of March. Shingle rose in front of her like rock-strewn sea-spray, and a sand-cloud gathered and swept out behind like mountain mists that are scattered before a Gale. The fisherman gasped for breath, for although the wind was blowing against his back when he mounted the mare, it blew fiercely in his face as he rode on. The mare went fast and far until she drew nigh to a precipice. Near the edge of it she halted suddenly. The fisherman found then that the wind was still blowing seaward, although he had thought it had veered round as he rode. Never before had he sat on the back of so fleet-footed a mare.

Said the stranger: "We have almost reached my master's dwelling."

The fisherman looked round about him with surprise, and saw neither house nor the smoke of one. "Where is your master?" he asked.

Said the stranger: "You shall see him presently. Come with me."

As he spoke he walked towards the edge of the precipice and looked over. The fisherman did the same, and saw nothing but the grey lonely sea heaving in a long slow swell, and sea-birds wheeling and sliding down the wind. "Where is your master?" he asked once again.

With that the stranger suddenly clasped the seal-hunter in his arms, and crying, "Come with me", leapt over the edge of the precipice. The mare leapt with her master.

Down, down they fell through the air, scattering the startled sea-birds. Screaming and fluttering, the birds rose in clouds about and above them, and down the men and the mare continued to fall till they plunged into the sea, and sank and sank, while the light around them faded into darkness deeper than the night. The fisherman wondered to find himself still alive as he passed through sea depths, seein naught, hearing naught, and still moving swiftly. At length he ceased to sink, and went forward. He suffered no pain or discomfort, nor was he afraid. His only feeling was of wonder, and in the thick, cool darkness he wondered greatly what would happen next. At length he saw a faint green light, and as he went onward the light grew brighter and brighter, until the glens and bens and forests of the sea kingdom arose before his eyes. Then he discovered that he was swimming beside the stranger and that they had both been changed into seals.

Said the stranger: "Yonder is my master's house."

The fisherman looked, and saw a township of foam-white houses on the edge of a great sea-forest and fronted by a bank of sea-moss which was green as grass but more beautiful, and very bright. There were crowds of seal-folk in the township. He saw them moving about to and fro, and heard their voices, but he could not understand their speech. Mothers nursed their babes, and young children played games on banks of green sea-moss, and from the brown and golden sea-forest came sounds of music and the shouts of dancers.

Said the stranger: "Here is my master's house. Let us enter."

He led the fisherman towards the door of a great foam-white palace with its many bright windows. It was thatched with red tangle, and the door was of green stone. The door opened as smoothly as a summer wave that moves across a river mouth, and the fisherman entered with his guide. He found himself in a dimly-lighted room, and saw an old grey seal stretched on a bed, and moaning in pain. Beside the bed lay a blood-stained knife, and the fisherman knew at a glance that it was his own. Then he remembers that, not many hours before, he had stabbed a seal, and that it had escaped by plunging into the sea, carrying the knife in its back.

The fisherman started to realize that the old seal on the bed was the very one he had tried to kill, and his heart was filled with fear. He threw himself down and begged for forgiveness and mercy, for he feared that he would be put to death.

The guide lifted up the knife and asked: "Have you ever seen this knife before?' He spoke in human language.

"That's my knife, alas!" exclaimed the fisherman.

Said the guide: "The wounded seal is my father. Our doctors are unable to cure him. They can do naught without your help. That is why I visited your house and urged you to come with me. I ask your pardon for deceiving you, O man! But as I love my father greatly, I had to do as I have done."

"Do not ask my pardon," the fisherman said; "I have need of yours. I am sorry and ashamed for having stabbed your father."

Said the guide: "Lay your hand on the wound and wish it to be healed."

The fisherman laid his hand on the wound, and the pain that the seal suffered passed into his hand, but did not remain long. As if by magic, the wound was healed at once. Then the old grey seal rose up strong and well again.

Said he guide: "You have served us well this day, O man."

When the fisherman had entered the house, all the seals that were within were weeping tears of sorrow, but they ceased to weep as soon as he had laid his hand on the wound, and when the old seal rose up they all became merry and bright.

The fisherman wondered what would happen next. For a time the seals seemed to forget his presence, but at length his guide spoke to him and said: "Now, O man! You can return to your own home where your wife and children await you. I shall lead you through the sea depths, and take you on my mare across the plain which we crossed when coming hither."

"I give you thanks," the fisherman exclaimed.

Said the guide: "Before you leave there is one thing you must do; you must take a vow never again to hunt the seals."

The fisherman answered: "Surely, I promise never again to hunt for seals."

Said the guide: "If ever you break your promise you shall die. I counsel you to keep it, and as long as you do so you will prosper. Every time you set lines, or cast a net, you will catch much fish. Our seal-servants will help you, and if you wish to reward them for their services, take with you in your boat a harp or pipe and play sweet music, for music is the delight of all seals."

The fisherman vowed he would never break his promise, and the guide then led him back to dry land. As soon as he reached the shore he ceased to be a seal and became a man once again. The guide, who had also changed shape, breathed over a great wave and, immediately, it became a dark mare with grey mane and grey tail. He then mounted the mare, and bade the fisherman mount behind him. The mare rose in the air as lightly as wind-tossed spray, and passing through the clouds of startled sea-birds reached the top of the precipice. On she raced at once, raising the shingle in front and a cloud of sand behind. The night was falling and the stars began to appear, but it was not quite dark when the fisherman's house was reached.

The fisherman dismounted, and his guide spoke and said: "Take this from me, and may you live happily."

He handed the fisherman a small bag, and crying: "Farewell! Remember your vow he wheeled his mare right round and passed swiftly out of sight.

The fisherman entered his house, and found his wife still there. "You have returned, she said. "How did you fare?"

"I know not yet", he answered. Then he sat down and opened the bag, and to his surprise and delight found it was full of pearls.

His wife uttered a cry of wonder, and said: "From whom did you receive this treasure?"

The fisherman then related all that had taken place, and his wife wondered to hear him.

"Never again will I hunt seals," he exclaimed. And he kept his word and prospered, and lived happily until the day of his death.

Poems are made by fools like me, but only God can make a tree. By studying the rings of an oak tree, it will give you a "knowledge of the oak", and from the tiny chestnut duth the mighty oak tree grow.

I was only Joking

Ever since I was a kid at school, I messed around with all the rules, Apologized, then realized, I'm not different after all. Me and the boys thought we had it sussed, Valentino's all of us, My dad said we looked ridiculous, But boy, we broke some hearts. In and out of jobs, running free, Waging war with society, Dumb blank faces stared back at me, But nothing ever changed. Promises made in the heat of the night, Creepin home before it got to light, I wasted all that precious time, And blamed it on the wine. I was only joking my dear, Looking for a way to hide my fear. What kind of fool was I? I could never win. Never found a compromise, Collected lovers like butterflies, Illusions of that grand first prize, Are slowly wearin" thin, Susie, baby, you were good to me, Giving love unselfishly, But you took it all to seriously, I guess it had to end. I was only joking my dear, Looking for a way to hide my fear, What kind of fool was I? I could never win. Now you ask me if I'm sincere, That's the question that I always fear, verse seven is never clear, But I'll tell you what you want to hear, I try to give you all you want, But giving love is not my strongest point, If that's the case, it's pointless going on, I'd rather be alone. "Cause what I'm doing must be wrong, Pouring my heart out in a song, Owning up for prosperity, For the whole damn world to see. Quietly now while I turn the page, Act one is over without costume change, The principal would like to leave the stage, The crowd don't understand.

Truth is stranger than fiction, and the truth is out there. Stay thirsty my friends.

Loch Lomond

By yon bonnie banks and by yon bonnie braes,
Where the sun shines bright on Loch Lomond.
Where me and my true love will never meet again
On the bonnie, bonnie banks o' Loch Lomond.

O ye'll take' the high road and I'll take the low road,
An' I'll be in Scotland afore ye;
But me and me true love will never meet again
On the bonnie, bonnie banks o' Loch Lomon'.

'Twas there that we parted in yon shady glen,
On the steep, steep side o" Ben Lomon'.
Where in deep purple hue the Hieland hills we view
An' the moon comin' out in the gloamin'.

O ye'll take' the high road and I'll take the low road,
And I'll be in Scotland afore ye;
But me and me true love will never meet again
On the bonnie, bonnie banks o' Loch Lomon'

The wee birdies sing and the wild flow'rs spring,
And in sunshine the waters are sleepin';
But the broken heart it kens nae second spring again,
Tho' the waefu' may cease frae their greavin'

O ye'll take' the high road and I'll take the low road,
An' I'll be in Scotland afore ye;
But me and me true love will never meet again
On the bonnie, bonnie banks o' Loch Lomon'.

Chronicum Holocenum

Come over the hills my bonnie Irish lass,
Come over the hills to your darling,
You choose the road love and I'll make the vow,
And I'll be your true love forever.

Red is the rose that in yonder garden grows
Fair is the lily of the valley
Clear is the water that flows from the Boyne
But my love is fairer than any.

Twas' down by Killarnies green woods that we strayed
When the moon and the stars they were shining
The moon shot its rays on her locks of golden hair
And she swore she'd be my love forever.

Red is the rose that in yonder garden grows
Fair is the lily of the valley
Clear is the water that flows from the Boyne
But my love is fairer than any.

It's not for the parting that my sister grieves
It's not for the grief of my mother
It's all for the loss of my bonnie Irish lass
That my heart is breaking forever.

Red is the rose that in yonder garden grows
Fair is the lily of the valley
Clear is the water that flows from the Boyne
But my love is fairer than any.

O ye'll take' the high road and I'll take the low road,
And I'll be in Scotland afore ye;
But me and my true love will never meet again
On the bonnie, bonnie banks of Loch Lomond..

Scotland the Brave

Hark when the night is falling
Hear! Hear the pipes are calling,
Loudly and proudly calling,
Down thro' the glen.
There where the hills are sleeping,
Now feel the blood a-leaping,
High as the spirits of the old Highland men.

Towering in gallant fame,
Scotland my mountain hame,
High may your proud standards gloriously wave.
Land of my high endeavor,
Land of the shining river
Land of my heart forever,
Scotland the brave.

High in the misty Highlands,
Out by the purple islands,
Brave are the hearts that beat
Beneath Scottish skies
wild are the winds to meet you
staunch are the friends that greet you
kind as the love that shines from fair maidens eyes.

Galway Bay

If you go across the sea to Ireland
Then maybe at the closing of your day,
You can sit and watch the moon over Claddagh
And see the sun go down on Galway Bay.

Just to hear again the ripple of the trout stream,
the women in the meadow making hay,
Just to sit beside the turf fire in a cabin,
And watch the barefoot gossons as they play.

Ooh

For the breezes blowing oer the sea's from Ireland
Are perfumed by the heather as they blow,
And the women in the uplands digging praties,
Speak a languge that the strangers do not know.

Yet the strangers came and tried to teach us their ways,
And they scorned us just for being what we are,
But they might as well go chasin after moonbeams,
or light a penny candle from a star.

And if there's gonna be a life hereafter
And faith somehow I'm sure there's gonna be,
I will ask my God to let me make my heaven,
In that dear land across the Irish sea.

I will ask my God to let me make my heaven
In my dear land across the Irish Sea.

Ooh.

In my dear land across the Irish Sea.

| 2500-3500 AD | Next "Bond Event" cooling is due |
| 3600 AD | The Earth is a giant yellow covered snowball. |

August 17, 2016

www.ingramcontent.com/pod-product-compliance
Lightning Source LLC
LaVergne TN
LVHW061335060426

835511LV00014B/1932